The Mystery of the Princes in the Tower: The Real Game of Thrones

Carolyn Noble

FIRST EDITION

Acknowledgements

Thank you to my beautiful family, Scott and Mia for always supporting and encouraging me.
Mum – thank you for being a legend and your never-ending patience

Table of Contents

Introduction

'But in the end, it is always far better to be left with an open question, to which we know we can offer no simplistic answer, rather than to be palmed off with an easy 'answer' for which, in reality, there is absolutely no historical basis.' John Ashdown-Hill[i]

On 9 April 1483, Edward IV, the King of England died leaving behind two young sons. What happened to those boys is a mystery that has captured the public imagination ever since. On news of the death, his eldest son at 12 years of age was proclaimed King Edward V. What happened next has long been a source of fierce debate between historians, both professional and amateur alike.

For within a matter of weeks, Edward V had been declared illegitimate, was living with his younger brother as a prisoner and had been replaced as king by his uncle Richard, the person trusted by their father to protect them. At the beginning there are accounts of the boys being seen regularly playing in the gardens and receiving visitors. This was not to last, soon contemporary writers claim that they were moved further within the Tower and their servants were dismissed, until ultimately rumours started to spread that they had disappeared or been murdered. Was Shakespeare's Duchess of York correct when she stated, '*Bloody thou art, bloody will be thy end*?'[ii]

Despite all this speculation, nobody was able to prove that the boys were dead or had been murdered and, if they were killed, who was responsible. The mystery was reignited in 1674 when workmen in the Tower are said to have discovered a chest or box containing human bones. Charles II declared them to be the bodies of the missing princes and ordered the bones to be placed within a memorial urn, erected close to the tomb of King Henry VII.

In 1933 the bones were examined and appeared to confirm that they were consistent with the details of the missing princes. However, further examination of the report has criticised the findings and suggested that the conclusions do not prove whether they are the bones of the princes.

Whilst, with the current evidence there is no way to prove what fate the princes ultimately met, one thing that many people think they know is: who was responsible for it. History is rarely written by the losers and this couldn't be more accurate in the case of Richard III.

One thing that cannot be disputed it that the Tudor dynasty wanted to portray Richard III as an evil tyrant. Blaming him for the murder of his own nephews, mere children, was inevitable.

The Tudor's were undoubtedly helped with this cause by the increase in printing and the power of the playwrights like Shakespeare, eager to content the monarch of the day as well as shroud their plays in as much drama as possible to keep the crowds coming.

The issue of Richard III is incredibly divisive. Many people believe the traditional image, that he was an evil tyrant who always intended to take the Crown for himself. Shakespeare has Richard declare, '*And thus I clothe my naked villany with old ends stolen out of holy writ; And seem a saint when most I play the devil.*'[iii] Whilst Thomas More explains that Richard was '*malicious, wrathful, envious, and, from afore his birth, ever forward.*'[iv] On the other side of the debate are those, such as the Richard III society who want to promote a more balanced picture of what they believe to be a much-maligned king.

This was the mystery that first got me hooked on history back when I was a child. My mum wanted to introduce me to history and would buy me a part-work series called Discovery to collect. Every issue would feature a different person from history and provide information about them and what life was like back in those times. It was through this collection that I first encountered figures such as Leonardo da Vinci, Elizabeth I and ultimately Richard III of course.

One issue of the series I received was a special edition containing a cassette tape. On the tape two school children travelled through time meeting all the characters I had been reading about. The part that has always stuck with me is where they talk to the Princes in the Tower, who were scared, and then to Richard III who I always felt was presented as somebody misunderstood and to be pitied. However, I was only eight and I accept that my interpretations back then may have been flawed.

My fascination with this subject started with the journey of those two school children on the tape and has followed me through my own journey, to writing the book that I felt needed to be written.

Although this is a mystery that has captivated historians at all levels, the discovery of the missing remains of Richard III have served to introduce the mystery to a new, wider audience. This has inevitably reignited the debate about Richard III and his character and ultimately whether he was responsible for the disappearance of his own nephews. The Looking for Richard Project aimed to find the remains of the king who had been quickly buried after the Battle of Bosworth in a friary that was destroyed by King Henry VIII following the reformation. and whose location had been lost. The founder of the project, Phillipa Langley secured support from Leicester City Council and commissioned the University of Leicester Archaeological Services in the search. On the first day of the dig, August 25, 2012, leg bones were discovered which led to the announcement on 4 February 2013, that the remains of Richard III had been found.

This find gave us unique insight into Richard III. The traditional image of a hunchback was confirmed to be untrue, revealing that he suffered from scoliosis, but this would have not been noticeable and would not have affected his ability as a soldier. Another revelation was the reconstruction of his head. The image produced was a much softer face than the portrait which has been confirmed as having been altered to make him look meaner.

Whilst the find opened the history of Richard III to a new audience and enthralled school children, one thing remained the same. When discussing Richard III most people would instantly respond with 'wasn't he the one who killed the boys in the Tower.'

Many books have been written both about Richard III and about whether he killed the Princes in the Tower, either decrying him as an evil villain or trying to rehabilitate his reputation. So why write another one? All accounts of Richard III must cover the mystery of the princes. Many separate books have been written just on the mystery itself. Did Richard kill them? Did they survive the clutches of the king Shakespeare records as saying, '*Since I cannot be a lover I am determined to prove a villain?*'[v]

The reason why I am writing this one is summed up in the quote at the beginning by John Ashdown-Hill. When reading books on this subject or watching documentaries I have found them to be informative yes, but also deeply frustrating with unsatisfactory arguments.

Many historians rely on contemporary accounts which, whilst they give an essence of life back in 1483, are all flawed and unreliable. Facts are incorrect, they are written by people who worked for the Tudor's but everything negative about Richard III is argued to be correct and reliable. Frankly, I don't buy it. Then there are statements with no explanation: They tell us it is clear Richard III was responsible but do not tell us why.

For established historians maybe no explanation is needed. To others it may not be so obvious, especially considering the underwhelming amount of evidence that has been produced against Richard III. As Ashdown-Hill states it is better to have no answer than to give an answer that we can't possibly know is correct. When I decided to write this book, I wanted one that answered the questions I encountered early into my research on this topic. We cannot answer the questions regarding the fate of the princes and the culprit for any sinister action against them.

What we can do is give people the information. Trust people to look at the evidence they have and make their own judgements and give people the information to open the debate. That is exactly what I aim to do with this book. I want to look at all the people around the time who met the vital criteria; means, motive and opportunity. Clearly other people benefitted from the disappearance. If there is insufficient evidence to definitively identify Richard III as a killer of these boys, we must look at the key people at the time and subject their evidence to the same scrutiny. Nobody I spoke to on this journey could name any other person that could have been responsible for their fate.

Chapter 1 – Richard III

Debated for centuries, the evidence pointing to Richard's guilt and the arguments proffered for his defence will be fully considered

It is not and probably never will be, possible to confirm the fate of the boys, now commonly referred to as the Princes in the Tower.

For centuries there was one thing that historians appeared to be certain about; that whatever happened to the boys, their own uncle, Richard III was behind it.

As early as the seventeenth century other historians started to question the traditional answer to this unsolved, yet captivating mystery, the version made famous by Shakespeare. Now, there is continued debate about it. Whilst there are still those who are passionate about demonising the former king, others are as vociferous in his defence. For a man who died centuries ago, Richard III continues to provoke fierce debate.

My aim is neither to defend or condemn Richard III. This is an assessment of the evidence pointing to guilt and the evidence suggesting innocence for the most famous suspect in the disappearance of two boys, Edward, and Richard in 1483.

Richard was born on 2 October 1452 at Fotheringhay Castle. He was the youngest son of Cecily Neville and Richard, Duke of York His father was a descendant from Edward III, as was the king at the time of Richard's birth, Henry VI. So, Richard was born into a noble family, but there was, at the time of his birth, a great distance between this new baby and the throne of England. Richard would have been raised as the son of a noble family and would not have been viewed or raised in the same way as a potential king in his younger childhood. There is little information about his birth and early years, but with the biological knowledge we have now it is certain that the claim of John Rous, written after Richard's death, that he was 'retained within his mother's womb for two years, emerging with teeth and hair to his shoulders'[vi] is untrue.

What we do know is that Richard and his siblings grew up in a period of conflict that would later become known as the Wars of the Roses. Their father, Richard Duke of York, and his supporters, had little faith in the ability of Henry VI to rule the country. He was weak and prone to extended periods of incapacity. This left the business of running the country to his French wife, Margaret of Anjou, who was not popular.

During his childhood Richard would witness his father being exiled from England, returning to England and being named the heir of Henry VI, and finally when he was eight he would be told that his father and older brother Edmund had been killed by the forces of Margaret of Anjou, in the name of King Henry VI, at the Battle of Wakefield, in December 1460. During the fighting and instability that followed, Richard and another of his older brothers, George, were sent away to the Burgundian Netherlands, by their mother, for their safety. They would remain there, away from their family until they heard that their elder brother Edward, Earl of March had defeated the royalist forces and on 4 March 1461 had been proclaimed King Edward IV of England.

With his brother now in charge, the boys were safe to return triumphantly to England as brothers of the new king. Due to his new status, young Richard was sent to live with a close kinsman, Richard, Earl of Warwick. He had supported the Duke of York and then Edward, in their bids for control of the kingdom and in return he was given the honour and responsibility of completing the education of the new king's brother.

It was whilst under the tutelage of Richard, Earl of Warwick that Richard would meet Francis Lovell, who would become a lifelong friend, and become acquainted with Anne Neville, Warwick's daughter, who would, in 1483, be crowned Queen of England, next to her second husband, Richard III.

Two things are clear regarding the character of this young man who would go on to become judged as one of England's best known villains: The first is that it was shaped against the background of intense, civil war, that saw him lose a brother and his father in battle. The second is that there are few figures, whom consideration of their nature, can cause such division and passion

There are those who believe that evidence shows Richard to have been a good lord who cared for the people he ruled. Thomas Langton, writing a private letter to a friend stated, 'He contents the people wherever he goes best that ever did prince; for many a poor man that hath suffered wrong many days have been relieved and helped by him and his commands in his progress. And in many great cities and towns were great sums of money given him which he hath refused. On my truth I liked never the conditions of any prince so well as his; God has sent him to us for the weal of us all.'[vii] This was written by somebody who had benefitted under the rule of Richard, but it was written privately, not a public show of support that he would have gained from.

Throughout his time in control of the north of England he appears to have demonstrated a commitment to fairness and justice, to the point of finding against his own people when arbitrating disputes.

As king he called only one parliament on which we can judge him. This was enough for Francis Bacon to describe him as a 'good law-maker.'[viii] He set up the Council of the North, to uphold the law and passed acts aimed at making the justice system fairer, giving accused people more rights and ensuring juries were picked fairly.
Considered objectively these appear to be the acts of a person who aimed to improve the lives of the people he ruled. However, Richard III was not universally liked, and other accounts paint him as a ruthless man, who ignored the law and rules of fairness when it was in his interest to do.
One example of this is the way that he is believed to have dealt with Elizabeth Howard, an elderly dowager duchess.

It was reported that Richard pressured the elderly lady into surrendering to him her estates. He was accused of using strong-arm tactics such as threatening to make her undertake a long and uncomfortable journey and it was said that he had made her cry in the way that he dealt with her. This appears to suggest that he was ruthless in obtaining what he wanted. However, the statements used were made years after the death of Richard, and therefore after the events that occurred. They were made at a time when the Earl of Oxford was trying to convince King Henry VII to return the lands to him, claiming his mother had not given up the lands voluntarily but under the duress of Richard. A certain amount of caution needs to be applied when evaluating these accounts.

A more damning example for Richard, is the way he treated his mother-in-law, Anne Beauchamp, Countess of Warwick. When Richard married Anne Neville, he would engage in a bitter dispute over the Warwick inheritance, with the Countess stuck in sanctuary, treated as though she were dead. Richard later, possibly to get the upper hand in the dispute, arranged for the Countess to be transported to his custody where she was kept under his control.

When considering the character of Richard, his supporters have a big battle to fight. Anything bad that he does is definite proof that he was the bad person portrayed to perfection by Laurence Olivier.
Any positive acts he carries out, are also argued as proving him to be the sinister villain he has been claimed to be. Positive acts are clearly an evil king trying to hide his ruthless and calculating character and to repair the damage to his reputation. When considering the acts of Richard III, he truly is damned if he does and damned if he doesn't.

As historians it is difficult to really know the intent behind anybody's actions and all we can evaluate are the acts themselves. After Richard was killed history was rewritten and he was subsequently accused of many acts, such as the killing of Henry VI, an accusation of which there is no corroborative evidence.

One thing that historians do seem to agree on to a certain extent is that Richard was always loyal to his older brother, King Edward IV. As noted, Richard was sent, in his youth, to complete his education under the instruction of Richard, Earl of Warwick, whose efforts to put Edward IV on the throne has earnt him the unofficial title of 'Kingmaker'.

However, Warwick was soon to lose faith with his kinsman and king, Edward. Whilst Warwick was negotiating a suitable royal marriage for the king, Edward had married a common widower, and mother of two sons, Elizabeth Woodville. The announcement of this secret marriage, and the favour shown to her large family, left Warwick humiliated.

Warwick quickly turned against Edward IV and began colluding with his brother, George, now Duke of Clarence, in an act that would ultimately lead to the downfall of himself, Henry VI and his Queen, Margaret of Anjou.

Despite his connection to Warwick, Richard never turned against his brother and when Warwick and Clarence gained the upper hand would again flee the country, this time with Edward, where they would regroup and form a new army to return to England and regain the throne.
Together the brothers prepared to face a new and unexpected threat. Warwick had formed an alliance with the Queen he had previously helped to depose, Margaret of Anjou. Having already married his eldest daughter to Clarence, he now offered his youngest daughter, Anne Neville to Edward, son of Henry VI and Margaret.

Throughout the lows and highs of his reign, Richard's loyalty to Edward did not crumble and Richard never showed any animosity to the Woodville family. The only sign of any disagreement between the two brothers was detected following the truce with the French at Picquigny. Edward had raised a significant amount of money to fund a war against their constant enemy, France. For Edward, the novelty of war seemed to wear off quickly and he was easily bought off by the French King. Richard was believed to be disappointed with this decision and didn't attend any of the meetings or celebrations. This appears to be the limit of any acrimony between the brothers.

Richard was certainly well rewarded by his brother the king, for the loyalty he displayed. The titles and power he received would inevitably make him powerful enough to launch his own campaign to be the King of England in 1483.

Following Edward IV's success, Richard continued to achieve more and more power. In October 1461 he was made Duke of Gloucester and this was quickly followed by him being elected to the Order of the Garter. By October 1469 he had impressed Edward and was rewarded with the title of Constable of England.

He was creating a power base for himself in the north of England and this was consolidated by him earning the title warden of the West March towards Scotland and Chief Steward of the northern lands of the duchy of Lancaster. Through his marriage to Anne Neville he would acquire a large share of the lands previously owned by the Earl of Warwick.

Richard also appears to have impressed Edward with his military ability as he showed complete confidence in Richard. On 14 April 1471 Richard was given his first military command at the Battle of Barnet and was later given charge of the vanguard that fought against Margaret of Anjou's forces at the Battle of Tewkesbury. Success in this decisive battle restored Edward IV as king and saw the final defeat of Margaret of Anjou on behalf of Henry VI. After the battle was over, it was Richard as Constable who oversaw the trial of the Duke of Somerset, one of the leading supporters of Margaret of Anjou.

Even critics of Richard have accepted his military skill, as Dominic Mancini stated, '*Such was his renown in warfare that, whenever a difficult and dangerous policy had to be undertaken it would be entrusted to his discretion and his generalship.*'[ix]

Regarding his marriage, Richard would have met Anne Neville when he was living with the Earl of Warwick, her father. When Warwick began to oppose Edward IV, they found themselves on opposite sides. Anne was used to seal the agreement between Warwick and Margaret of Anjou when she was offered as a bride to her son Edward of Lancaster. Margaret of Anjou was finally defeated at the Battle of Tewkesbury where Edward of Lancaster, son of Margaret, and husband of Anne, was killed. At this time Anne would have been reunited with Richard. Why the marriage between Anne Neville and Richard, Duke of Gloucester took place is also subject to fierce debate. Ricardians would argue that the couple met as children when relations between the two families were closer.

They may, or do, see Richard as rescuing Anne from her ill-fated marriage to Edward of Lancaster, a marriage she may not have wanted, and they could finally be together, a true love match. Evidence to support this view would be the fact that she was always by his side when he needed support, they were crowned side by side and despaired over the death of their only son together. It was also due to Richard that Anne's mother was able to leave sanctuary and was reunited with her younger daughter. Together they would go on to have one child who would ultimately become Prince of Wales before his young death.

However, the match could be viewed as something far more calculating. Marrying Anne brought Richard a lot of lands previously held by the Earl of Warwick as well as increasing his popularity and securing him the support of those that had previously been loyal to the Earl of Warwick.

The marriage was a further thing that caused division between the three brothers. George, Duke of Clarence had married Anne's elder sister Isabel as part of the rebellion against Edward IV. George wanted to keep control of Anne so that he didn't have to share the Warwick estates. This caused a bitter dispute between George and Richard which ultimately led to Edward IV intervening, causing further resentment between him and his less loyal brother George.

The period that defines how most people view Richard III is that which follows the death of his brother. King Edward IV died at the age of 40 on 9 April 1483. Richard had always been unwaveringly loyal to Edward, which explains why, leaving a court full of factions and disputes he left the care of his sons and heirs to Richard.

Yet on 6 July 1483, it was Richard and his wife Anne that were being crowned, not his 12-year-old nephew, who had been deposed and remained languishing within the walls of the Tower of London, with his younger brother Richard, Duke of York.

Although there was no history of conflict between Richard and the Woodvilles it was clear that his nephew would be under the significant influence of the Woodville family. Edward had, as Prince of Wales, been sent to Ludlow with his own court, which was led by his other uncle, Earl Rivers, Anthony Woodville.

The Woodville's were already rumoured to have been behind the execution of George, Duke of Clarence and so it may have been that Richard feared the rule of a Woodville dominated, boy-king, despite the deathbed wishes of Edward IV. This is supported by Mancini who claimed that Edward V's stepbrother said 'we are so important that even without the King's uncle we can make and enforce our own decisions.'[x]

And so, it began, the battle for control of England. On one side the Woodvilles, claiming control over the 12-year-old king and on the other Richard and those who were no friends of the king's maternal family.

Ultimately it was Richard who successfully outmanoeuvred his opponents. On 22 June1484 a sermon was given where it was declared that the sons of Edward IV were illegitimate. It was claimed that when Edward IV married Elizabeth Woodville he was already pre-contracted to marry another, thought to have been Eleanor Talbot.

The Duke of Buckingham guided the leading citizens of London to draw up a petition asking Richard to take the Crown and on 6 July he was crowned King of England.

As historians are divided over the fate of the boys so too are they divided regarding how Richard became king, debating whether he was forced to act due to the threatening behaviour of Elizabeth Woodville and her relatives or whether he always coveted the crown his brother wore.

After this, the sons of Edward IV, kept in the Tower, started to be seen less and less until rumours about their fate began to circulate, starting a mystery that still endures.

Chapter 2 – The Case Against Richard III

We will now consider the evidence that supports the argument that the princes were murdered by their uncle, Richard III. When the police are looking for a suspect, they will examine three key criteria, who had the means to commit the crime, who had the opportunity to commit the crime and ultimately, who had a motive.

The prosecution could state that Richard's motive for killing the princes was that they were a threat to his new position as King of England. One of the most famous of Richard's accusers, Thomas More, claimed *'And forsomuch as his mind gave him that, his nephew living, men would not reckon that he could have the right to the realm.'*[xi] Richard had only become king by deposing his young nephew, Edward V. Whilst they were alive, supporters of Edward IV could lead rebellions in the name of Edward V.

The reality of this concern for Richard appears to be confirmed by another chronicler, Polydore Vergil. Writing after the death of Richard III he claimed there were many people who wanted to free the princes and an attempt was believed to have been made in July 1483, around the same time as the last reported sighting of the boys.
Richard had declared them to be illegitimate due to King Edward IV having been pre-contracted to another lady before he married his future Queen, Elizabeth Woodville. It was also claimed that he had it reported that his brother, the late king was also illegitimate, the result of an adulterous affair between Richard's mother and an archer in France.
If this was the case, the boys were illegitimate and the sons of a man who should never have been the rightful king.

Surely, once the king made the boys illegitimate and crushed the attempts to free the princes he was as secure as possible. However, Richard III would have been all too familiar with the story of William I, also known as William the Conqueror and William the Bastard. William's illegitimacy had not prevented him from invading England to pursue a claim to be king and ultimately taking and keeping power. It was not impossible that Edward V, despite the claims about his birth could appear as a figurehead for opponents of Richard III.

Another possibility that threatened Richard's position was that the illegitimacy against the boys could have been repealed, as was done after Richard's death, by his successor, King Henry VII. It wasn't just the sons of Edward IV that were declared illegitimate; his daughters would also carry that stigma. The eldest daughter Elizabeth of York would, through marriage to Henry VII shake off the allegations of her status and become Queen of England.

Although it can be claimed that Richard became king legally, after being petitioned to take the throne, it cannot be denied that this was only due to the accusations of illegitimacy against the king's children and they clearly still posed a threat to Richard's reign.

Richard will also have been aware of the actions of two kings that may have led him to murder the boys. The first to be considered is King John. He murdered his young nephew to secure his position. Although this lost him some of his supporters, most people understood the brutal reality that King John had been faced with. It can be argued that Richard found himself in a similar position and may have believed, following the precedent of King John, that this was a legitimate course of action.

The other king to look at is King Henry VI. King Henry VI was only a small child when he became king. Due to this, Humphrey, Duke of Gloucester was named Protector until Henry was old enough to rule in his own right. As the king got older and surrounded himself with his own men, Duke Humphrey fell out of favour and was eventually killed, probably by his own nephew, the king. The similarities between this scenario and the situation Richard faced, especially as he was also Duke of Gloucester, surely could not have been lost on him. This could have been the factor that led him to believe that if the princes were alive, his own future and life were in significant danger.

In an Act of Parliament in 1475, Richard was given control of the remaining Neville lands if a male heir of John Montagu survived. There was one male heir, George Neville and Richard secured custody of the boy, whose survival was necessary for Richard's political and financial stability. Disaster struck for Richard in May 1483, a key event that might have affected Richard's decision to seize the throne. George Neville died. Losing these lands would destroy the power base in the north he had created for himself and he would be reliant on the goodwill of a Woodville dominated boy king to restore the lands to him and it was clearly not in the best interests of the Woodville family, to restore Richard to the status of most powerful person in the kingdom after the king.

Another factor that needs to be considered is that the last time the boys were seen they were under the 'protection' of Richard III. When Richard and the eldest of the boys, called Edward V arrived in London, Edward was sent to the Tower. He was later joined there by his younger brother. At the time, the Tower was considered a royal palace and it was normal for kings and queens to stay in the Tower prior to their coronation, so this did not in itself cause any concern.

It is likely though that this was not a normal stay in the Tower. Ultimately the boys had limited freedom as they were protected by the guards of Richard III and Henry Stafford, the Duke of Buckingham. Ultimately it was King Richard III that took responsibility for the welfare and security of the boys. Even if Richard cannot be found guilty of their murder, he must bear some responsibility, as their safety was his responsibility. If he did not murder them, he had certainly failed to protect them.

The response of Elizabeth Woodville, the mother of the princes, also suggests that there was a fear of how Richard would treat the family if he had power. On hearing that Richard had gained control of the young king and had his closest advisors arrested, Elizabeth collected as many belongings as she could and took her remaining children into sanctuary. This was the second time they had been forced into sanctuary. The first time she was awaiting Edward IV coming to rescue them and retain his kingdom. This time there was nobody to rescue her and she was isolated and waiting to see how events unfolded around her.

Richard had people watching sanctuary and so she had limited access to visitors and therefore to information about what was going on outside the walls of her self-imposed prison.

One visitor that she did receive was a physician called Lewis Caerleon. He was also the physician of Margaret Beaufort, the mother of Henry Tudor, who had been in exile for years as he was the closest thing to an heir that the House of Lancaster had left.

Margaret Beaufort used this contact to gain support from Elizabeth Woodville for a plot to overthrow Richard and replace him with her son, Henry Tudor. To encourage Elizabeth to support this plot it was agreed that Henry Tudor would marry the eldest daughter of Elizabeth and Edward IV, Elizabeth of York. This would restore Elizabeth Woodville to her role of Queen's Mother.

Some historians believe that Elizabeth Woodville would never have acted in this way unless she believed that her sons were dead. They also point to the fact that Richard had already killed one of her older sons and her brother, Anthony Woodville. Therefore, it would not be difficult for Elizabeth to accept that Richard could kill her younger sons to secure his position as King of England. Certainly, her involvement in the plot showed that Elizabeth Woodville wanted to bring down the king who had usurped her young son, by whatever means necessary.

This argument is weakened by consideration of the future conduct of Elizabeth Woodville. In 1484, after receiving a promise from Richard III that herself and her daughters would be safe, they emerged from sanctuary and the daughters attended Richard's court.

There has been a significant debate over why Elizabeth did this. It can be claimed that she would never have done this if she believed that he had killed her sons. If he had been ruthless enough to seize the Crown and kill the two young boys that posed a threat to him, why would she believe that his promise to not harm them would keep them safe?

The other side of the argument is that Elizabeth Woodville had no alternative. Richard III was a young king and could rule for decades whilst her and her family remained in sanctuary. She needed to make amends with Richard to give her daughters a chance of a decent future. Elizabeth Woodville may have also wanted to improve her own position. She had been Queen of England and now she was in sanctuary, living off charity. She would also have been aware that it was her own husband who had set a precedent when he breached the safety of sanctuary following the battle of Tewkesbury.

The burden of keeping the royal family in sanctuary may also have been becoming too much and this may have forced Elizabeth Woodville to come to terms with the new king.

Whilst there may have been practical factors that led to Elizabeth and her daughters coming out of sanctuary, it also has to be considered that at this point, Henry Tudor was still a real threat to Richard III, so there was still hope that Richard would be overthrown and they could emerge from sanctuary sure of their safety.

As well as sending her daughters to Richard's royal court, Elizabeth Woodville also wrote to her adult son who had sought safety in exile with Henry Tudor, advising him to abandon Henry Tudor and come back to England and join Richard. If we accept that she had no choice but to release her daughters into Richard's care, that in itself does not explain why she encouraged her remaining son to leave safety and return to the cause of the man who killed his brothers. We must also consider that Elizabeth Woodville never publicly blamed Richard III for the death of her sons, even after his death, when such an accusation would have helped to secure the future of Henry VII and his Queen, Elizabeth of York, Elizabeth's own daughter.

There are also no records of Elizabeth Woodville ordering funeral masses for the boys after 1483. If they had been subject to a murder it would have been more important than ever to ease the passage of their troubled souls through purgatory. Yet we can find no record that this was put in place. A further motive to be considered in the case against Richard relates to the execution of his brother, George, Duke of Clarence. George had a difficult relationship with Edward IV, Elizabeth Woodville, and his younger brother Richard. He had conspired with The Earl of Warwick to take power for themselves and even to restore Henry VI as king. Despite Clarence being reconciled to the family, relations remained tense.

The mutual hatred between Clarence and the Woodvilles increased and ultimately his behaviour became so erratic that he ended up being tried for treason and found guilty. He was sentenced to death and it is believed that he could choose the manner of his death.

Edward IV had now ordered the death of his own brother and the brother of Richard. Could Richard have ordered the death of his nephews as an act of revenge against the family he believed to be responsible for his own brother's death?
The chronicler Mancini seems to imply this when he tells us that Richard was overcome with grief and vowed to avenge the death of his brother, Clarence. He stated that Richard stayed in the north after this event to avoid the jealousy of the Queen.[xii]

This reaction to Clarence's death appears to be supported by a letter that was sent to James Fitzgerald, Earl of Desmond.[xiii] In the letter it is believed to have stated that he had to keep his inward feelings hidden.

Not everybody believed that Richard was as devastated about Clarence's death as Mancini would have us believe. Richard went on to benefit more than anybody else from the death. This does not mean that he wasn't upset about it, but Thomas More goes further than highlighting the benefit to Richard by claiming that he helped bring about the death in the first place.[xiv]

There is no evidence to suggest that this is true; but it is true that the brothers had their own difficulties. The decision to collude with Warwick caused a gulf between the three brothers that could never be truly healed.

A further source of tension was the distribution of the Neville lands. At the height of his conspiracy with Warwick, George married his daughter, Isabel. Isabel's sister Anne had been married to Margaret of Anjou's son, Edward, Prince of Wales, who had been killed in battle at Tewkesbury. Following this, George secured custody of his sister-in-law to allow him to control her share of the inheritance.

When Gloucester decided to marry Anne Neville, this was opposed by George who knew that the lands he wanted to control would be shared. This was the start of a major dispute that would require Edward IV to step in and take control. On this basis, revenge over the death of Clarence does not appear to be a strong motive for killing the Princes in the Tower.

The main evidence implicating Richard III in the murder of the princes comes from chroniclers writing in the fifteenth and sixteenth centuries. Many of these Chroniclers report that it was believed the boys had been murdered by the cruel uncle. There are four main chroniclers that we shall consider as part of the case against Richard.

The first one to look at is Dominic Mancini[xv] as he was in England at the time of the events he was reporting on. Mancini was an Italian, believed to have been sent to provide reports back to the French on events in England.

He arrived in England sometime in late 1482 or early 1483. He had produced other pieces of literature and was considered an objective narrator of events. As an Italian, he is not considered to have any allegiance to any of the key figures involved in the shocking events occurring in London. Therefore, the prosecution would assert that the work of Dominic Mancini is an impartial, balanced account.

Mancini also appears to have good, inside knowledge, providing information given to him by Dr John Argentine, the physician of Edward V. Argentine is reported as telling Mancini that Edward 'Like a victim prepared for sacrifice, sought remission of his sins by daily confession and penance because he believed that death was facing him'
Mancini also tells us that he saw grown men moved to tears at the thought of what had happened to the boys. It could be claimed that this impartial account of events supports the case that Richard killed the princes.

However, when relying on this text there are several factors that need to be taken into consideration. As a native of Italy, it is likely that Mancini spoke little English and therefore may have relied on rumours among the Italian merchants for the information he gathered.

Mancini's account also contains errors such as the date of the death of Edward IV, placing it two days earlier than it happened. Errors such as this limit the weight that can be placed on it as evidence of the events that occurred.

Mancini also lacks significant detail in his account. There is a lack of many other dates provided in his work and although he repeats the words of Dr John Argentine, few other sources are named and therefore it would be hard to verify the accuracy of the narration he has provided.

Mancini left the country and returned to France shortly after the coronation of Richard III and completed the work later that year. Although it could be claimed that it was completed in a timeframe that still makes it relevant as an eye-witness account, Mancini himself had admitted to errors in his memory and writing after the event could have caused inaccuracy in his version of events.

Another problem with Mancini's account is that it might not be as objective as initially believed. One of the few sources we know he consulted was Dr John Argentine who cared for Edward V and could be considered a biased source, considering Richard III had deposed the boy he was looking after. The lack of detail regarding this encounter with Dr John Argentine is also important. He states that Edward believed he was facing death. If you combine this with the fact that he had a doctor in attendance could this mean that at least one of the boys was ill? Child mortality was a significantly different issue in 1483 than it is today.

In terms of allowing us to identify whether Richard III was guilty of murdering the boys, the account does not take us much further. At no point does he confirm what has happened to the boys.

The next writer we shall consider is Polydore Vergil.[xvi] Vergil came to England in 1502 and wrote his history for Henry VII in 1506. Vergil gives us more information on the fate of the Princes than Mancini did. Vergil states that Richard '*by any kind of meane he determynyd by death to dispatche his nephews, because so long as they lyvyd he could never be out of hazard.*'[xvii] This appears to confirm the motive of Richard III; he thought his nephews would always be a threat to him whilst they were alive.

Vergil also indicates that Richard III was capable of this act by giving details of other acts he was responsible for. For the first time, he is accused of murdering Henry VI whilst he was a prisoner in the Tower. Richard is also accused of killing Edward of Lancaster, not on the field of battle, but in cold blood after the fighting had stopped.

Vergil's account clearly shows Richard III to be ruthless and calculating and easily capable of despatching his nephews to obtain the prize of becoming King of England.

A further accusation is made against Richard by Vergil. According to this account Richard had it publicly proclaimed that his late brother was not fit to be king because he was the result of an adulterous affair that their mother had and was illegitimate. Vergil tells us of the upset that Cecily Neville felt and how she complained of the slander that was done to her by her own son. Not only is this account new, it differs completely from the version of Mancini, who claims it was Cecily herself who had claimed Edward IV was illegitimate. When assessing the evidence provided by Vergil, we must remember that he was not in England when these events happened and must have been basing his history on second-hand accounts.

Vergil had been recommended to Henry VII and was asked to write the history for him. This reduces the importance of this piece of work as he was acting for the person who had killed Richard III and taken the throne for himself. Vergil would have been eager to please his patron. The Tudor dynasty was new and based on a tenuous claim to the throne, the worse they could make Richard look, the easier it would become to justify the way they came to power.

One thing that is noticeable in the account of Vergil is the clear knowledge he appears to have of the inner thoughts of Richard, a man he can never have met. At one point he claims, *'Richard duke of Gloucestre who thought of nothing but tyranny and crueltie'*.

Is Vergil reporting on events that have become clearer over time or is he an example of how much a legend can grow based on rumour, propaganda, and political allegiance?

The third commentator to be considered is Thomas More.[xviii] As a child growing up learning about the Tudors, to me Thomas More was the principled man of government who died for his beliefs, refusing to recognise Henry VIII as head of the Church of England.

More was also responsible for producing Utopia, a piece of writing that won him critical acclaim. Therefore, his History of Richard III must be given serious scrutiny.

As with Vergil, More goes on to give extra information about the disappearance of the princes and the crimes and bad acts of Richard III. In More's account, whilst on progress, Richard sent word to the Constable of the Tower, Robert Brackenbury that he wanted him to murder the boys. Brackenbury was horrified and refused the request of his king. In response somebody pointed out James Tyrell to Richard and said he would carry out the task. So, James Tyrell was sent to the Tower with an order for Brackenbury to hand over the keys for one night. He enlisted the help of two others and the boys were suffocated and buried under a staircase in the Tower.

More's account goes on to claim that Tyrell was knighted for these murders and many years later confessed to the deed. More expands further on Richard's evil nature, now claiming that he was pleased that his brother George was killed and describes Richard as *'malicious, wrathful and envious'* More's account therefore appears to clear up both what happened to the princes and that it was indeed Richard who was guilty. Not as far as the defence is concerned. When relying on this account as evidence it must be remembered that this was written in 1513, 30 years after the disappearance, when More himself had been only eight years of age.

Again, it appears as though this account must have been based on second-hand information passed down to him. One of the people More was familiar with was Bishop John Morton. Morton had been accused of plotting against Richard III in 1483 and would certainly not have had anything positive about the former king to pass on to More.

Again, there are significant errors in the account. At the very beginning More states that Edward IV died at the age of 53, when we know he died at the age of 40. More claims that Tyrell was knighted for killing the princes, but he was knighted by Edward IV after the Battle of Tewkesbury. More also claims that Brackenbury was horrified by the order of Richard to kill the boys. However, despite this, Brackenbury remained loyal to Richard and died at his side fighting for him at Bosworth. It is also strange that there is no record anywhere else of the confession of James Tyrell. The only record of any confession is in this account. It was never published to the benefit of Henry VII and to secure the Tudor dynasty. He also notes that another one of the killers, Dighton confessed and was released. This account would have us believe that James Tyrell and Dighton both confessed to killing a king, a king who was the brother of Henry VII's Queen, and one was released without any penalty and Tyrell was executed for a separate offence.

The final writer that I shall consider is John Rous,[xix] the Neville family chronicler. He had always been an admirer of the Earl of Warwick and wrote flatteringly of Anne Neville.

During the reign of Richard III, Rous described him as, '*The most mighty prince Richard by the grace of God*', who ruled his subjects well and punished offenders of the law. Following the defeat of Richard III and accession of Henry VII after Bosworth, Rous began to sing a much different tune. Now Richard as king was excessively cruel and he stated that Cecily Neville was pregnant with Richard for two years and when he emerged, he had teeth and hair down to his shoulders.

This is the most obvious example of history being written by the winners. Writers at the time wanted to please the ruler. When Richard III was king, Rous was full of praise, but when Henry VII took over, those words of praise became embarrassing and dangerous to Rous, who, accepting the reality of the situation, could be considered to have fallen in line with the new version of events, and version of Richard, that the new Tudor dynasty were happy to present.
What is clear is that when considering the evidence from chroniclers, all may not be what is seems. Although they appear to agree that Richard was responsible, they differ regarding what he did, some give no detail, while others give detail without giving any real sources for their information. While chroniclers were happy to place blame with Richard, others believed the boys had been removed to safety, others believed it was the Duke of Buckingham. One rumour was displaced by another. Both suspects were dead and could not defend themselves at a time when propaganda was increasingly being used.
Richard III had previously used it to try to destroy support for Henry Tudor, using illegitimacy in his family line against him.
 Whereas stories that Richard killed his nephews could have been used to make his followers revolt and join the rebellion.

Chroniclers were writing based on supposition as there were no hard facts on which they could rely. Whilst it may be argued that those rumours were an indication of what the public believed, it still amounts to gossip, which is unreliable, and designed to influence opinion.

After considering the evidence against him, it is considered that Richard clearly had the means, motive, and opportunity to commit the crime. It is also clear that he has been the main suspect in this case based on circumstantial evidence and speculation.

We will now consider the evidence in defence of Richard III.

Chapter 3 Richard III – The Case for the Defence

Having considered the evidence used to support the claim that Richard III killed the Princes, we will now assess the evidence that is used to show that Richard did not commit the act he has been accused of for over 500 years.

In the prosecution case it was noted that the motive for the murder was that the boys were a threat to Richard III as king. If this was indeed the motive for Richard killing them, we must consider why he killed the two boys and left seventeen other potential threats alive. Edward IV had five daughters who were still alive and surely posed a similar threat to Richard. If the illegitimacy against the sons could have been repealed, so it could also have been repealed against the daughters. We already know that plans were being made to marry Elizabeth of York to Henry Tudor to strengthen his claim to the throne which would have made her a real threat to Richard.

Another threat to Richard was from the son of George, Duke of Clarence. Edward, Earl of Warwick had a stronger claim to the throne than Richard III but had been prevented from taking the throne due to the attainder against his father. As with the legitimacy of the princes, the attainder could have been reversed. When Clarence had joined forces with Richard, Earl of Warwick and ultimately Margaret of Anjou, he passed on to his heirs a claim to the throne through the House of Lancaster.

Rather than treating his rivals ruthlessly there is evidence to demonstrate that he treated family rivals with great care. In March 1484 Richard made assurances to Elizabeth Woodville that he would take care of her daughters and herself if they came out of sanctuary. Despite the plotting to marry Elizabeth of York to Henry Tudor, young Elizabeth was received at court and Richard was believed to be working on suitable marriages for her and her younger sister Cecily.

Edward, Earl of Warwick also prospered under Richard III's reign. Edward was knighted by Richard, in York, in September 1483 and some historians have suggested that he was named as Richard's heir following the sudden death of his only son, Edward, Prince of Wales.

When Richard created the Council of the North to administer justice, he left it under the control of another nephew, John de la Pole, Earl of Lincoln. This gave Lincoln a clear chance to create a northern power base as Richard himself had done before becoming king.

All seventeen family rivals went on to outlive Richard III. Does it make sense that Richard would kill two threats and treat others with favour?

The prosecution may choose to argue that Richard did not see the daughters of Edward IV as a threat. England had never had a successful female heir and may not have feared that the people would rise in rebellion to put one of Edward IV's daughters on the throne in his place. This argument is flawed by the very fact of Elizabeth of York's proposed marriage to Henry Tudor, considered to be the Lancastrian heir and gaining considerable support for his invasion.

Maybe Richard killed the boys but was haunted by what he had done or was aware of the rumours regarding the boys and how bad it was for his reputation. Maybe this forced him to change strategy. To avoid further bloodshed, he decided to keep those that posed a threat to him close so that he could monitor them and treat them with favour to give them less reason to turn upon him. This is a popular strategy amongst politicians nowadays most strikingly when Tony Blair was forced to make his great foe Gordon Brown Chancellor of the Exchequer or when Teresa May was forced to allow Boris Johnson to join the Cabinet to try and keep enough support to retain her power.

Another piece of evidence to be used in Richard's defence is the fact that he never confirmed their deaths. If it is accepted that his motive was that the boys posed a threat to his reign, couldn't this threat only be truly extinguished if it were well known that the boys were dead?

If people still believed that there was a chance that they were still alive, there was still the opportunity for people to rebel in their names and try to overthrow Richard III. He gains no benefit from killing them unless it is widely known that they are dead and can no longer be used to replace him. Yet he appears to have neither acknowledged their disappearance nor announced their deaths. The threat from the princes was still very real.

Richard's behaviour can be compared to that of his successor, Henry VII. During his reign he was confronted with Lambert Simnel, considered to be an imposter, claiming to be Edward, Earl of Warwick. To stop this threat from gaining momentum, Henry VII removed the real Edward, Earl of Warwick from the Tower and presented him to his court so people knew that Lambert Simnel was a fake.

There were options available to Richard at this point. He could have claimed they had died of natural causes, which was far more plausible in 1483 than it would be now. This would give him the opportunity to gain sympathy from the public for the loss of family members whilst allowing him to avoid any blame for their deaths. In Thomas More's account he states that before giving up her youngest son from sanctuary Elizabeth Woodville stated, *'if the child in his sickness miscarried by nature, yet might he run into slander and suspicion of fraud.'*[xx] We also know from Mancini that Edward was under the care of Dr John Argentine and believed he was facing death.

Richard could have been honest and admitted they had been killed. He himself had grown up in a ruthless period of conflict and could have claimed that he took necessary action for the stability of the country. King John had previously killed his young nephew for the same reason and whilst some people were appalled by the act, they understood the reasoning behind it. Although it was a risk, Richard could have been seen in that time as a strong king who had eliminated opposition for the sake of his country and people. Importantly it would have stopped the rumours and put an end to the speculation once and for all, instead of maintaining an enduring mystery which is still debated all these centuries later.

Against this it could be argued that he was vulnerable having just taken the throne from the son of a late, popular monarch. If he admitted to killing those boys, it was equally possible that the people and the supporters he relied on to keep him in power would have turned on him.

Maybe Richard believed that the best way forward for his future and reputation was to hope that if the boys were out of sight people would forget about them and he wouldn't then have to make the announcement that could ruin his future and reputation. Here was a king that was faced with the choice of staying quiet and being plagued by fear of rebellion in their name or facing the possibility of becoming known as the hated child killer, he has pretty much been presented as since 1485. If Richard believed it was too risky to announce that he had killed the boys, he was given a perfect opportunity in November 1483.

Henry Stafford, Duke of Buckingham was complicit in the events that led to Richard being offered the Crown and was considered one of Richard's closest allies. He did well under Richard. He had been excluded from royal favour under Edward IV and felt humiliated when he was forced to marry one of Elizabeth Woodville's sisters. He was from an important noble family and believed the marriage was beneath him.

In September 1484, a rebellion against Richard broke out. It would later be called Buckingham's Rebellion, but the initial aim had been to reinstate Edward V as king. During the rebellion, rumours would start that the boys had been killed and the aim of the rebellion would change to support Henry Tudor's challenge for the throne.

Buckingham was betrayed and Richard succeeded in destroying the rebellion. The Duke of Buckingham was captured and executed on 2 November 1483. This execution gave Richard a golden opportunity. He was outraged at the betrayal and with Buckingham dead, he could have confirmed the rumours of the boys' deaths and pinned the blame squarely on his former ally. Richard could emerge free from the threat of Edward V that had caused the rebellion and more importantly, free from blame.

Although the rebellion had started in the name of Edward V, it ended up championing Henry Tudor. Blaming Buckingham could also lead to the inference that Henry Tudor was involved and cause the Yorkist support he had gathered to desert him.

On the other hand, it could be argued that this was not an option open to Richard. If he tried to blame Buckingham and by implication Henry Tudor, Richard's opponents would fight back, still claiming that it was Richard who had them under his control and he was the one who had killed them. It is unlikely that if Richard did kill them, he would have done it himself so there would be people out there that knew the true story of what happened to the boys. The betrayal of Buckingham would have left Richard sure that he could trust nobody and that those involved could also turn against him. Surely, the only reason for Richard not blaming Henry Stafford was that there was nothing to blame him for; that Richard still believed the boys were alive.

One piece of evidence the defence would rely on is the reaction of Henry Tudor when he was successful at the Battle of Bosworth and became King Henry VII.

Once Henry entered London as king there was plenty of time for him to order that the Tower be extensively searched for any sign of the boys or their fate. There is no record of this happening.

There was time for Henry VII to order an investigation into their fate, again there is no record of such an investigation. Again, this was the perfect situation for Henry VII. He could declare them to be dead, preventing any further rebellions, against his weak claim to the throne, in the name of the boys. He could also use it as a massive publicity stunt to blacken further the name of Richard III; but he chose not to.

At this point Henry Tudor had the most to lose by the boys being alive. He knew that his claim to the throne was weak and wanted to strengthen it by marrying Elizabeth of York. To do this effectively he needed to repeal the Titulus Regius and make the children of Edward IV legitimate again. Henry would have been aware that if he did this, he would also be acknowledging that her brothers were legitimate and therefore had a much stronger claim to the throne.

If he knew or believed that Richard III had killed the boys, his failure to make it public and strengthen his position makes little sense.

However, The Act of Attainder against Richard does mention the shedding of infants' blood. The prosecution would argue that this is his declaration that Richard III killed his nephews. Maybe Henry was sensitive to the instability in the country since the death of Edward IV and wanted to focus on the future. He wanted people to focus on the new reign of the Tudor's rather than reopen speculation and rumour regarding the deaths of the boys who should be occupying the throne he now sat on.

Richard's relationship with his mother also indicates that he was not responsible for killing the boys who were her grandchildren.

Although claims are made that Cecily Neville complained about Richard slandering her by claiming that Edward IV was the result of adulterous relationship there is evidence that this was not the case.

Letters between Richard and his mother after he took the throne demonstrate affection and respect between the pair. A lot of the meetings that led to Richard III taking the crown took place at the home of his mother and this suggests that the events had her support and that she had a prominent role in events. Clements Markham goes further and states *'Richard so far as appears, can have given his mother neither anxiety nor sorrow.'*[xxi]

Cecily Neville never supported the marriage between Edward IV and Elizabeth Woodville and may have felt that the lesser of two evils was to support her son over a child who had been dominated by his overbearing Woodville relatives.

The prosecution could also argue that she may have been forced to sanction Richard's actions. If we believe that he was an evil tyrant who pressurised women out of lands and could kill his own nephews, is it not also possible that he forced his mother to accept his rule and the murder of her grandchildren whether she liked it or not?

Religion is another factor that needs to be considered at this stage. Richard III was a pious man. Michael Jones states that Henry VII recovered Richard's Book of Hours and gave it as a present to his very pious mother, Margaret Beaufort.[xxii] He also planned to set up a large chantry at York Minster. The size of this would mean that masses were virtually continually being said for his soul. Although this can be argued as the acts of a truly devout man, another motive for the chantry can be constructed.

The size of the chantry may not have been a demonstration of his religious beliefs, it could have been a sign that Richard had committed unspeakable acts and knew that his soul would need as much help as possible.

Certainly, at the time, people believed that religion demonstrated Richard III's guilt. The death of his young son was seen by his opponents as divine retribution as was his own death at Bosworth. In the fifteenth century people believed in the divine right of kings. Richard's death, the end of his reign, was God's judgement on him and on the new, deserving king, Henry VII.

After assessing all the evidence regarding Richard III's involvement in the murders of his nephews he did indeed have the means, motive, and opportunity to kill the boys. What else is clear though, is that there are no substantial pieces of evidence to support the long-held belief that Richard III killed them. There is nothing that appears to justify the impassioned arguments of innocence or guilt still fiercely debated today. We are reliant on the representations of people like Mancini, Vergil and More, whose accounts grow ever more dramatic and sensational like the tabloid newspapers of today. These accounts need to be treated carefully. It is possible that these accounts were true, and these narrators accessed relevant documents and sources to uncover the truth of what happened to the princes. It is equally possible that they did not.

On 17 December 2010, a landscape architect disappeared in Bristol. On Christmas day her body was found, and it was confirmed that she had been murdered. During the search and following the recovery of her body her landlord was arrested and released without charge. The tabloid press started to print stories about her landlord and suddenly they were buying stories of his alleged strange behaviour. He soon changed from an individual quietly living his life to villain. He was vilified purely because of his appearance and the way he lived his life. The press interest in him led to his life changing overnight. He later complained to the Levenson enquiry and was successful in all lawsuits against the papers concerned.

Subsequently, her killer was found, convicted, and sentenced. Her landlord was exonerated completely. If they had not found the killer would the accounts of the British newspapers be used the same way as Mancini, Vergil and More's accounts may have been, to condemn in the court of popular opinion, an innocent man?

Chapter 4 Margaret Beaufort - Background

Could a mother's love and regal ambition for her son lead her to murder another mother's sons in the game of thrones?

Although she is considerably less infamous than Richard III, Margaret Beaufort was another figure that people have strong opinions about.

Margaret Beaufort was a 13-year-old widow when she gave birth to her only child, Henry Tudor, who was forced into exile for most of his life by the House of York. Margaret's devotion to her son was obvious Here we will examine whether regal ambitions for Henry, and her vital connections through her last husband, forced her to stack the deck in her son's favour. Would she take the cruel step of murdering the boys or would her pious devotion allow her to use the power of prayer to let God's will play out?

Margaret Beaufort, the ultimate founder of the Tudor dynasty was born on 31 May 1443 at Bletsoe Castle. Her mother was Margaret Beauchamp, the daughter of Sir John Beauchamp. Before marrying Margaret's father, she had previously been married to Sir Oliver St John with whom she had seven children before he died.

Margaret Beauchamp's second marriage was to John Beaufort, the Duke of Somerset. He was the grandson of John of Gaunt and Katherine Swynford. John of Gaunt married Katherine many years after the children were born so John Beaufort, Margaret's grandather was illegitimate. Efforts had been made to legitimise the status of the children. Richard II declared them legitimate in statute in 1397.

Henry IV would later amend this to add words that would exempt the Beaufort family from claiming the throne and it is doubtful that anybody saw the Beaufort's as any threat to the king.

By the time he met Margaret Beauchamp, John Beaufort was bitter and disillusioned. He had been caught and held for ramson which had not been paid for many years. Over the years Beaufort had continually been disappointed, the release he thought was close never coming.

Things appeared to be changing for John Beaufort. He was married, had a daughter and was due to lead a military expedition into France, with the high esteem of the king. It was not long before what became known as Fortune's wheel took another turn. Margaret Beaufort was not yet one when her father returned from France in disgrace, considered an embarrassment. He would soon die, with some suggesting he took his own life.

Margaret would now become a wealthy heiress but still had to weather the storm of her father's dishonour. The first issue that needed to be resolved was who would be granted the wardship of the young heiress now her father had died.
The king decided that responsibility for Margaret should be given to his most favoured councillor, Willian de la Pole, the Duke of Suffolk, although she was allowed to continue living with her mother, rather than being sent to live with William and his family. Aware of the value of her estates, William de la Pole arranged for Margaret to be married at the age of six, to his own son who was only eight years old himself.

It would not be long before Margaret would have to navigate her way out of another scandal, as Suffolk was accused of *'marriage of Margarete, daughter and heir of John the late Duke of Somerset, purposing her to marry to heis said sonne, presuming and pretendying her to be nexte enheritable to the corone of this your realm.'*[xxiii] Suffolk was exiled from England, and on his journey was intercepted and murdered.

Margaret was again vulnerable, and again, had to wait for her fate to be determined, as the king decided who to award her wardship to for a second time. Before making this decision Henry VI invited Margaret and her mother to court. During this visit Henry VI made arrangements for Margaret that would ultimately change the course of English history. Margaret's wardship was given to Edmund and Jasper Tudor, the king's own half-brothers. She now moved closer to the throne and would receive an intensive education.

Edmund and Jasper Tudor were related to the King of England, but were themselves, wholly lacking in English royal blood. Following the death of Henry V, his young widow had entered a secret marriage with Owen Tudor. Together they had three children, Edmund, Jasper and Owen. Despite the disapproval the marriage had caused, Henry VI cared for his half-brothers, raising the status of Edmund and Jasper as Earl of Richmond and Earl of Pembroke, respectively.
Edmund and Jasper had gained significantly through the patronage of the king, but they would both have been aware of the estates, the wealthy heiress Margaret Beaufort could bring them, and Henry VI indicated that he would like Margaret to marry Edmund Tudor.

For Margaret this was a problem. She had already been married at the age of six to Suffolk's son and now she wrestled with what she should do and sought spiritual guidance from St Nicholas. Margaret would claim that at night she was visited by St Nicholas who advised her she should marry Edmund Tudor.[xxiv] Her childhood marriage was annulled and on 1 November 1455, now aged 12, she married Edmund Tudor and became sister-in-law to the King of England. Keen to produce an heir and secure the estates of his young wife, Edmund insisted on consummating his marriage to the slight 12-year-old immediately.

Despite his efforts to produce an heir and claim his wife's estates, Edmund Tudor would not live to see the son he had so desired. As troubles escalated between the ruling House of Lancaster and the disgruntled House of York, Edmund was captured. Although he would be released, he was struck down with illness and died on 1 November 1456.

Margaret Beaufort now found herself widowed, heavily pregnant and vulnerable again when she was still only 13 years of age. Margaret sought protection from Jasper Tudor at Pembroke Castle. It was here that her son Henry Tudor, the new Earl of Richmond was born on 28 January 1457. Aware that she required some form of protection from the turbulent forces taking hold of the country, and with a new son to protect, Margaret knew she needed a new husband and she needed to find him quickly. There was one nobleman in the country that was almost as powerful as Richard, Duke of York and that was Humphrey Stafford. Jasper Tudor and Margaret Beaufort headed for Stafford's house where they would arrange what would be Margaret's third marriage. As soon as the required period of mourning for Edmund Tudor was completed, Margaret would marry Humphrey's second son Henry Stafford. The couple were married on 3 January 1458 and the couple are believed to have resided together at their residence in Bourne, Lincolnshire.

Margaret clearly arranged this marriage for purposes of practicality and safety, but there were also signs of affection between the couple, who would have no children together. Fortune's wheel would continue to taunt Margaret as the Wars of the Roses continued to tear the country apart. Margaret witnessed the deposition of Henry VI, her brother-in-law, and the crowning of Edward IV from the House of York. Her husband had fought for the king at Towton, and although he was ultimately on the losing side, he survived the battles and was subsequently pardoned by the new king.

Early into her second marriage to Henry Stafford, the new couple would certainly have had cause to worry when the House of Lancaster was deposed and Edward, Earl of March, from the House of York was proclaimed King Edward IV. Edward was clearly aware of Margaret Beaufort and Henry Tudor and their close affinity to Henry VI. He had pardoned Henry Stafford for fighting against him at Towton. There can be little doubt that Margaret feared for her future and what fate had in store for her. Her concerns could only have increased when Edward announced that he was confiscating her son's estates and the wardship of her young son was given to Lord Herbert, a close ally of the new king. She would now have to cope with her child being raised at the centre of the suspicious Yorkist regime. Although it appears that she could visit Henry, she would have had to accept that she now had little control of or knowledge of Henry's upbringing and childhood.

With regards to Margaret and her husband, Edward IV appears to have been more generous. Although he was likely suspicious of Margaret and her connections to Lancaster, and may not have fully trusted the couple, he did not take any active measures against her and even showed then limited favour.

Edward granted Margaret and her husband a manor in Woking which she would use to her full advantage. It was here that she would lavishly entertain the man who had taken pleasure in eliminating the rest of her family and who posed a threat to her only son.

All the good work Margaret had done cultivating the favour of the king would be tested by yet another reversal of fortune. In 1470 it was King Edward IV who had been forced to flee his kingdom at the hands of Henry VI and the man who had played an essential role in raising Edward to the throne, the Earl of Warwick.

As Henry VI began his second term as king, Margaret was reunited with her son. Confident that he was back for good, Margaret arranged to take young Henry to meet his uncle the king, who would apparently claim that one day Henry would himself be king. In the Wars of the Roses, Margaret was clearly nailing her colours to the Lancastrian mast.

Her husband however was not easily convinced. Despite her efforts to persuade him to fight for Henry VI, he was not to be swayed, and in 1471, he would fight alongside a reinvigorated Edward IV, determined to restore his own position once and for all.

This was a costly decision for both Henry Stafford and Margaret. During the fighting he was seriously injured and never fully recovered. He died in October 1471. He left behind Margaret, widowed a second time and at the hands of a regime that knew she could not be trusted. She had lost the only protection she had and to make matters worse, with Henry VI and his only heir, Edward of Lancaster dead, Edward IV's only rivals now were Margaret and her son, Henry. Acutely aware of the danger, Margaret asked Jasper Tudor to take Henry into exile with him. Without the protection of her husband, and with her son in exile, Margaret was truly alone.

As before, Margaret needed a marriage and she was going to make sure that she took control and found a husband who could protect her from the reach of the ever-suspicious Edward IV. The man she chose this time was Lord Thomas Stanley. He was considered a trusted supporter and more importantly, had established such a power base for himself in the north of England that any king would be wary of crossing him.

This marriage was a wise strategic move for Margaret and may have helped ease Edward's fears about her loyalty. Her interests were now entwined with his own success.

Stanley was increasingly gaining the trust and respect of the House of York and was rewarded with more authority and Margaret reaped the benefits, She was given an important role in the reburial of Richard, Duke of York and at the christening of the king's youngest daughter Bridget in 1480.

Gaining in confidence Margaret began petitioning the king to allow her son to return to England and to claim the lands owed to him as Earl of Richmond. In 1482 an agreement appeared to have been reached and there were even talks regarding a possible wedding between Henry Tudor and the king's daughter, Elizabeth of York. However, the agreement would come to nothing due to the untimely death of King Edward IV on 9 April 1483.

So close to achieving her wish of being reunited with her son, Margaret's hopes were dashed when the king's brother stunned everybody by deposing his nephew and becoming King Richard III.

For Margaret this was indeed a setback, but she appears to have immediately reopened negotiations with the new king. She was given the opportunity through the favour the new king showed to herself and Lord Stanley, who both played roles at the coronation.

However, Margaret may have never fully trusted Richard who was believed to be negotiating with Brittany, to have Henry Tudor handed over to him. At some point she started plotting against Richard and the flawed, failed rebellion of Buckingham, clearly exposed her role in the intriguing.

Margaret was named in a bill of attainder and she risked being sent to her death. Richard was aware of how much he needed to maintain Stanley's support, and this may explain why she escaped with being put under the guard of her husband and losing her properties to him. Stanley was expected to keep tight control over his wife so she could no longer communicate with rebels and ultimately her own son.

Despite these restrictions Margaret continued to correspond with her son and to raise support for his invasion. Her usually cautious husband appears to have given her significant leeway, despite the concerns of the king.

Whilst her marriages may have been based on strategy and navigating her way through the turbulent times facing her and the country at large, there can be no doubt that her relationship with her son was based on absolute love and adoration.

From the moment she gave birth to Henry Tudor, on 28 January 1457, she would devote her life to promoting the interests of her only child, her *'dearest joy in the world.'*[xxv] Even then, she was barely 13 and a widow, yet she moved quickly to secure a new marriage that would protect both her and her son. Margaret was only of slight build and a young teenager when she gave birth. The birth was incredibly difficult, and the religious Margaret may have believed that the fact that they both survived the ordeal was a miracle and a sign that Henry was destined for great things.

It has been claimed that after the birth, Jasper Tudor had the boy christened as Owen, after his own father. Margaret was annoyed by this and had him christened again this time named after his royal relative, the king.[xxvi] Whatever great fate awaited Henry; Margaret may have believed it was connected to his royal uncle.

Although Henry survived the birth, according to his first biographer Bernard Andre he was a weak and fragile child, who thrived under the care and devotion of his mother.[xxvii] It would be this lavish care that made him the man he became. To protect her son, Margaret had to enter a marriage that may have kept her apart from her son, who was raised under the stewardship of Jasper Tudor.

It was this arrangement that left Margaret desperately waiting for news as battle raged between the Houses of York and Lancaster in Wales, the home of her child. Her greatest fears would have appeared to have been confirmed when she heard that Jasper had been forced to flee and the close ally of Edward IV had taken control of Pembroke Castle and of an unsuspecting Henry Tudor.

Realising the significance of the young child, Herbert offered a substantial amount of money to the king for the wardship of the boy. Margaret's dear boy was now in the hands of Yorkist enemies and she was powerless to intervene, even as he was stripped of his estates.

Margaret was now a bystander to the upbringing of her own child and being able to choose his tutors and visit him occasionally would be small comfort to a mother who needed to be in control. Caroline Halstead would go on to claim that 'the personal sufferings of both parent and child were greatly aggravated by a premature and hopeless separation.'[xxviii]

Despite the distance between them, Henry was always her greatest focus, and every decision calculated to work in his best interests. Never was this more apparent than during the brief restoration of Henry VI. Margaret was delighted to be reunited with Henry, and of vital importance to Margaret was that she take Henry to meet his uncle, the king. Probably since they both survived his difficult birth; Margaret would have believed her son had been saved because he was destined for greatness. We cannot begin to imagine then, how Margaret would have felt if Henry VI did indeed prophesise that one day the kingdom of England would be ruled by the young boy in front of him.
By showing her loyalty to the House of Lancaster, Margaret undoubtedly took a calculated risk that would not end well.

Through her actions she had exposed her son to danger. Following the death of Henry VI and his son, Henry Tudor was now a key rival to Edward IV. This time she could not afford to take the risk that he would be well treated by the king. To protect him, she persuaded Jasper Tudor to take him out of the country into exile. This separation would be more difficult for both mother and son, but ultimately Margaret would have known it was the only way to guarantee his safety. Not only was she separated from her dear boy, but he was essentially a prisoner, dependant on the goodwill of the Duke of Brittany and the foreign policies of France and England towards Brittany.

Again, during this enforced separation, Margaret would prove to be unstoppable when it came to promoting her son. She was in contact with him, raised money and support for him and was probably responsible for warning him that Edward IV was proposing a marriage between him and the king's daughter Elizabeth as a trick to get custody of him.

There is no doubt that during 1483, she played a significant role in presenting Henry Tudor as a credible and potential candidate for the throne. Under suspicion by Richard III she would risk her own life to raise support for his cause and inevitable invasion.

By the time Henry Tudor became King Henry VII he had spent most of his life away from his mother. This did not stop them from being as close as any other mother and son. On landing in England and preparing to face Richard III in battle, Henry knew the person he should turn to for advice and immediately wrote to his mother. It was also to his mother that he turned following his victory at Bosworth, staying with her at Woking for two weeks.

The letters between the two show the depth of their affection for each other, with Margaret declaring Henry to be *'her greatest joy in the world'* and writing to the *'sweet and most dear King.'*[xxix]

Margaret was overwhelmed with emotion when she witnessed the coronation of another king, her beloved son. During the reign of Henry VII, Margaret, as the king's mother was often recorded to be at his side at formal events, at court and when the king was travelling. At one residence in Woodstock, they had adjoining rooms.

The biggest test of their relationship must have been when it was discovered that William Stanley had declared that he would not fight against Perkin Warbeck if it were believed he was truly the younger of the princes. William Stanley, Margaret's brother in law was executed for treason. Margaret and Thomas Stanley left court to deal with the loss. Margaret was soon joined by her son who travelled to Lathom to comfort her and assure her of the affection he still had for her and her husband.

Margaret was there for her son to the very end, moving in to help him deal with his grief when his wife, Elizabeth of York died.

Whilst most people would agree that she was devoted to her son and determined to find a great place for him in the English court, people are far more divided when it comes to the character of the woman who would become the mother of the Tudor dynasty.

Especially in later life, Margaret took pleasure in normal pursuits such as entertaining, playing chess and choir recitals. Margaret also took a lot of trouble to make sure she was immaculately presented.

Whilst people may disagree about the level of Margaret's piety, with some arguing that it bordered on fanatical, it is certainly true that she took her religious devotions more seriously than others. Delivering her funeral eulogy, Bishop Fisher claimed, *'she was not vengeful or cruel, to the church and God.'*[xxx]

Her religious piety may have started when she was a child, when both herself and her mother were admitted to Croyland Abbey, situated not far from the home of her mother. In Margaret's household, daily life and routine revolved around her religious devotions, with some claiming that she prayed so much that she injured her back and knees.

Her religious devotion may also explain her charitable work. Contemporary writers also claimed that Margaret was mindful of the suffering of others, given how much she had been through in her life, she may have been able to relate to the struggle others were enduring. It was claimed that she took responsibility for maintaining twelve poor people[xxxi] and even used part of one of her houses as a hospital wing to help the sick.[xxxii] There is significant evidence of a woman who used charity to improve the lives of others and to avoid conflict.

Whilst religion and charity clearly were important to Margaret and show us one side of her character, it is also clear that Margaret Beaufort was capable of being ruthless and determined when required. This side to Margaret appears to be demonstrated in the tale of her son being christened with the name Owen without her knowledge. Margaret was only 13 years old when she challenged Jasper Tudor, the person who she had turned to for protection, following the unexpected death of her husband.

Throughout her life she was the victim of the absurd twists and turns of fate. Yet, the way she went about arranging her marriages; marriages that offered her significant political advantages and protection show that she must be considered one of the most strong-willed and determined women of that era. She took absolute control of the destiny of herself and her only child.

When Henry became king, he sent the young Edward, Earl of Warwick to his mother, where she was in effect his guard. She was aware of the suffering her own son had endured as a captive of the Duke of Brittany. Yet, to protect her son and the new dynasty they were creating, she was ruthless enough to allow another innocent child to be jailed and to suffer an uncertain imprisonment.

The way Margaret navigated the political strife of the years up to 1485 clearly show that she was a woman who was astute and strategic. The marriage to Henry Stafford gave her protection from one of the greatest nobles in the kingdom. Her marriage to Thomas Stanley placed her at the heart of the Yorkist regime at a time when the king was suspicious of her motives and loyalty. When Richard III was crowned, she may already have been plotting against him in favour of her son. Despite this she entered negotiations with him to allow her son to return and played a prominent role alongside her husband at the Coronation ceremony.

As part of her intriguing she was able to persuade Elizabeth Woodville to become her ally and to allow her daughter to marry Henry Tudor when he invaded and took the throne for himself. George Buck in his defence of Richard III believed that Margaret was manipulating nobles and kings to secure her desires, accusing her of dissembling in her negotiations with Richard III.[xxxiii] Humphrey Brereton went even further describing Margaret of being treacherous.[xxxiv]

Throughout her life Margaret would indulge in behaviour which would lead to her being described as acquisitive, a trait that she would be noted as sharing with her son. Margaret was not only politically astute but demonstrated exceptional financial awareness.

As the king's mother she would actively pursue a family debt dating back nearly one hundred years. Her acquisitive nature also shows in the fact that whilst pursuing this long-standing debt she sued for more than was owed to her.

As she got older it may have been expected that Margaret would take a more passive role in the finances of her estates, but this was not the case for Margaret. Despite her charitable nature, Margaret would actively pursue the widows of servants who owed her money. Henry VII granted his mother the wardship of the Duke of Buckingham's sons who were incredibly wealthy. Margaret would use this to the advantage of herself and her own family.

The charge of acquisitiveness would be one faced by different generations of her family. Her father the Duke of Somerset was accused of using his excursion into French territory to improve his own finances. People writing about her son, following his reign, would also accuse him of being acquisitive and miserly.

When she became the mother of the King of England, Margaret entered the second phase of her life. After the struggles of the first, this phase would see her become the second most powerful woman in England.

On his accession to the throne, Margaret became the Countess of Richmond and Derby. Margaret played a pivotal role in making her son king of England and the evidence suggests that once she achieved this, she was not prepared to be a background figure. She was regularly at court or with her son, and when they were apart, they remained in close contact. The extent of her influence at court disappointed some. At one of her properties she created an administrative centre and acted as a Justice of the Peace.[xxxv]

Evidence of Margaret's life as mother of the king suggests that rank and status were important to Margaret. She was a keen supporter of Queen's College, as Margaret of Anjou, Elizabeth Woodville and Anne Neville had been before her.
Margaret spent a lot of money on her houses. In one of her properties she called the main room the Queen's Chamber and had her arms placed in the windows of Coldharbour house.[xxxvi]

During the reign of her son, she would wear identical clothes to the Queen, including crowns at special events and changed her signature to Margaret R, which could have been short for Richmond, but was believed to be a change to a more regal status. In what could be a symbol of the control Margaret liked to exert, she put down in writing several ordinances to be followed for certain occasions. This included births, marriages, and death, and interestingly, the king's mother was to wear everything like that of a queen.

Margaret's tumultuous life came to an end on 29 June 1509. She had outlived all her husband's and her son the king and she had created a dynasty that was now in the hands of her grandson, King Henry VIII. Would Margaret, the woman who injured herself praying so much take the step of killing two innocent boys to further the interests of herself and her beloved son?

Chapter 5 – The Case Against Margaret Beaufort

The main piece of evidence that requires the inclusion of Margaret Beaufort on the suspect list for the murder of the princes is her motive. Margaret Beaufort was a woman determined to advance the interests of her only child. Margaret was only a young teenager when she survived the difficult birth of Henry Tudor, a birth that Margaret did not expect to live through. Given her religious nature and tender years, Margaret may have considered their survival a miracle, a sign that her son was destined for a great role in the country and that she was needed to play an active role in bringing this about.

Margaret had previously shown herself susceptible to a more supernatural, mystic sense of religion, when she had to choose between marriage to William de la Pole's son and Edmund Tudor. History has it that Margaret asked for guidance and was advised to pray to St Nicholas. The next day she claimed that during the night he had appeared and told her she should marry Edmund Tudor.

The vision of St Nicholas and the miracle of the birth was followed by another incident that may have confirmed her thoughts about Henry's future. In 1470, when Henry VI was briefly restored to the throne, Margaret took her son to meet the king. At this meeting, the king apparently prophesised that one-day Henry Tudor would rule the kingdom.

Whether this is an accurate record of what was said, this may have been the point when Margaret started to believe and work towards the possibility of making Henry a credible heir to the throne. Although at this time Henry VI already had an heir, his son Edward of Lancaster.

The evidence we have of Margaret clearly shows that Henry was Margaret's greatest focus and she would never stop working towards making the best life possible for her son.

We have seen that she was a ruthless strategist when required and this combined with her devotion to Henry were a dangerous combination for anybody who stood in the way of what Margaret wanted for her son. Margaret 'fought like a tigress to advance the fortunes of her only son.'[xxxvii]

When Edward IV was restored to the throne, Margaret clearly believed that Henry Tudor and his Lancastrian ancestry posed a significant threat to the York dynasty. This is demonstrated by the fact that she did not believe that he was safe in England and persuaded Jasper Tudor to take her precious kin into exile with him.

It is also clear that through her plotting with Elizabeth Woodville, the Duke of Buckingham and those still loyal to the House of Lancaster, Margaret Beaufort was the person responsible for presenting Henry Tudor as a credible candidate to become the King of England. During what became known as Buckingham's rebellion the focus of the rebellion changed from rescuing the princes to preparing for an invasion led by Henry Tudor, aided by rumours of the death of the boys.

The key factor in Margaret's plot was that Henry Tudor would marry the eldest daughter of Edward IV, Elizabeth of York. This would strengthen Henry's tenuous claim to be a royal heir, and unite the Houses of York and Lancaster behind Henry's bid for power. Richard III had declared the children of Edward IV illegitimate in his parliament of 1484. For Margaret's plan to be most effective she would need the act declaring the children as illegitimate overturned. This would make Elizabeth of York a legitimate heir to the crown.

However, this posed a problem for Margaret, by restoring the legitimacy of Elizabeth of York, they would also be making her brothers, the princes legitimate. This would mean there were two people with a much stronger claim to the throne than both Henry and Elizabeth. For Margaret's plan to be effective, the princes needed to be dead.

After the failed rebellion of 1483 Margaret Beaufort was attainted for treason and was supposed to be kept under tight control by her husband Lord Stanley. It was clear Margaret was plotting and her motive clear; 'the throne of England for her only son.'[xxxviii]

Despite being in danger, Margaret continued to contact Henry, raise money for his invasion and encourage people to support his cause. She had already escaped with her life once and must have known that if she were caught again, she would not be so lucky a second time.

Chroniclers at the time were aware of the ambitious nature of the Beaufort family. The ruthlessness with which they would achieve their aims was demonstrated by the Duke of Somerset, when he burned down a church full of women and children who had opposed him.

Could a leading figure of the Beaufort family kill two boys to ensure the will of God was achieved and her son was proclaimed king, despite the stigma of their illegitimate line? As the king's mother, Margaret took on a very regal status of her own. It is also possible that she had always yearned to become royalty and knew that females were not trusted to rule kingdoms in medieval England. Therefore, she became the mother of a new dynasty, revelling in her new regal power. Although it is clear that Margaret's ardour in pursuing the best interests of Henry provide a clear motive for the murder, the idea of a Lancastrian revival after the deaths of Henry VI and Edward of Lancaster was still highly unlikely and only became a reality later in 1483.

Whilst this means that Margaret may not have been planning for this in advance, it doesn't rule out the possibility that she saw an opportunity and seized it at any cost. She had shown excellent strategy in her choice of husbands and dealing with the turns of the Wars of the Roses. It is not impossible that she saw the opportunity and did what was necessary to exploit it.

It could also be argued that we are reading too much into the talk of marriage between Henry Tudor and Elizabeth of York. Although such a union would undoubtedly help garner support for a Tudor invasion, it was also the case that Edward IV had previously entered into talks with Margaret regarding such a marriage. Although it is possible that Margaret was always planning and waiting for the right opportunity for Henry Tudor to make his move, it also has to be accepted that maybe she saw this marriage as good advancement for her son and was genuine in her desire to merely secure the return of Henry into England.

Although it may be the case that Margaret was genuinely negotiating for Henry's return, it cannot be denied that things changed significantly when Richard deposed his nephews and became Richard III. Any rumour of discontent amongst the people could have been seized upon to promote Henry as a credible candidate for the throne.

Another point in Margaret's defence is the support she received from Elizabeth Woodville. The only reason she could have had for supporting the invasion of Henry Tudor would be if she knew her boys were dead. However, given that her and Margaret Beaufort shared a physician, Lewis Caerleon, it would not have been difficult for Margaret to convince Elizabeth that the boys were dead, and that Richard was to blame. Elizabeth Woodville was in sanctuary, possibly guarded by Richard's forces. She would have had limited visitors and information about what was happening outside her shelter.

It also has to be taken into consideration that Elizabeth Woodville ended up reaching an agreement with Richard III and tried to get her son to return from exile and support the existing king. Could Elizabeth have realised that it was not Richard who had planned the execution of her sons, but the woman she had joined forces with, in a bid for the Crown for Henry Tudor? Was Margaret Beaufort able to convince Elizabeth because she knew that the boys were dead?

Another motive for the involvement of Margaret is her loyalty and support for the House of Lancaster. Margaret herself was from the illegitimate line of John of Gaunt and had married the half-brother of King Henry VI, Edmund Tudor. Despite appearing to accept the accession of the House of York, Margaret showed her true loyalty when Edward IV was forced into exile and Henry VI restored to the throne. Margaret used this as an opportunity to introduce her son to the Lancastrian king. Whatever happened at that meeting clearly Margaret began to see her son's destiny entwined with the fortunes of the House of York. Margaret may have felt required to avenge the death of Henry VI and his son and a duty to restore the line of Lancaster. As such she may have viewed herself as completely absolved from allegiance to the House of York and its heirs.

Despite the way that the House of Lancaster and her only Beaufort family had been eliminated by Edward IV, Margaret would also have been aware that whilst he was a ward of the Herbert's, Henry had been well treated and she had been allowed to visit him. She may have resented the fact that his estates were confiscated, but before the disappearance of the princes she had negotiated an agreement with Edward IV which would have seen Henry Tudor return to England and receive his estates. Edward IV had shown leniency to the child that was a threat to his security. Would Margaret have returned the favour to his sons?

There is also a question about Margaret's loyalty to the House of Lancaster. Political expediency had seen Margaret seek favour with the ruling house at the time. She received favour from the king and even entertained him at her manor in Woking. Through her marriage to Stanley she became a trusted figure in the Yorkist court and played a prominent role in the christening of Edward IV's youngest daughter Bridget. Margaret appears to have made peace with the new king, but was clearly skilled at hiding her true affiliation, except when it came to her son.

Another factor that may have caused Margaret to remove the boys, was the fear of Fortunes wheel. Belief in and fear of Fortune's wheel dates back to Cicero and was prevalent in medieval times. Fortune's gifts could be fleeting and withdrawn at any time. Fortune would spin her wheel at random and some would prosper whilst others suffered misfortune. Those favoured by Fortune knew this could be temporary and the next spin of the wheel could change their lives again.

Margaret's life appears to be a perfect example of Fortune's wheel dating back, before she was born, to the Battle of Bauge in 1421 when her father was captured and kept prisoner for 13 years. Margaret would constantly have to battle with the whims of Fortune, from the rumoured suicide and disgrace of her father, to becoming a vulnerable widow, forced to send her only child away into exile.

John Fisher captures this fear of Fortune's wheel in his eulogy of Margaret where he stated, '*Dare I say of her, she never yet was in that prosperity, but the greater it was the more always she dredde the adversyte.* [xxxix]
During her life she had seen herself in great favour, close to the king, only to see her Beaufort family and the King, Henry VI, eliminated.

Despite her fear of the whims of Fortune, Margaret always fought. When she was vulnerable, she decided to create her own fortune and created strategically important marriages that protected her and Henry Tudor.

Margaret knew how Fortune could turn and how kings were as susceptible to the gifts of Fortune as anybody else. Margaret had witnessed the defeat of Henry VI as he was replaced by Edward IV. She was actively aware of events that led to the restoration of Henry VI, whilst Edward IV was forced into exile. Again, Margaret appears to have been well informed of events throughout England as Edward IV returned from exile, fighting to be recognised as the rightful King of England once and for all. After this Edward IV had taken no more risks and eliminated the two main threats to his leadership, Henry VI, and his son. Events of 1483, where uncle would depose nephew took everybody by surprise and may have forced Margaret to act.

At some point Margaret started plotting to make her own son king. She was aware of the threat the young princes could pose to her son in the game of thrones, at the mercy of Fortune and her own games.

Margaret had shown she was willing to take the fight to Fortune, by facing misfortune head on, making decisions to further the interests of herself and her son. Margaret may have seen the killing of the princes as a way of righting the wrongs of the wheel of fortune and of giving her son the best chance to fulfil the prophecy of the late king

At the coronation of Henry Tudor and later at the marriage of her eldest grandson, Margaret is recorded as weeping uncontrollably. This has been considered to be the fear of how Fortune could take everything she had achieved away. The prosecution would argue that the uncontrollable emotion was the burden she was carrying of the steps she had been forced to take to make those pivotal ceremonies a reality.

When considering whether Margaret Beaufort had a motive to kill the Princes in the Tower, revenge must be an important factor. Although Margaret's son was still alive, because of Edward IV she had been forced to endure a long and painful separation from him.

She had missed out on most of his childhood, relying on second-hand accounts of his progress and being left entirely helpless when the battle for the throne of England engulfed Wales where her son was being held. When Edward IV became king, she had felt as though she had no choice but to send him in to exile with Jasper Tudor. Here, Fortune intervened again, in the form of bad weather, forcing Jasper and Henry into Brittany where, although treated well, they were ultimately captives of Duke Francis. Margaret could do little to ease both their sufferings whilst Henry was passing the prime of his life in hopeless exile.

Margaret would also have witnessed the pleasure and determination with which Edward IV pursued and eliminated the rest of the Beaufort family. As well as executing remaining members of her family, Edward IV confiscated the possessions of their elderly and vulnerable relatives. An Act of Attainder was passed in 1468 which may have clearly highlighted to Margaret the depth of his anger with the Beaufort family, and the danger both herself and her son still faced.

As Edward IV had been determined to eliminate the remaining members of her family, had Margaret exacted a similar revenge on the York family, by removing two of their own sons and plotting to replace them with her own son?

Although this is possible, it must be remembered that at the time the princes disappeared, their father, the architect of the downfall of both Lancaster and the Beaufort's was dead and any act of revenge against him would ultimately have come too late.

We must also consider whether this type of revenge is in-keeping with the character of Margaret herself. It has been noted that she could be ruthless when required so this suggests that a plot of revenge is possible. However, during the reign of the York dynasty there is no evidence of Margaret plotting against them. She found herself a safe marriage at the heart of the York regime and appeared to negotiate and come to an accommodation with the young king. It was only after the death of Edward IV and possibly after the disappearance of the princes that we see Margaret actively plot against the reigning king.

Whilst an argument can be made that Margaret Beaufort did indeed have a motive to kill the boys, we must also decide whether she had the means and opportunity to carry out this crime. First, we must consider Margaret's position. She had chosen for her husband, one of the most powerful men in the kingdom, trusted by the inner circle of both Edward IV and Richard III's court. Thomas Stanley was Lord High Constable and would have had little difficulty securing access to the boys at the request of his wife.

Stanley had managed to find a way through the Wars of the Roses without having to commit to either side or take any action to put himself or his men into danger. This did mean that there was a limit on how much he was trusted by the ruler of the day, but they needed him on side and both Edward IV and Richard III had showered him with greater trust and responsibility. Both Stanley and Margaret would play prominent roles in the coronation of Richard III and his wife, Anne Neville.

This plan would rely on the support of her husband who had proven himself to be risk averse in previous years, yet Margaret had other people she could turn to if her husband could not be convinced to come out in support of her son.

Margaret had two trusted servants Reginald Bray and William Hussey. They were loyal to Margaret and her promotion of her son. They were fixers, who got things done without Margaret questioning how they had achieved it. Could they be trusted to commit this most awful crime and show complete loyalty to their Beaufort mistress? Reginald Bray would often undertake dangerous, important missions on behalf of Margaret and Henry Tudor, and was himself rewarded with the top honour of the Order of the Garter.

Margaret also had an important connection that she could have used to help her gain access to the Tower, and ultimately the boys. Margaret Beaufort was related to Henry Stafford, the Duke of Buckingham. Henry Stafford played a significant role in the events that led to Richard becoming King Richard III and as a result became the second most powerful man in the kingdom. There is no doubt that at some point, Henry Stafford grew dissatisfied with the reign of his former ally, Richard III. Buckingham would act in accord with supporters of Margaret Beaufort and Henry Tudor to try to depose Richard, only a few months after his coronation. His power and titles after July 1483 gave him easy access to the boys and as we will discover later, Henry may have had his own motives for wanting the boys out of the way.

In his defence of Richard III, George Buck stated that he had seen a manuscript which stated that Margaret and Dr Morton, contrived the death of Edward V and resolved it by poison.[xl] It is true that Margaret had an important knowledge of medicines. Towards the end of his life, Margaret moved in with her son to look after him when he was ill. It is also reported that in later years she would use part of her household as a hospital wing. It is credible therefore that she would have had knowledge that may have allowed her to poison the boys. We must, however, treat the comments of George Buck with a certain degree of caution. George Buck believed Richard III did not kill the boys and needed alternative suspects. The manuscript he mentions as describing the death of Edward V by Margaret's hands was not cited in his work and there is no other record of the accusation against Margaret.

After examining the evidence against Margaret, she did indeed have the required motive, means and opportunity to commit the crime. This of course does not mean she is guilty, and we must now consider the case for the defence for Margaret Beaufort.

Chapter 6 – The Defence of Margaret Beaufort

When considering whether Margaret Beaufort could have committed such an act as the murder of two young boys, attention must be given to her religious devotion. One thing that biographers of Margaret agree on is that religion was particularly important to her. We have already seen how it was claimed that after praying to St Nicholas, she was visited by him and advised to marry Edmund Tudor.

This was a woman whose day was supposedly built around her religious observances and who prayed so much that she would injure her back and knees.

Margaret's Confessor, Bishop John Fisher described her as 'to Gode and the Churche full obedient and tractable.'[xli] She was an incredibly pious woman, who may have taken her religious devotion further than many of her peers.

Therefore, is it plausible that this woman, aware of the commandment thou shalt not kill, would commit such a terrible sin to promote the regal interests of her son?

We have already seen, in the case of Richard III, that being considered pious did not prevent him from being considered a major suspect in this crime. So, although it is accepted that Margaret took her religion very seriously, this may not be enough to rule her out as a person of interest.

There were two things that were especially important to Margaret: her son and her religion. Since her death, she has been described, rightly or wrongly, as obsessive and zealous in pursuit of both these interests. She was determined to bring about the best possible outcome for her son.

It is possible that her obsession with securing the best future for Henry combined with her religious ardour. Margaret has already been portrayed as being prone to the more supernatural elements of medieval religion, as in the vision she claims to have had of St Nicholas who urged her to marry Edmund Tudor, father of Henry. When King Henry VI was introduced to a young Henry, it is believed that something the king said led Margaret to believe that he had prophesised that one day her son would be King of England. At this period, kings were considered to rule by the will of God. Rather than ruling Margaret Beaufort out as a suspect, it is possible that the obsessive love for her son combined with her religious devotion, and she may have believed that it was God's will that Henry Tudor become king. Both Margaret and Henry had been lucky to survive a difficult birth and she may have believed that they had both been spared to fulfil a great destiny. Henry to be king and Margaret to help bring this about. Could somebody so religious justify the deaths of two boys if it were to bring about the will of the God she served?

Religion had certainly not prevented a Cardinal named Adrian from plotting to kill Pope Leo, after Adrian received a prediction 'that one should succeed Pope Leo, whose name should be Adrian.'[xlii] If religion was not enough to prevent Cardinals from plotting against the Pope, then religion itself cannot rule Margaret out of this crime.

This is especially so when considering the practical nature of Margaret Beaufort when dealing with the Church. Although Margaret was well known for her support for religious houses, she had always developed a reputation for being acquisitive and pursuing self-interest. Whilst it was acknowledged that she was generous towards religious institutions, some believe that there was always expected to be something in return for Margaret or her son and she would engage in litigation with the church when she felt as though she had been wronged by it.[xliii]

During her life Margaret arranged for a large number of masses to be said for her soul when she died. Masses for the soul were common in medieval England to ease the passage through purgatory. The fact that Margaret ordered so many could be a sign of the piety that she was famed for, or it could be that there was a terrible sin that Margaret's soul needed help with particularly.

Another point that should be raised in defence of Margaret Beaufort is whether she would have taken such risks and committed such an act, when the chances of her son becoming king were so low.

It could be argued that in 1483, Henry Tudor was a very unlikely contender for the role of King of England. Margaret Beaufort was descended from an illegitimate line of John of Gaunt, through his mistress Katherine Swynford. Although they had later married and had the children legitimised, Henry IV had made it clear that these children had no right to claim the throne.

Henry's father, Edmund Tudor had been the half-brother of King Henry VI, but was of no English royal blood. When Henry V died, his widow married a servant, Owen Tudor and together they had a son, Edmund, who would later become the father of the first Tudor King.

As well as the issues regarding his dubious lineage, there was also the issue that Henry had been in exile in Brittany since he was a child and was therefore not very well known within the powerful families in England. This would make it difficult for him to gain support from these families who would be instrumental in bringing down Richard III and supporting his replacement.

When trying to raise support for Henry Tudor, Margaret would also have had to overcome the fact that the Yorkist line had been in power for over two decades, apart from a short period, where Henry VI had briefly regained the throne before being overthrown by Edward IV for a second time. This period had allowed the Yorkists to gain credibility and provide stability to the country. During this time, the Yorkist line was accepted as having a legitimate right to rule. Removing a Yorkist King and replacing it with an unknown, illegitimate Lancastrian may have risked plunging the country back into civil war. If Margaret did kill the boys to improve her son's chances of becoming king, she was committing a horrendous act with little chance of it paying off.

Removing Richard III from power and killing the princes did not make Henry Tudor the best contender. There were at least two people still alive with better claims to the throne. Edward, Earl of Warwick was the son of the attainted Duke of Clarence, and nephew of Richard III. Richard III also had another nephew, John de la Pole, son of Richard's sister. They would both have continued the stability offered by the Yorkists and were well-known and could act as figureheads for the Yorkists.

Although it can be argued that Margaret would not have killed the boys as it was not a realistic prospect that he would become king, there is also evidence that the prospects of Henry Tudor were not as remote as first appears.
Although Henry IV had stated that the Beaufort's had no claim to the throne, this change was never enacted by parliament and therefore did not carry the force of the law.

In the fifteenth century the stigma associated with illegitimacy also appeared to be lessening. When considering the strength of Henry Tudor's claim to the throne, the key players would all have been aware of the successful claim to the throne by William the Conqueror, despite his illegitimacy.

In 1424, more than sixty years before the disappearance of the princes, the Beaufort family tried to offer Joan Beaufort as a bride to the Scottish King. This was evidence that they had regal ambitions and saw themselves as close to the throne. Even then in 1424 they didn't feel as though the illegitimacy of their line was an obstacle to the highest offices.

The importance of the Beaufort family, in their relationship to the royal family was further demonstrated when Margaret Beaufort herself was just six years old. She had been married to the son of one of the king's closest advisors, The Duke of Suffolk. Suffolk was later accused of marrying his son to Margaret as he knew she was a close heir to the throne, and of plotting to put her and his son on the throne. This suggests that the Beaufort family were considered to have a claim to the throne, many years before Henry Tudor was born.

When evaluating whether there was any realistic chance of Henry Tudor becoming king, we must also consider the actions of Edward IV and Richard III. Both kings appear to have felt threatened by Henry Tudor as they both entered negotiations to try and get him transferred to their custody.

Although in 1482 Margaret Beaufort appeared to reach an agreement with Edward IV for him to return to England, and possibly discussed marriage to Elizabeth of York, on a previous occasion she had warned him not to accept such an offer from Edward, fearing what would happen to her son if he was in the control of the King. The way that the Kings tried to get Henry Tudor under their control suggests that they perceived him to be some sort of threat to their security. Although it appears that Henry Tudor was an unlikely contender to be king when the boys disappeared, clearly the kings and the Beaufort family did not believe the threat he posed to be unrealistic. One thing cannot be denied: the rumours that the boys had died certainly shot Henry Tudor to prominence as the contender who would save England from the tyranny of Richard III.

The evidence of Margaret Beaufort negotiating with both Edward IV and Richard for her son to return to England and regain his titles and land are also evidence that she had accepted both the legitimacy of the Yorkist line and her son's position in that regime.

Margaret had managed to reach agreement with Edward IV, firstly that Henry could inherit some estates on the death of Margaret Beaufort and then in 1482, that he could return to England safely. Although this agreement could not be concluded due to the unexpected death of Edward IV, Margaret immediately opened negotiations with Richard III, to allow her son to return.

Even when King Henry VI was briefly restored to power, Margaret did not use this as an opportunity to try and improve Henry's position, rather she entered negotiations with George, Duke of Clarence who had been given his estates.
Although the negotiations appear to show a mother who is asking for no more than the safe return of her son, this doesn't rule her out of the murder of the boys.

Although she appeared to be working towards an agreement with both Edward IV and Richard III, we do not know how serious she was about these negotiations or to what purpose she was trying to secure his return to England. George Buck believes that she was not genuine in the negotiations and suggests that maybe they were to distract from the plotting she was involved with to improve her son's position.[xliv]

Certainly, with regards to her discussions with Richard, it is believed that she started plotting to overthrow him almost immediately after she had asked him to allow Henry Tudor to return. We know that she was involved in plotting and intrigue throughout Richard's reign, first supporting rebellion in the name of the young princes, before highlighting the claim of Henry Tudor.

It was Margaret Beaufort who in 1476, well into negotiations with Edward IV, advised Henry Tudor not to return to England based on a promise from the king that he could marry one of his daughters. It appears that during the negotiations neither side was convinced of the other's intentions and may both have been trying to outmanoeuvre each other.

Although the negotiations could appear to suggest that Margaret Beaufort was happy for her son to return to England as Earl of Richmond, again this evidence is limited due to our lack of knowledge of when Margaret Beaufort realised Henry could be king – after the disappearance of the boys or when they were alive and an obstacle to the founding of the Tudor Dynasty.

It is also important, as with Richard III, to look at the way that Margaret Beaufort treated other potential rivals to the throne. As previously stated, Edward, Earl of Warwick had a strong claim to the throne. He was the son of Richard III's older brother and although Clarence had been attainted, this was an obstacle that Yorkist supporters of Warwick could overcome. When Henry Tudor was successful at the Battle of Bosworth and became King of England, one of his first acts was to secure the custody of Warwick and place him in the custody of the one person he knew he could trust absolutely, Margaret Beaufort.

No harm came to Edward, Earl of Warwick during the short period of time that he was with Margaret, before being transferred to The Tower of London as a prisoner. Warwick stayed there until as an adult, he was executed. Although it is true that he came to no harm with Margaret, he did spend his whole childhood a prisoner until he was executed. The decision to execute him would ultimately have fallen with the king, possibly influenced by his most trusted advisor, Margaret Beaufort

Henry also trusted Margaret to take control of the two sons of Henry Stafford, Duke of Buckingham, who had been executed by Richard III. They too had royal lineage and could have been considered a threat to the new king. Whilst it may be the case that Margaret exploited their wardships to benefit her own family as much as possible, both survived their time with Margaret and the way she managed their estates left them as very wealthy adults.

The daughters of Edward IV could also be a threat to Margaret's plans for her son. To marry Elizabeth of York he would have to repeal the illegitimacy of the daughters. This meant that her sisters could then pose a threat to the new king. Yet, Margaret appears to have had a good relationship with the girls, especially Cecily. Cecily was married to one of Margaret Beaufort's half-brothers and Margaret took active steps to protect a widowed Cecily when she undertook a secret second marriage without the authority of the king. Margaret also contributed to the costs of Cecily's funeral. The way that Margaret Beaufort treated these threats makes it hard to believe that she would have taken such ruthless action against the young princes.

The young Tudor dynasty was forced to take drastic action against Edward, Earl of Warwick and a man called Perkin Warbeck who had tried to lead a rebellion against the king, claiming to be the younger of the Princes in the Tower. Both Warwick and Warbeck were ultimately executed. What role Margaret Beaufort played in these executions depends on how much influence she had over the decision making of Henry VII. Did she, as claimed by the Spanish Ambassador,[xlv] influence the young king considerably or, did Henry not really listen to his mother as claimed by Francis Bacon.[xlvi]

We saw with Richard III that he was blamed by chroniclers who were writing shortly after his death. When considering Margaret Beaufort as a suspect it is interesting to note that no chronicler blamed her or indicated that she was involved in the disappearance of the boys. So, whilst the accusations of chroniclers have been used to point the finger at Richard, the lack of accusations regarding Margaret could be used to suggest that her innocence.

We must remember though that these chroniclers were writing their record of events whilst Margaret's son was King of England. Rather than risking incurring the wrath of Henry VII they would have been trying to please him. Certainly, one of the chroniclers, Thomas More had learnt a valuable lesson when his father was punished for criticising the king. Whilst Henry had grown up separated from his mother, his treatment of Margaret Beaufort, as the king's Mother suggests that he expected her to be treated with the highest honour.

It is important to remember that Margaret Beaufort was a woman in a world dominated by men. It could be argued that this would have prevented her from having the power to access the boys, let alone kill them and cover her tracks effectively. Although women were not treated as equals, we cannot underestimate the determination and ability of Margaret Beaufort. Despite being a woman Margaret Beaufort worked to arrange marriages for herself that would guarantee her safety and security and was instrumental in creating a power base for Henry Tudor that would allow him to secure for himself the role of King of England.

What is clear from the evidence is that we cannot prove whether Margaret Beaufort was involved with the disappearance of the boys. What we can declare, with certainty, is that she certainly had the means, motive, and opportunity to make her a legitimate suspect in this mystery.

To many of us, living in the twenty first century, it seems incomprehensible that a woman would go to the lengths of killing two young boys to further the interests of her own son. In Japan as recently as twenty years ago, Mitsuko Yamada pleaded guilty to the murder of her neighbours two-year-old daughter.[xlvii] One explanation given for the murder was that the girl had passed an exam to get into a much sought after, private kindergarten, which Yamada's child had not secured entry to. It was claimed that the young girl was murdered so that Yamada's child could get the place. Yamada later claimed that it was to punish the mother who had caused her five-year-old son to be ostracised.

Whichever reason turns out to be the truth, it does make us look at the case of Margaret Beaufort. If in the twenty first century mothers are willing to kill children to secure a school place or because of the way her son has been treated, it certainly does make it possible that back in a more ruthless age, Margaret Beaufort could have killed the two boys to gain for her son the ultimate prize of King of England. It must also be remembered that the family of the boys did a lot more than ostracise Henry Tudor. He was stripped of his lands and titles, forced into exile, living under guard and in fear of being handed over to his enemies.

In a mystery that seems likely to never be solved it is only right that Margaret Beaufort take a prominent place on the list of potential suspects.

Chapter 7 – Cecily Neville – Background

Could a mother-in-law detest her daughter-in-law – the queen – so much that she would kill her grandsons to prevent her retaining power?

Cecily Neville was only too aware of how dangerous the Wars of the Roses could be. She had lost her husband and son in battle against the forces of Henry VI and witnessed her own son, Edward, proclaimed king. Her pride in her son was apparently replaced by rage at his choice of bride. Could Cecily have destroyed her own grandsons to prevent her daughter-in-law retaining power, or was she herself, a victim of the events of 1483 and the tyranny of her youngest son, Richard III?

On 3 May 1415, within the walls of Raby Castle in County Durham, another baby girl who would grow up to be a formidable woman and play a significant role in the events of 1483 was born.

Cecily Neville was the youngest child of Ralph Neville, the Earl of Westmorland, and his wife Jean Beaufort, who were approximately fifty and thirty-six years old respectively at the time of her birth. The family she was born into was as large as it was important. Cecily Neville had nine full siblings and ten half-siblings. The Neville family was large and one of the most important dynasties in fifteenth century England. Cecily herself was the great granddaughter of Edward III.

Whilst nobody could have predicted on this May day in 1415 that by the time of her death, she would have been the mother of not one, but two kings of England, the fact that a prosperous future awaited her would have been beyond doubt. Cecily Neville was a beautiful and proud young lady earning the nicknames the 'Rose of Raby' and 'Proud Cis.'[xlviii]

The act that sealed Cecily's fate and set her on the path towards the unbelievable events of 1483 was the introduction of Richard Plantagenet into her household. In December 1423, Cecily's father, Ralph Neville bought the wardship of Richard, whose father, the Earl of Cambridge had died. Ralph Neville had a large family that he needed to find spouses for. Richard would later inherit the Dukedom of York and the title of Earl of March from his disgraced uncle. At the age of nine years old Cecily Neville was betrothed to Richard Plantagenet.

Although Ralph Neville would not live to see the marriage take place, his wife Jean was committed to seeing the marriage through, once Cecily was of an appropriate age. In the fifteenth century this was at the age of 12, so the marriage to Richard would have taken place after May 1427.

The marriage between Richard and Cecily was the start of a successful union that would last until the death of Richard in 1460 and produce eleven children. Although we do not know when the marriage took place it will have been some time after Cecily turned 12 in 1427. Certainly, records indicate that they were married by 1429 when they were given permission to choose a confessor together.

Although this marriage would be blessed with eleven children, the first recorded child is Anne who was born at least ten years after the marriage in 1439.

The actions of both Cecily and Richard, suggest that their marriage was a close one with Cecily supporting her husband through good times and bad. When Richard, Duke of York was given a position in France, Cecily moved to set up home there with him in Rouen and it was here that her eldest sons, Edward and Edmund were born and christened.

During the marriage, Richard, Duke of York was one of the most powerful nobles in the country and concerns regarding the ability of king Henry VI to rule led him into conflict with those advising the king and most importantly the Queen, Margaret of Anjou. These conflicts would see the fortunes of Cecily and Richard fluctuate from being stripped of office and humiliated to being confirmed as Protector when the king was ill and unable to rule.

These spins of Fortunes wheel led to increasing tensions within the country which would erupt into the Wars of the Roses. Although the conflict would see Cecily's two sons become king, Cecily would be left devastated when Richard, Duke of York and her son Edmund became fatalities of the feud.

Due to the frailties of the king a compromise had been reached where Henry VI would remain king. However, it would be Richard, Duke of York and his sons who were to be his heirs at the expense of his own son, Prince Edward. This was a compromise that Margaret of Anjou could not accept and so the battles escalated, and armies were formed and took position.

In December 1460, York and his son Edmund were possibly tricked into leaving the safety of Sandal Castle where they were outnumbered. York was killed in the Battle of Wakefield and Edmund tried to flee but was captured and executed at the hands of the Queen's forces. Cecily Neville found herself a widow, grieving for her son and forced to protect her younger children. In a further blow she suffered the humiliation of finding that the heads of her husband and child had been placed on spikes in York as a warning to others.

This was the precursor to a new stage of her life where she would be Cecily Neville, the king's Mother, as her eldest son Edward, Earl of March avenged the death of his father and brother and defeated Margaret of Anjou before becoming King Edward IV. This was also the start of a period of her life that would see her relationship with her husband called into question.

Histories of the events that led to Richard III becoming king claim that at some point, to justify his actions he claimed that Edward's sons could not be king because Edward IV was not the legitimate son of Richard Duke of York.

Whilst some historians believe that this was a cynical move by Richard to destroy support for the young Edward V, which upset and offended his mother Cecily Neville, others have the accusation coming directly from Cecily Neville herself.[xlix]

Some accounts have Cecily Neville making the accusation in response to finding out that Edward had secretly married a woman of low birth, causing considerable anger and distress to 'Proud Cis'. It has also been stated that Cecily Neville was so adamant about this claim that she was willing to acknowledge it before a public enquiry and was happy to be cross-examined about it.

Whilst it is not certain where the accusations came from, rumours regarding the paternity of Edward IV appeared to be circulating around 1469. Two of Cecily's sons were now on opposite sides of the Wars of the Roses and George, Duke of Clarence was now being proclaimed a suitable king due to the fact that their mother had had an affair with an archer called Blaybourne and so Edward IV had no right to rule. These rumours appeared to have reached the French King around this time.

Most people consider this to be a slander against a pious and proud woman to discredit the rightful king, or the wild outburst of a woman angry at the choice of bride, her son, the King of England had chosen for himself.

When Edward was born, he was the eldest son of Cecily Neville and Richard, Duke of York and was christened in a small private chapel in Rouen Castle. When looking at whether the affair rumours are true, some historians have pointed to the comparison between this christening and the christening of the second eldest son Edmund. Edmund was born in 1443 and his baptism took place on 18 May with significantly more magnificence than that of Edward. His parents obtained the use of a sacred relic and the service itself took place in Rouen Cathedral. This could indicate that Edmund was being treated as the eldest son of Richard, Duke of York and certainly Richard preferred to be accompanied by Edmund as at the Battle of Wakefield.

However, these issues are not proof. The nature of Edward's christening may have been determined by other factors such as whether Edward was a sickly baby and they wanted to get him christened quickly. His father being accompanied by Edmund rather than Edward could also have been a practical issue. Even now there are rules about the next two heirs to the throne travelling together. Maybe Edward was kept separate from his father so that he could lead a counterattack, in the event of his father's death, which is exactly what happened after the Battle of Wakefield. Whilst debate over the issue of Edward's paternity continued, there were no obvious signs that Richard, Duke of York doubted his paternity and the first record of these rumours come years after the death of York.

After the Battle of Wakefield, Cecily Neville was grieving and vulnerable. Her husband, whom she had given her full support had failed in his bid for power and now she was at the mercy of King Henry VI and his Queen. Within weeks though Fortune's wheel had spun again, and Cecily Neville was to see her eldest son named King of England. This meant that she was now the most important lady in the land.

This was a role she appeared to cherish, as she exerted influence over her young son. Whilst Edward IV was away from London, consolidating his power in the country, Cecily acted as his representative and it was believed that she had control over the king. As king, Edward was generous to his mother, granting her all his late father's estates and indulging her lavish lifestyle.

Edward though had fought for the power to rule as he saw fit and is believed to have tired of being advised by his mother and cousin, Warwick, and the influence they exerted over Edward IV started to crumble.

It was one of the decisions that Edward would make on his own that would have the biggest impact on his relationship with his mother. Whilst Warwick was trying to negotiate a foreign marriage for Edward, he secretly married a low born widow, the mother of two children.

When the marriage was revealed, Cecily Neville was furious. She was proud of her heritage and status in society and believed that her son should have been married to somebody of a similar standing or background to himself. Descriptions have been given of vicious rows between mother and son, about plans by Cecily to break the marriage and of claims of Edward's illegitimacy. One thing that is obvious is that this secret marriage to Elizabeth Woodville changed the relationship between Cecily and her eldest son.

Whilst he was single, Edward is believed to have spent a considerable amount of time in the company of his mother. After his marriage, Cecily appears to have spent less time at the royal court. Certainly, she is not recorded as being present at the coronation of her new daughter-in-law.

This change in the family dynamic may have been responsible for creating an insecurity in Cecily Neville who changed the way she was known from 'My Lady the King's Mother' to 'Cecily, the King's Mother and Queen by right.

The change in the relationship is believed to be behind the decision of Edward to give his mother the residence of Berkhamsted as her main residence. Fotheringhay had been the Neville family home where Cecily Neville had raised her children and now she was forced to give it up and move to a new place that was not very well maintained and not up to the standard that she would have been used to. This has been seen as a sign of Edward's displeasure at his mother for the way he treated his Queen, Elizabeth Woodville.

The increasingly fractious relationship between her two sons, Edward and George, Duke of Clarence would serve to put further strain on this now fractured relationship.

Cecily had observed helplessly the breakdown in relations between the king and Clarence. When Clarence tried to overthrow Edward, first in favour of himself and later in favour of King Henry VI, he had committed the ultimate betrayal. Yet, it was Cecily Neville, who with the assistance of her daughters sought to bring about a reconciliation. This appeared to be complete when Clarence's co-conspirator and Cecily's nephew, Warwick was killed. The reality was that the relationship between the brothers would never be the same. Disputes over the marriage of their third brother Richard to Anne Neville, and how the Neville estates would be distributed made matters worse. Clarence continued to unravel, and his erratic behaviour resulted in Cecily Neville receiving the ultimate blow. Her son the king had sentenced her other son, Clarence, his own brother to death. All that she could do was plead with the king to change the method of execution to something less unbearable.

What Cecily thought of her son's death we can only guess, but rumours that it was Elizabeth Woodville who was responsible for it may help explain the behaviour of Cecily Neville in 1483 when another son would take the crown from one of her Woodville grandsons.

Cecily Neville would live to be the mother of not one King of England, but two. A lot less is known about her relationship with the son who would go onto become King Richard III of England.

Written after his death, we have claims that Cecily Neville was pregnant with Richard for two years and that when he was born, he had teeth and hair down to his shoulders. This created an image of the villain we have come to know him as, although we now know this to be untrue.

We do know that Cecily Neville was forced to send her young son, Richard, away to the Burgundian Netherlands when he was only eight years old. This was following the death of his father and elder brother. Cecily wanted to protect him, and George and they remained there until they could return as brothers of the new King of England.

We do not know a lot about their relationship until the major events of 1483 when we then must evaluate vastly different claims. The most accepted interpretation of events would have us believe that Richard had it publicly declared that his mother had been involved in an adulterous relationship that had resulted in the conception of his brother Edward IV. Cecily was apparently terribly upset about this accusation and complained for years after about the conduct of her youngest son.[i]

When we look at the relationship after he usurped the throne however, we see a relationship between mother and son that still appears to be close and affectionate.

Many of the events that led to Richard usurping the throne from his 12-year-old nephew took place at the residence of his mother. Although this doesn't mean that she was involved in the meetings, or even agreed with his action, it is strange that, if there was any tension between them, they were held here where people could surely notice the tension in the relationship.

Cecily Neville was a formidable woman, who had fought to support the interests of her late husband and her children and yet there are no records of any furious rows with Richard about his actions, the way there were when she so visibly disapproved of Edward's choice of wife, suggesting that Richard acted with the blessing and maybe even advice of his mother.

There is little written correspondence between the two that has survived but one letter shows the same affection between the two after 1483 as years before. Whilst trying to navigate the unprecedented events of 1483, it was to his mother that Richard appealed for advice and guidance. Indeed, it would be from his mother's residence in Berkhamsted that Richard would advance to meet his rival and ultimate death at Bosworth.

The relationship Cecily Neville enjoyed with her sons give us insight into the character of the woman who found herself at the centre of the political upheaval of the Wars of the Roses.

As with Margaret Beaufort, Cecily Neville stands out as a formidable woman. She found herself alone with a family to protect when her husband was forced into exile and despite the precariousness of her position, was able to plead for her husband, claiming he was supportive of the House of Lancaster when he was actively plotting against it. Cecily had stood up to her own son, the king when she disapproved of his marriage. Cecily would risk all to intercede on behalf of Clarence to prevent him from being hung, drawn, and quartered.

There are two other aspects of her character that Cecily Neville is famed for. The first is her piety. Cecily Neville was considered very pious, especially in her later years. At Berkhamsted her daily routine was balanced between religious observance and managing her estates. Edward IV obviously knew the importance of religion to his mother as he used this to his advantage when trying to get his mother's blessing for his marriage to Elizabeth Woodville. During the turbulent years of the Wars of the Roses, it may have been her religion that allowed her to deal with the losses she suffered, and the uncertainty of what Fortune's next move would be.

The second aspect of her character she is famous for is her extravagance. Cecily Neville came from one of the most prominent families in fifteenth century England and is believed to have enjoyed the trappings that came with her position.[li] This first appeared to become an issue when she set up home in Rouen with claims that Richard, Duke of York had to employ somebody to keep an eye on her spending.[lii] Claims of her indulgence appeared again during the period that her husband was named Protector of England, when she was known to give audiences in the throne room, as though she were already queen.

In defence of Cecily Neville, this was really part of the role she had to play. She was the wife of the second most powerful man in the kingdom and a certain amount of extravagance and ceremony were expected. This increased as her own position did. When Edward IV became king, he did not have a wife and she was the closest thing the country had to a queen and would have been expected to act as one.

Her claim to be Queen in her own right and wife of the rightful inheritor of the realm of England also could be considered to demonstrate Cecily's obsession with status and appearance. However, as it coincides with the introduction of Elizabeth Woodville and therefore a threat to her position, this could have been borne out of insecurity, rather than greed.

In August 1485, Fortune's wheel played its last game with Cecily Neville. All her sons were dead. One of her sons was vilified as the murderer of two of her grandsons and Henry Tudor sat on the throne. Cecily Neville was still the grandmother of the new Queen, Elizabeth of York but played less of a part in the politics of royal life than she had previously. This was the time when Cecily Neville could devote more time to her religion and lived out the most peaceful chapter of her life until her death in 1495.

Having considered the life and character of Cecily Neville we must now consider whether she has any case to answer in the disappearance of the two princes, her own grandsons.

Chapter 8 – The Case Against Cecily Neville

It may seem a controversial decision to add Cecily Neville to the list of suspects in the disappearance of the two boys who were ultimately her own grandchildren. However, the purpose of this book is to look at the different motives people had and what they gained from the disappearance. Cecily Neville's position was more complicated than any other in the battle for the crown. In 1483 she was witnessing her son challenge her grandson. This was a woman who had already been forced to watch on as two sons fought each other until one was left with no choice but to execute the other. Now, her family was battling itself again. Was she a passive observer or did she favour her son over a Woodville grandchild?

We have already identified that the marriage of Edward IV to the mother of the princes caused tension in the relationship between Cecily and her son, as concerns about the influence of the Woodvilles increased. The new king was 12 years old and had been surrounded by his Woodville kin for his whole life.

When Cecily Neville found out about the marriage, she made it clear that she was not happy about it and that she did not consider Elizabeth Woodville to be fit to be Queen of England. Thomas More tells us that 'she devised to disturb this marriage.'[liii] We also understand that there is debate about whether the rumours surrounding Edward IV's own paternity may have been started with herself, when she was in the position of having to choose which son, George, or Edward she would support. Mancini claimed that she was so against the marriage that she was willing to submit to a public enquiry.[liv]

'Proud Cis had endured a lot during the years. She had come so close to becoming Queen before having that future torn away from her when her husband was killed at the Battle of Wakefield. She may have feared that the low born Woodvilles posed a threat to the future of the Yorkist dynasty.

Another sign that Cecily Neville would not accept Elizabeth Woodville and her family as members of the royal family was that she was not recorded as being at the coronation of England's new Queen. Another significant event that Cecily Neville was not recorded as attending was the reburial of her beloved husband and son. Cecily Neville had the most reason to be at this event. but her presence was not recorded. Some historians believe that this is a sign that she was not prepared to attend an event where she would be of lower importance than Queen Elizabeth Woodville.

Cecily Neville, on return from Rouen, had raised her family at Fotheringhay. That was their family home. In 1469 Cecily left this home and moved instead to a residence at Berkhamsted. This property was not in the best state of repair and would have been less grand than what she had been used to at Fotheringhay. The reason for this move has also been considered as evidence of a breach between Edward IV, his wife and Cecily Neville. Cecily Neville was a woman who cared about status and it is unlikely that she would have chosen to leave her family home for a less grand property. This could be a sign that Cecily Neville was being punished for her attitude to Elizabeth Woodville.

This evidence indicates that Cecily Neville was seriously opposed to the common Elizabeth Woodville becoming England's Yorkist Queen and gives her a motive for wanting to remove her Woodville children from the line of succession and promote the superior lineage of her own son.

It is suggested that she may have been behind two different claims that would have barred the boys from ruling, firstly, that their father was illegitimate and secondly that they themselves were illegitimate. By siding with Clarence it may have been that she felt as though she had cut her losses with Edward and his family and knew that when Edward died she had to remove the boys who posed a threat to her only remaining son, before he was a victim of their ruthlessness like Clarence had been.

Before making a judgement on this evidence it is important to consider that not all the evidence suggests that there were issues in the relationship, certainly not issues between Cecily Neville and her grandchildren. Cecily was the sponsor of Edward's first child, Elizabeth of York and is recorded as attending family events such as christenings and the wedding of the youngest of the princes, Richard, when he was married to Anne Mowbray. Even if she had issues with Elizabeth Woodville, the attendance at these events suggests that she accepted her grandchildren and they were important to her.

This is supported by Edward's behaviour when he returned from exile to regain his Crown. It was to his mother's residence that he moved his family when he was able to free them from sanctuary. They stayed there whilst Edward consolidated his grip on the country and finally defeated his former ally, Warwick.

In a letter in 1476, Elizabeth Stonor reports a meeting between Cecily and her son which she described as 'a very good sight.'[lv] This was years after the move to Berkhamsted, when the two appeared to be on friendly terms.

So, whilst it is true that Cecily Neville's disapproval of Elizabeth Woodville may have provided her with a motive for wanting to remove the princes there is no evidence to suggest that she disapproved of her grandchildren.

Another motive for us to consider with Cecily Neville is revenge. The Woodvilles were believed to be responsible for the different breaches that had occurred within the family. The first casualty was Cecily's nephew, Richard, Earl of Warwick. Warwick had supported Richard, Duke of York in his disputes with King Henry VI and Margaret of Anjou. Warwick had managed to flee to safety, whilst his father was killed with Richard, Duke of York, and Edmund. Warwick was a key ally of Edward IV and fought to avenge the deaths of both their fathers and make Edward IV the rightful King of England.

Due to his marriage Warwick held a lot of power and land and his support was vital to Edward IV, as he established his power in the country. Edward IV wanted to make his own decisions, culminating in his secret marriage. Whilst Edward was hiding the secret of his new marriage, Warwick was trying to negotiate a foreign match for Edward that would benefit the country. When the news was announced that he had already married, Warwick was humiliated. This was the start of Warwick losing his influence as Edward began to turn to the large family of his new wife for support. The last straw for Warwick was when his request for his eldest daughter Isabel to marry the king's brother, Clarence was refused.

Clarence and Isabel were married, against the wishes of the King, on 11 July 1469 and there is reason to believe that Cecily Neville may have been present. This marriage was a signal for all out rebellion against the king. Warwick, Clarence, and their armies were too strong for Edward IV who was captured. Warwick tried to rule in Edward's name but soon realised that this would not work. Edward secured his freedom and Warwick and Clarence were forgiven.

The peace did not last; Warwick and Clarence rebelled again. This time Edward was prepared, and it was Warwick and Clarence who found themselves forced into exile.
Cecily Neville would have been devastated to learn that the tension within her family had escalated to a point where Warwick and Clarence would join forces with the wife of Henry VI. Warwick reached an agreement with Margaret of Anjou, where his youngest daughter Anne would marry Prince Edward and Warwick would throw his support behind restoring Henry VI as King of England.

The tension between Warwick and Edward would reach its climax on the battlefield Whilst Clarence would once again be reconciled with his family, Edward would be forced to end his feud with Warwick in battle. Cecily Neville's son had killed her nephew and it was the Woodvilles that were being blamed.

The next victim of the family feud would be Clarence. Although he was formally reunited with his brothers, the betrayal had caused issues within their relationship. The fragile relationship between Edward and Clarence would escalate when the recently widowed Anne Neville was married to Richard, Duke of Gloucester. Clarence wanted to control his sister-in-law and therefore her share of the Neville inheritance. A bitter dispute between Gloucester and Clarence ensued, which would require the intervention of the king.

It would be another proposed marriage that led to the ultimate downfall of Clarence, believed to be the favourite son of Cecily Neville. When Clarence's wife Isabel died, his sister Margaret proposed that he could marry her stepdaughter. Given Clarence's betrayals this was a move that the king would not tolerate and Clarences' behaviour became more erratic, accusing a servant of poisoning his wife. King Edward IV was no longer able to ignore the behaviour of his brother and he was arrested, tried, and sentenced to death. Cecily Neville was now informed that her eldest son would be responsible for executing his own brother. All she could do was try to ease Clarence's suffering and it is believed that she was responsible for the death sentence being changed. He would not be hung, drawn, and quartered and his execution would be private.
Cecily Neville had now lost a nephew and another son, and it was widely reported that Cecily and Richard blamed Elizabeth Woodville for the losses the family suffered. Elizabeth Woodville had cost her a son, and the murder of the princes would show Elizabeth Woodville how it felt.

Whilst this appears to be a strong motive, Warwick and Clarence were adults who were responsible for their own actions. It may have been the marriage to Elizabeth Woodville that initially caused the problem in the York family, but it was the decisions of Warwick and Clarence that led them to escalate to the point that Edward had no choice but to take decisive action. This seems clear to us over 500 years later, but Cecily Neville was a mother who had lost another son and may not have been as rational in deciding where the blame for the deaths lay.

Cecily Neville may also have genuinely believed that her 12-year-old grandson, influenced by his mother and his Woodville dominated council posed a real threat to her remaining son. On the death of Edward IV, Richard, Duke of Gloucester was expected to be named Protector, whilst his nephew, Edward V was a child.

Mutual distrust between the families meant that the Woodvilles may have feared for themselves if Richard was allowed to assume power and control and they tried to convince the council that he should not be Protector.

Cecily and Richard's concerns appeared to be confirmed when Elizabeth Woodvilles' son from her first marriage started issuing orders and papers in the name of the king, with Dorset going on to state 'we are so important, that even without the King's uncle we can make and enforce these decisions.'[lvi] It looked as though a battle for control was beginning, with both sides fearing the consequences of losing.
If Richard believed that during his time as Protector, he could build a relationship with the young king and gain some measure of control or influence, then the attitude of Edward V on their first meeting after Edward's death would have shown him he was wrong. Richard arranged for Anthony Woodville, the boy's uncle to be arrested and informed the new king of this. Edward V was defiant in his trust of both his uncle and his mother. Edward V had been surrounded by Woodville relatives and it was now clear that their hold over him would be difficult to break.

The actions of Elizabeth Woodville, after hearing that her son was in the custody of Richard, Duke of Gloucester, would also have alarmed him and his mother. Elizabeth Woodville collected her belongings and children and fled into sanctuary again, reportedly taking the treasury with her.

Richard produced cartloads of weapons to justify the action he had taken at Stony Stratford as he tried to convince the nation that his life had been under attack from the Woodvilles. Cecily Neville may have believed that she had to take ruthless action against Edward V to secure the safety of Richard, Duke of Gloucester. The boys were declared illegitimate and therefore some people no longer saw the boys as a threat to Richard.

As she observed events, Cecily Neville may have been concerned to learn, not long after his coronation that there had been an attempt to free the princes from the Tower. Having taken the throne from Edward V, there would be no forgiveness for Richard, if the boys were released and a rebellion successful in their names. This may have been the moment that Cecily Neville realised that if the boys lived, her son was not safe.

It was not only her sons' position that was at risk if the Woodville family gained control of the young king. Cecily Neville had been treated well by her son initially after he became king. He had given her lands and income and indulged a luxurious lifestyle. Cecily had made it clear that she did not approve of Elizabeth Woodville as her son's queen and may have been forced to give up the home she loved as a consequence. If Edward V were king, she would be replaced in the role of king's Mother, by Elizabeth Woodville. Cecily Neville would be reliant on the goodwill of the woman whose marriage she tried to end. Losing her status and lifestyle would be something that would be difficult for somebody as proud as Cecily Neville. Losing it all at the hands of the woman she didn't believe good enough for her son and whom she blamed for the troubles her family had gone through may be too much to bear.

At this stage in her life though, Cecily Neville was becoming increasingly pious and as she got older, she lived a more monastic life. Possessions and status may have become less important to Cecily as she retired to Berkhamsted to lead a more pious, quiet lifestyle. Based on her piety, this would appear to not be a strong motive.

Clearly, Cecily Neville did have motive to commit the crime of killing the boys. Next, we need to consider whether she also had the means and opportunity to commit the crime.

Certainly, Cecily Neville came from a large family and had many powerful connections that could have helped her with a task as sensitive as this one. One of these connections is a man whose name comes up regularly when talking about these murders. James Tyrell has famously been named as the person who carried out the orders of Richard III to kill the boys. Thomas More gives a detailed description of the murder based on a confession Tyrell is supposed to have made and the evidence of whether he was involved will be considered in more detail later in this book.

James Tyrell did not only have a connection with Richard III. His connection with Cecily Neville dated back to his childhood. After Edward IV became king, he gave his mother the wardship of the infamous James Tyrell. Whilst Tyrell's alleged involvement in the murder of the princes has been explained as him carrying out the orders of his king, it also has to be possible that if he was involved, it was at the request of somebody else. Cecily Neville had a connection with the man widely accused of the crime. If James Tyrell killed the boys, then this gives Cecily Neville the means and opportunity to make her a viable suspect in this case.

Cecily had proved that she was willing to get involved in the politics of the time and there is evidence that she was involved in plotting with her husband, Richard, Duke of York, whilst also proclaiming loyalty to Margaret of Anjou and King Henry VI. She may also have been involved with plotting with her son Clarence, maybe giving him the information about Edward's paternity. She is believed to have been with Clarence when he married Isabel against the king's wishes. This may have been an attempt to talk him out of the action that could tear her family apart or it could be evidence that she was complicit in an attempt to replace a king with another son.

The evidence above appears to confirm that Cecily Neville had the means. motive and opportunity to kill her grandsons. Next, we will look at the evidence that suggests that Cecily Neville was not involved in one of the country's most enduring mysteries.

Chapter 9 – The Defence of Cecily Neville

There is no doubt that Cecily Neville was one of the strongest, formidable women of her time. We have already identified that she had the means, motive, and opportunity to kill the Princes in the Tower. But could the Yorkist matriarch really have killed her two grandsons?

As with Margaret Beaufort, Cecily Neville was famed form her pious lifestyle. Certainly, when she moved to her residence in Berkhamsted her life revolved around her religious devotion and she enrolled as a Benedictine oblate. In her biography of Cecily Neville, Amy Licence tell us that 'Cecily rose at seven in the morning. Her chaplain was waiting to say matins while she dressed and, when she was ready, he administered the Mass. This would be followed by a visit to the castle chapel to hear divine service, followed by two more low Masses. She then went to dinner and, while she ate, listened to religious readings, usually from the Lives of the saints or reflective, contemplative texts.'[lvii]

In 1566 the bodies of the Duke and Duchess were discovered, having been moved during the reformation. On Cecily Neville they found a papal indulgence, used for the remission of earthly sins. Her being buried with this indulgence is a sign of how important her religion was to her when she was alive. Given the significance of religion to Cecily Neville, it is hard to comprehend that she was unaware of the commandment, 'thou shalt not kill'. This could be used in the defence of Cecily Neville to state that she would not have been involved in any murder of her grandsons.

This would be to ignore the fact that religion can be used to justify any act if people view it as God's will. Before, during and after battles, those fighting, and their families would pray for God's blessing. Cecily Neville had been one of those waiting back home praying for God to favour her husband and sons during the battles fought during the Wars of the Roses. All would have known as they waited for their prayers to be answered that they were hoping for the death of all those on the other side. Being religious and being ruthlessly pragmatic in medieval England were not mutually exclusive.

Another issue affecting whether we believe Cecily could have committed such a crime was when she developed her pious nature. Certainly, she was very pious in her later years, living in Berkhamsted, dedicating her life to serving God. This doesn't mean that she was always as pious. This could have been something that developed later in life, maybe when she needed comfort and forgiveness for some of the acts, she committed to promote the interests of her husband and sons.

Her piety has also been used to suggest that the rumours regarding her alleged adultery could not be true. We have however, seen that these rumours are reported by some chroniclers as actually starting with Cecily herself. If these reports are true not only was Cecily claiming to be guilty of the sin of adultery, but she was also prepared to publicly recognise her behaviour.

Another issue that needs to be considered is her relationship with the boys. People were prepared to kill and eliminate threats to their position, but these were two young boys. They were not just nameless threats or obstacles to the promotion of the Yorkist cause; they were her grandsons. Whilst she may have supported her only remaining son, this does not mean that she would do so at the cost of her grandchildren's lives.

Cecily Neville had lived through family disputes, especially the feuding between her sons. Yet, at these times it was Cecily Neville who tried to bring the brothers back together again. Although she may have been involved with Clarence's decision to marry Isabel Neville without the permission of the king, when the two sides were poised for battle, it was Cecily who worked to broker a reconciliation, rather than lose one of her sons. Wouldn't she have taken similar action in this latest instance of family tensions, rather than sacrificing one family member for the benefit of the other?

We also know that despite any issues Cecily Neville had with her son and daughter-in-law, she was present for important functions relating to her grandchildren. She was Elizabeth of York's sponsor and even attended the wedding of the youngest of the princes, even though she was trying to come to terms with the fact that her eldest son, Edward IV had sentenced another of her sons to death. Here she is recorded as sitting with the king, queen, and her grandchildren. Cecily's behaviour suggests that she had a good relationship with her grandchildren and makes it difficult to believe that in the space of a matter of weeks, following Edward's death, she would have wanted the boys' dead.

It is also notable that she left her grandchildren bequests in her will.[lviii] This is except for the children of Clarence, which suggests that it may have been Clarence that she had issues with, not Edward and Elizabeth Woodville.

What we do not know is what Cecily Neville's motivation was when dealing with her grandchildren. Whilst we know that Cecily attended the christenings and weddings of her grandchildren, we cannot be sure why she attended them. Whilst it is possible that she was a loving grandmother who wanted to join in family celebrations, it is also possible that she was there because she had to be. During the early years of Edward IV's reign, it is believed that she was able to exert a lot of control over the new king, but as he got older, he wanted to make his own decisions. If the king told her that he wanted her to attend, would she have had any choice?

We know that she did not attend the coronation of Elizabeth Woodville, but we do not know what the consequences of that decision were for Cecily Neville. She was later forced to leave her family home for a less grand, new residence. If this was a punishment, it was because she had annoyed the king. Could she risk irritating him further and facing more consequences?

Cecily Neville's position and status depended on her relationship with Edward, the father of her grandchildren. It is also believed that Cecily was involved in intrigue against both Margaret of Anjou and Edward IV during the rebellion of Clarence. What was important to Cecily Neville was the Yorkist regime. Although she may not have been pleased with Edward IV and the decisions he was making, they needed to present a united front, to allow Edward IV to be perceived as the leader of a strong dynasty that could offer support to the divided country.

Cecily's concern for the Yorkist dynasty could also point to her being a danger to her grandchildren. One of her objections to Elizabeth Woodville was that she was a low-born widower. Although the boys were her grandchildren it is possible that she saw their bloodline inadequate for the role of furthering the Yorkist cause.

Of concern to Cecily Neville and everything she had hoped for would also have been the age of her grandson as he faced the responsibility of becoming King of England. Edward V was only 12-years old. Kings were supposed to lead their armies in battle and inspire confidence. England was still recovering from the rule of Henry VI who had inherited the throne as a young child.

Under his rule England lost all their French territories and tensions within the country rose as different nobles tried to manipulate the young king for his benefit.

England was still reeling from the divisions caused by the Wars of the Roses and if the House of York was unable to produce a strong candidate to lead the country, other contenders would make their move. The House of York was vulnerable and needed stability and strong leadership. Whilst Edward V may not have been the ideal candidate, Cecily Neville had watched as Richard remained unwaveringly loyal to Edward IV and may have seen her son as the answer to the new dynasty's problems.

Whilst Richard's usurpation could be achieved without any bloodshed, keeping him on the throne would be a lot harder to achieve if the boys were alive. The threat to the House of York could have caused Cecily Neville to take whatever action was necessary. The fifteenth century was a vastly different time when family loyalties may have suffered when there was a need for ruthless pragmatism.

The relationship Cecily Neville had with her grandchildren would also have been quite different to the relationship most grandparents now enjoy. This is especially the case with regards to the elder of the boys, Edward. As a young boy Edward was sent to Ludlow as Prince of Wales. Here he was joined by his own council headed by his uncle Earl Anthony Rivers. It is probable that Cecily and the young Edward did not have much contact with each other for most of his short life. Given the geographical and emotional distance between the two family members it would have been possible for Cecily Neville's dislike for Elizabeth Woodville to extend to her children.

When looking at whether Cecily had motive to kill the boys, I considered whether she saw them as a threat to her son Richard. This would only be a satisfactory motive if we accepted that she had a good relationship with him and was supportive of the action he took against his nephews in 1483.

Not everybody, writing after the events of 1483 was convinced that this was the case. Stories about Richard's birth appeared stating that there was something wrong with him from birth, emerging after a two-year pregnancy with hair down to his shoulders. It was also reported that Cecily was angry with Richard for publicly claiming that she had committed adultery and felt nothing but 'horror and revulsion'[lix] when she thought of her youngest son. This does not sound like a woman who would commit such a horrific act as killing two young boys, to his benefit. What we also know though is that Cecily Neville may have been complicit in the rumours of her adultery, maybe starting them herself in a fit of pique, following the marriage of her eldest son.

A lot of the events that took place between the death of Edward IV and Richard's coronation took place at his mother's residence of Baynard's Castle and so it has been concluded that she must have either agreed with or participated in the decisions that were made during this time. Yet, his mother had other residences and we do not know that she was at Baynard's Castle when these meetings were conducted.

Even if it is accepted that Cecily Neville was supportive of the actions that put Richard on the throne this does not mean that she agreed to or was complicit in the murder of the boys. It only proves that she believed her son to be a better candidate to rule England than a 12-year-old boy she barely knew and could hardly hope to influence.

When considering the character of Richard, his treatment of the Countess of Oxford was considered. Here he was accused of using strong-arm tactics to coerce the Duchess to give him what he wanted. If he could use fear and intimidation here, he could have used it against his mother, and she may have been another victim of Richard's ambition.

She would have witnessed the way Richard arrested and executed Anthony Woodville and heard about the events of the Council meeting where Hastings was arrested and executed without trial. As with Edward IV, she was reliant on the goodwill of the king. As formidable as Cecily Neville had been, she may not have been in any position to stand up to the son who was set upon becoming king. The choice of her residence to plan the usurpation may not have been something she had any choice over. The affection and goodwill that appeared between mother and son may have been nothing more than a coping strategy, as was placating Margaret of Anjou, whilst her husband planned the downfall of the House of Lancaster.

This is not in keeping with Cecily Neville's character, as she was never really considered a passive observer to the events that occurred around her. Certainly, Richard had previously shown himself keen to comply with the wishes of the formidable matriarch. Things were certainly different now as he sought to become the most powerful man in the land, she may have been unable to challenge his actions. Again, the fact that Edward IV was king did not stop her from aggressively condemning his secret marriage, clearly not fearing the consequences of standing up to her son.

This argument could be supported by the lack of Cecily Neville's name in the records of those present during the coronation of Richard III and the celebrations that followed. This was in keeping with her behaviour during the coronation of Elizabeth Woodville who she clearly didn't think was fit for the role that was being celebrated.

Another indicator of her feelings for Richard could be that she doesn't mention him in her will. This contrasts with Edward IV who is mentioned twice. It has been suggested that he has been omitted from this document because of the way he treated his mother. Yet, her will was written during the reign of the man who had killed Richard III and declared himself the rightful King of England. The omission of Richard's name could have been due to the political sensitivity of the time rather than an accurate representation of her feelings for her son. Edward IV who was mentioned twice, was, at the time the will was written the late father of England's Queen. Elizabeth of York. Elizabeth and Henry were now secure on the throne and Richard was dead. Nothing was to be gained by the inclusion of Richard.

Another event that Cecily Neville is not recorded as attending is the reburial of her husband and son. It has previously been suggested that this was due to issues with Elizabeth Woodville attending. It is worth noting though, that the Chief Mourner at the reburial was Richard, Duke of Gloucester. Yet at this stage he had not accused his mother of adultery and is not known to have caused any anguish to Cecily Neville at this point.

An important piece of evidence in the defence of Cecily Neville is that nobody has ever blamed her for the deaths. No chroniclers stated or implied that she had been in any way involved. It must be remembered that they were writing at a time when it was convenient for the king to have the blame placed squarely on Richard. This painted Henry as the hero who had liberated England from the rule of the tyrannical child killer. Although she was no longer Cecily Neville, the king's mother, she was still Cecily Neville, grandmother of the much-loved Queen of England and to disparage her was to risk upsetting the royal family.

At the time they were writing, Cecily Neville had become famed for her piety and would have seemed an unlikely suspect at that point.

Another significant point is that no modern-day writers have tried to pin the blame on her either. As groups and society try to rehabilitate the character of Richard III, other people have been named as potential suspects from Margaret Beaufort who has already been considered in this book to John Howard, Duke of Norfolk. Recently, new theories regarding the sister of the princes, Elizabeth of York have emerged and will be looked at later.

Despite the need to try and find other people who could be blamed for the fate of the missing princes, the omission of Cecily Neville speaks volumes. The case against Cecily Neville is significantly weakened by the complete lack of evidence regarding her involvement. Suggestions of her involvement are based on nothing but speculation. Yet this has been enough to condemn her son for over five hundred years.

In the twenty-first century it seems unbelievable that a grandmother could be suspected of any form of involvement regarding the murder of her two grandsons. Yet this is something that still happens in the modern age we live in. In February 2012 Joyce Hardin Garrard was convicted of the murder of her granddaughter in the United States of America. Garrard believed the nine-year-old girl had lied about sweets she had taken from a school friend. As a punishment she made the girl run. The girl was not allowed to stop. After three hours the girl became sick and later died.[ix] Over five hundred years after the possibility that a grandmother may have killed her grandsons to secure her son the ultimate prize of becoming King of England, a grandmother was prepared to kill her grandchild because they may have lied over some sweets.

Whilst we will probably never know what happened to the princes, it is possible that Cecily Neville has given us a significant clue as to whether she was guilty or innocent.

When she wrote her will she left a legacy to a Master Richard Lessey who would prove to be involved in a plot to put Perkin Warbeck, claiming to be the younger of the princes, on the throne in the place of Henry VII and Elizabeth of York. There were also legacies to people connected to Margaret of Burgundy, believed to be instrumental in the plot.

Coincidence? Or was Cecily Neville helping people who could help replace Henry VII, with her own grandson? Was Cecily Neville telling us that she couldn't have been responsible for murdering the boys because she knew that at least one of them was still alive and ready to challenge Henry VII?

Chapter 10 – Henry VII – Background

When Henry VII became King, he decried the evil acts of the tyrant Richard III and the shedding of infant's blood. Genuinely horrified or did he protest too much?

The next suspect deserving of our attention is Henry Tudor, the man who went on to become known as King Henry VII. Here is another key player who would gain significantly from the disappearance of the two boys.

When he was born, it is far from likely that anybody could foresee the way that his future would unfold.

On 28 January 1457, the walls of Pembroke Castle witnessed the difficult birth of a young boy. His mother was a13-year old widow who would go on to be the ancestor of every future monarch in England.

The baby's father had died before his birth, imprisoned by the Yorkists as the Wars of the Roses developed, he had been released before dying, possibly of the plague. Henry Tudor was now in the care of his mother Margaret Beaufort and his uncle Jasper who would become a lifelong ally and confidante.

What little evidence there is of Henry's early years suggest that he was a sickly child. He is described as a puny and delicate baby with a sickly constitution.[lxi] At this stage there is no sign of the triumphant invader who would win the Battle of Bosworth and kill the incumbent king.

Margaret Beaufort's love for her son is often described as bordering on obsessive and so if there were any health problems or weaknesses with Henry as a child, we have to believe that Margaret would have dedicated herself to nurturing her only child.

If she believed that the survival of herself and her son through a difficult birth was something of a miracle, then her obsessive love for her child and her religion would have crossed paths. She would have believed she had to make Henry thrive so he could fulfil the great destiny that awaited him.

The first major change in Henry's fortunes came when he was only four years old. The battles between the Houses of York and Lancaster were now in full swing and momentum had turned towards the House of York. In Wales, Jasper Tudor found himself forced to flee England. He left Pembroke Castle and joined Margaret of Anjou and Henry VI, who had also been forced to flee. As Pembroke Castle was forced to surrender, Henry Tudor found himself at the mercy of the Yorkist forces.

William Herbert, a loyal ally of the new King, Edward IV, quickly realised the value of the young child in his care and bought his wardship off the king for a £1000. Although Henry Tudor was considered a threat to the king and was attainted by him, he seems to have had a comfortable childhood. He is believed to have been educated by Oxford graduates and his mother could visit him during this time.

As Henry grew up and became increasingly aware of the divisions tearing the country apart, he could not have been prepared for the next turn of Fortune's wheel. Although Henry and his mother would have been worried about Henry being in the hands of the Yorkists, he had been well looked after and protected by the Herbert family.

At the age of 12, Henry Tudor was old enough to ride out with Herbert at the Battle of Edgecote. Momentum had now turned against the Yorkists and the reinvigorated Lancastrians took control at the Battle of Edgecote, killing Henry's guardian, William Herbert.

This time the future seemed brighter for Henry and his mother. Edward IV was in exile and Henry VI was King of England again. Henry Tudor was reunited with his mother, hoping for the continued reign of the House of Lancaster.

It was at this time that Henry Tudor was introduced to the king for the first time, where the king is believed to have foreseen that one day the kingdom would be ruled by the young boy in front of him.

Despite the prophecy from King Henry VI, many people at the time would have had difficulty believing that the young Tudor boy would indeed go on to become King Henry VII. Henry Tudor was connected to the royal line by both his mother and father, but both bloodlines had issues that made him an unlikely candidate to be king.

Henry's mother Margaret Beaufort was the granddaughter of one of Edward III's younger sons, John of Gaunt. The issue with this bloodline was that John of Gaunt had not been married to Katherine Swynford when she gave birth to Henry's grandfather. He had been in a relationship with Katherine for many years and she had four children with him.

John of Gaunt did marry Katherine Swynford, but many years after the children were born and the children were declared legitimate both by the papacy and King Richard II. Although this was a dubious start for the Beaufort line, the marriage and interventions of king and Pope appeared to address the issues of their status.

This was not the end of the matter and the Beaufort's would suffer a real blow when Richard II lost his throne to Henry IV. Henry was another son of John of Gaunt, but by his first wife Blanche of Lancaster. He accepted the legitimacy of his half-siblings but added the important, significant caveat that they were not considered legitimate heirs to the throne. Although this was clearly his will and was well-known, it was never passed by parliament. This made the position of the Beauforts unclear and lacking security.

Henry's connections to royalty through his father's line were also complex. His father, who he never had the opportunity to meet, was the half-brother of King Henry VI. Henry VI was the son of Henry V and his young wife Katherine de Valois. In events that were all too familiar to Margaret Beaufort and Henry Tudor, Henry V would die leaving a young widow alone to raise her infant son. Katherine became involved with a servant named Owen Tudor. She secretly married Owen and they produced three sons together, Edmund, Jasper and Owen.

Clearly Henry VI was fond of his half-siblings and he took care of them. Edmund became Earl of Richmond and Jasper became Earl of Pembroke. When the wardship of the wealthy heiress, Margaret Beaufort became available for a second time, he gave it to his two oldest half-brothers, Edmund, and Jasper. Shortly after this, Edmund married Margaret Beaufort. Clearly, Henry Tudor had connections to the royal family but Owen Tudor, his grandfather, had no royal heritage and his grandmother Katherine although a member of the French royal family was only Queen of England through her marriage to the King, Henry V.

There can be no doubt that Henry's claim to the throne, as the Wars of the Roses erupted around him, would not have been obvious or likely. As King, Henry would have to find a balance between using his marriage to Elizabeth of York to strengthen his claim to the throne whilst asserting his right to rule by himself.

When Edward IV was forced into exile and Warwick helped to restore Henry VI as King of England, Margaret Beaufort and Jasper Tudor made clear their delight at this unexpected change in fortunes. Margaret may have found a way to live with a Yorkist King, but she was always loyal to the House of Lancaster.

The Readaption, as the Lancastrian restoration is known, was short-lived. As Edward IV reclaimed his crown, he was now all too aware that some Lancastrian supporters would never accept him as king. The threat was reduced by the death in battle of the Lancastrian heir Edward of Lancaster, and the unexpected and convenient death of Henry VI in the Tower of London. Having removed two major figureheads for rebellion, he would now have been fearful of more remote relatives such as Margaret Beaufort and her Tudor son.

Jasper Tudor held out as long as he could but soon realised he was beaten and that he would have to flee to France. At this point Margaret, fearing for the safety of her son asked Jasper to take Henry into exile with him. As she did so, she would not have known that she would not see him again for fourteen years.

When they left Wales, Jasper and Henry were intending to head to France, but stormy weather blew them off course and they ended up in Brittany. Brittany was reliant on English support and the arrival of these two high-profile exiles caused a diplomatic issue for Duke Francis.

Whilst in Brittany they appeared to have been treated well by Duke Francis, it was clear to Jasper and Henry that they would not be free to leave. Duke Francis promised Edward IV that he would keep the two arrivals more secure and restrict their movements. This led him to move them from his own palace to a secluded chateau.

The two exiles were allowed to live comfortably and were given a generous allowance for their households, but as the years passed, conditions must have begun to feel more oppressive, Initially, the young nephew was allowed to stay with his uncle. At some point during their enforced stay, the decision was taken to separate them. They would also see their English servants removed to be replaced by Breton guards.

Henry Tudor would later tell the French chronicler, Commynes that 'from the time he was five years old he had been always a fugitive or a prisoner' and that he had endured an imprisonment of fifteen years or thereabouts in Bretagne, by the command of the late Duke Francis.'[lxii]

During their long exile, Jasper and Henry Tudor would also have felt a limited amount of security. Edward IV would negotiate with Duke Francis to try to get Henry Tudor into his custody. At one-point Margaret Beaufort sent a warning to her son that any promise from Edward IV of a marriage to one of his daughters was a trick, leading Henry to a narrow escape from being handed to English guards.

The death of Edward IV did not end the threat to Henry. Richard III had divided opinion in England by declaring his nephews illegitimate and making himself the new king. He was insecure and vulnerable. He also needed to eliminate any threats and promised the Treasurer of Brittany 1000 archers in return for Henry Tudor. Again, Henry's supporters were able to give him warning and despite their attempts, Edward IV and Richard III were never able to gain custody of Henry.

Polydore Vergil tells us the following about Henry VII, 'His spirit was distinguished, wise and prudent, his mind was brave and resolute and never even at moments of greatest danger, deserted him. He had a most pertinacious memory. Withal he was not devoid of scholarship. He was gracious and kind and was as attentive to his visitors as he was easy of access.'[lxiii] Supporters of Henry tell us he was a fair man who wanted to end the violence of the civil war and bring peace to England. This was a man who favoured the wife of William Herbert who had been given his wardship, despite feeling like a prisoner through those years and felt obliged to look after his supporters following the Battle of Bosworth.

Certainly, Vergil never met Henry VII and may have formed his opinions of him based on the narrative of the good king saving the country from the tyranny of Richard III. Another important fact is that not everybody agreed with Vergil.

Bacon's view of Henry was that of 'a dark prince and infinitely suspicious, and his time full of secret conspiracies.'[lxiv] Historians and biographers tell us of a harsh man, who could be ruthless and would take any steps necessary to protect himself. As with Richard III, words such as tyrant and despot are used to describe Henry, offering us a picture of a cold, calculating king, determined to rule and strengthen his position.

Descriptions of Henry as being miserable also colour our view of the first king in the Tudor dynasty. It has been claimed that he did not enjoy the usual frivolities of court life, such as banquets and dances, describing him as joyless and desperate to spend as little money as possible.

Yet, Henry clearly had interests that did bring him joy. He was believed to have been a fan of dicing and playing cards. He shared with his daughters a love of music and was a keen sportsman, with a love of tennis and playing chess.

Descriptions of Henry also depict him as quite a serious man who possessed many skills that would assist him as king. He is believed to have been able to converse in different languages, no doubt aided by his time in Brittany and France during his exile. His preparations for the invasion and subsequent battle at Bosworth would have taught him about the need for careful planning, attention to detail and the need to fund adequate resources to fulfil the task at hand.

When confronted with threats to himself and his family he would show himself capable of taking swift, decisive action, whether it be sending troops to face rebels or putting pressure on the French to withdraw support for rival candidates for the throne.

Regarding Henry's character there is one trait that he is believed to have inherited from his Beaufort relatives that he continues to be associated with. Henry VII has always been considered a miser. His mother Margaret had been accused of being acquisitive as had other members of her family. When Henry VII inherited the throne, the Treasury was empty, and Henry dedicated a significant part of his time to balancing the books and improving the royal finances. This may be partly responsible for the reputation he has developed. On top of that, the lack of frivolity at the court may have been due to his character but could also have been through a need to not spend money on extravagance. Whilst Henry may have felt an obligation to the people who had supported him both in exile and at Bosworth, he was determined not to make the same mistakes as former kings by rewarding them too much and making overmighty subjects. This would have caused resentment as people felt they had not been rewarded sufficiently for their assistance.

As with most people of this era, religion played an important role in Henry's life. One way this is displayed is by the desire of Henry to get his late uncle, Henry VI canonised. Although he ultimately failed to achieve this, the ardour with which he pursued it led some to believe that his piety was as strong as that of the uncle he appeared to revere.

The division caused by the usurpation of Richard III, presented Henry Tudor with a unique opportunity. To gather support from those Yorkists that had been loyal to Edward IV and subsequently Edward V, it was proposed that he should marry Edward IV's eldest daughter, Elizabeth of York. This would gain him the support of both Lancaster and York and allow him to present a credible threat to the new King of England.

Henry was also able to secure the support of an unlikely ally. For fourteen years, Henry Tudor and his uncle Jasper had been captives of the Duke of Brittany.

Following the accession of Richard III, Duke Francis was convinced to support Henry Tudor in his invasion of England and agreed to provide him with ships.

As planning for the invasion continued, supporters of Henry Tudor urged him to start using the title of king, in another attempt at convincing the public that Henry was a serious contender and threat to the tyrant, Richard III.

Back in England, Margaret Beaufort was working hard to help her beloved son. She was spending her time writing to influential people, encouraging them to support Henry when he invaded and securing funds that would be sent to Henry to fund his plans.

It is believed that Margaret Beaufort may have played a role in convincing Henry Stafford, Duke of Buckingham to switch allegiance to Henry Tudor and get involved in what became known as Buckingham's Rebellion.

The plan was ultimately that Richard would be attacked on two fronts. The first would be from inside England, when Henry Stafford would lead the country into rebellion against the king. At the same time Henry Tudor and his army would be sailing to England, ready to attack.

The force led by Stafford was no real challenge for the royal forces and he was easily beaten, before being betrayed by his own followers. He was handed over to Richard's men and executed on 2 November 1483.

Sailing from Brittany, Henry Tudor was unaware of this and prepared to land. When he spotted soldiers, they tried to convince him that they were Stafford's men, but his instinct was not to trust them. He decided not to land and was forced to retreat to Brittany.

Here he would have to regroup and devise a new plan for taking control of England. His mother was in danger as she was known to have supported the failed attempt and her contact with the outside world was supposed to be prevented by her husband.

Despite the suspicion surrounding her, Margaret Beaufort was once again able to help Henry Tudor prepare for a further invasion attempt. On 7 August 1485, Henry Tudor and his troops landed at last at Milford Haven. They started a march toward Haverford West, and ultimately to battle, trying to gain as much support as possible on the way. Henry would also write to his mother to seek her advice and counsel as he prepared for the fight of his life.

It was on the 22 August 1485 that the two forces eventually would meet at the Battle of Bosworth. Both leaders would still have been unsure about who would declare for each side as the fighting got underway.

The fighting was ferocious and as the day continued, both Richard and Henry would have been aware that the influential forces of the Stanley family were showing no signs of intervening. Nobody knew whose side they would ultimately decide to take.

At one point in the fighting, it is believed that Richard saw an opportunity to end the threat from Henry Tudor once and for all. Henry Tudor was separated from his main force and Richard charged at him. By taking out the leader of the rebellion, he believed he would end it completely. It was at this point that William Stanley and his troops entered the battlefield, charging towards Henry and Richard.

It was as Richard was about to strike at Henry Tudor that William Stanley's forces attacked Richard, killing him. The death of Richard III ended the fighting almost straight away, with Henry Tudor being declared, King Henry VII.

Henry believed that his victory was God's will and knelt to the ground to give thanks for the victory he had achieved. If God had helped him to become king, he would certainly need help with the challenges ahead.

At the age of 28, Henry found himself king of a land and people that he barely knew. He had spent the first half of his life in Wales, miles away from the machinations of the royal court. The second half of his life had been spent in exile, out of England, a captive of the Duke of Brittany.

So, whilst he knew little of the land or people, he was now responsible for, it is certain that he knew even less about the life and responsibility involved with the kingship of England

To gain support for the invasion, Henry had promised to marry Elizabeth of York, considered to be the Yorkist heir. One of his first acts following the Battle of Bosworth was to secure custody of his proposed bride. Before getting married, Henry had a more pressing celebration to prepare for. Having won the right to be king through battle, Henry wanted to establish his own right to rule and so ensured his coronation took place before his wedding.

Having secured control of the country, the wedding could take place. The couple were married on 18 January 1486. Outwardly the marriage appeared to be a success. The king and queen presented a united front and provided heirs to continue the Tudor dynasty, most notably a son Henry, who would become one of England's most infamous king's, Henry VIII. Yet historians are divided on whether the marriage was a personal success.

Evidence from key events suggests that it was a happy marriage and that the couple were fond of each other. This was most evident in the way that they grieved together when their eldest son, Arthur died. Henry Apparently got the news first and was distraught, this led to his wife coming to him to comfort him. When she left Henry, she struggled to cope with the news, and it was Henry's turn to comfort his wife.

The reaction of Henry to the death of his wife also suggests that they shared a close bond. Elizabeth died in February 1503, following the birth of a premature daughter. Henry was shattered by the death and became reclusive, shutting himself away from everybody. Henry's mother, Margaret Beaufort had to move in with him and help him come to the terms with his loss.

Despite these displays of affection, historians still believe that this was not a happy marriage. Francis Bacon describes the relationship as poor and stated that Henry was not a good husband to Elizabeth of York. It has also been suggested that Henry was disappointed by the rumours circulating whilst he was still in exile, regarding Richard III's plans to marry Elizabeth. Some believed that Henry genuinely wanted to marry Anne of Brittany but had to marry Elizabeth to secure the safety of the new Tudor dynasty.[lxv]

Whilst we can never understand the true thoughts and feelings of Henry and Elizabeth, we can interpret their actions. Certainly, the marriage was initially proposed as a political strategy, but the couple were often together and found comfort in each other during the challenges they faced.

Opinion of Henry VII as man and husband are divisive so it should come as no surprise that people are conflicted in their opinions of whether he was a good king. Henry VII's coronation took place on 30 October 1484. He ruled until he died on 22 April 1508. He achieved three of the aims that are believed to have been important to him. Firstly, he brought peace and stability to England following decades of civil war.

Secondly, he managed the finances and left the country in a solid financial position for his son and heir, his third achievement; an heir to continue the Tudor dynasty.

Supporters of Henry VII claim that he was a brave king who was strong but preferred to work for peace. It was his wisdom that made him successful and his tolerance and lenience to those who opposed him that was key to his success. Although he had to sentence his stepfather's brother to death, his followers claim that this was the only example of Henry VII dealing severely with anybody who posed a threat to him.

As groups fought to establish that Richard III was maligned by his Tudor successors, they have also sought to do so at the cost of Henry VII's reputation. Clements Markham goes as far as to claim that it was Henry VII who was the tyrannical leader, the despotic king feared by his subjects. He paints a picture of a greedy, mean man who was ruthlessly trying to eliminate anybody that could be viewed as a possible threat to him.[lxvi]

One thing that is not clear about Henry VII as king is how much influence his mother had on him during his reign. Margaret Beaufort had sent her son into exile when he was fourteen years old for his own safety. He had remained exiled, separated from his only parent for another fourteen years, when at times his cause would have seemed hopeless. How much influence could the matriarch hold over the son she hadn't seen for such a long time?

Certainly, Francis Bacon was dismissive of Margaret's hold over her son suggesting that although he may have listened to his mother, he paid what she said little attention.[lxvii] Yet, there are many indications that this was not the case. When Henry VII landed In England, one of his first acts was to write to Margaret Beaufort for her guidance. Here he appears to be relying on the person who had made the invasion possible at all.

Once he became king, Henry promoted his stepfather, making him the Earl of Derby, despite his initial lack of public support in the lead up to the Battle of Bosworth. This could be an indication of his mother's influence, as could the fact that he also allowed his mother to act as a single woman when dealing with her own affairs. The only sign of any tension between mother and son was when Henry forced her to give up her Woking estate, a decision she reversed immediately after her son's death.

That Henry relied significantly on his mother appears to be supported by the Spanish Ambassador who claimed that she had significant control over her son's decisions.[lxviii] It is also demonstrated by the fact that she spent so much time with her son, and she was trusted as executor of his will.

Towards the end of his reign, Henry appeared to have been worn down by the responsibility he had actively sought. He had been haunted by people claiming to have a better claim to the throne than himself, and ultimately by the death of his son and heir and his wife.

Chapter 11 – The Case Against Henry VII

Whilst Henry was certainly out of the country, biding his time in exile, when rumours regarding the disappearance started, it cannot be denied that he was the one who would go on to benefit the most from their mysterious removal from the line of succession.

With the boys out of the way there were two less obstacles to his own coronation and the opportunity to gain the support of Yorkists through marriage to the young Elizabeth of York. Therefore, he must be considered a viable candidate for any crime committed against the young princes.

One of the first pieces of evidence that must be investigated when looking at Henry VII, is the way he dealt with other, rival candidates from the House of York. The most significant of these figures was the young Edward, Earl of Warwick, son of Clarence and another of Richard III's nephews.

Warwick was now one of the most senior members of the House of York. More importantly he also could claim to be a Lancastrian claimant. When his father, Clarence had defected to the Lancastrian cause. he had been rewarded with a place in the Lancastrian succession. Following the deaths of Henry VI, Edward of Lancaster and Clarence, Warwick could be considered the valid heir to the throne.

Henry VII was clearly aware of this. The first thing he did following the Battle of Bosworth was to send his followers to secure the custody of two important rivals. The first was his fiancé, Elizabeth of York.

The second was the young Edward, Earl of Warwick. Once in the new king's custody, Edward was kept under the control of Margaret Beaufort for a short period of time, before being sent to the Tower where he would remain as a prisoner. Whilst a prisoner, rumours circulated that Henry would have the boy put to death. This caused concern throughout the kingdom and people were quick to realise the similarities between the case of Edward, Earl of Warwick and his two cousins, the princes.

Once Edward, Earl of Warwick came of age, he was accused of treason and executed. The reason for this decision has been disputed. Whilst some may argue that he was discovered to be plotting against Henry VII, the timing of his death was certainly beneficial for the future of the Tudor dynasty. Henry VII had been planning a marriage with the daughter of Ferdinand and Isabella, the Infanta Catherine of Aragon, to his heir, Prince Arthur. Following plots against Henry VII and imposters claiming to have a better claim to the throne than Henry, Ferdinand was hesitant about agreeing the match. He felt the threats to the Tudor's were too significant. To ensure the match went ahead, Edward, Earl of Warwick had to be eliminated as a threat.

Francis Bacon, and the recent historian Sarah Gristwood go further in their opinions of Henry VII's behaviour. Bacon claims he had an ardent desire to eliminate all important persons from the York line,[lxix] whilst Gristwood accused him of achieving this goal with 'chilling efficiency.'[lxx]
Whether it be the death of Edward, Earl of Warwick or the illegitimate son of Richard III, John of Gloucester, Henry VII certainly appears to have attempted to wipe out those that could be considered a figurehead for rebellion.

We do not know when the princes disappeared. All we have is speculation. We therefore must assess how Henry VII would have reacted if having reached London as the new king, ready to marry Elizabeth of York he had found the princes safe and sound. We know that he was responsible for the death of one of Richard III's nephews, Warwick. It must be accepted therefore that Henry VII is a credible suspect in this medieval mystery.

We have already identified that Henry Tudor did not have a particularly strong claim to the throne, a claim that would be significantly weaker if the princes were to reappear. Of course, this does not mean that Henry committed the crime, but it would certainly give him a valid motive. Whether this provides us with a legitimate motive depends on whether you accept the weakness of his claim to the throne.

Arguments in favour of his claim being poor include the fact that he did not come from a legitimate, royal bloodline. It was believed that his mother's family had been excluded from the throne and since the death of Henry VI and his only heir, it appeared to be widely accepted throughout the country that the Yorkist claim to the throne was superior to any other. When Henry Tudor succeeded at Bosworth there were several nobles in the kingdom who were considered to have a stronger claim to the throne than him. It is also noted that it was by conquest that Henry Tudor became king, as with William the Conqueror, rather than any line of succession. Senior members of the House of York, such as the missing princes could be used as figureheads for rebellion against Henry, as they had been used in plots against Richard III before him.

Henry Tudor, on becoming king, challenged anybody who believed they had a right to be king to come and claim it and we can only speculate as to what would have happened if the princes had been located.

However, we must also consider the 'prophecy' of Henry VI. We are told that when Henry Tudor first met Henry VI as a young boy, Henry VI declared that one day the young man in front of him would be King of England. Whilst we do not know for certain what was said at this meeting, it appears as though something was said that led Margaret Beaufort to believe that a great destiny awaited her son. It has also been suggested that maybe Henry VI was considering nominating Henry Tudor as a potential heir in case anything happened to Edward of Lancaster. This weakens the motive of Henry if he believed in his right to be king. Certainly, Edward IV and Richard III tried desperately to get Henry Tudor into their custody, suggesting they saw him as a threat.

Once Henry VI and Edward of Lancaster died, Henry Tudor can be considered a significant member of the House of Lancaster. Once Henry Stafford, Duke of Buckingham, was executed more rebels started to look to Henry Tudor as their only hope. Certainly, the rumours of the deaths of the princes led to an increased level of support for Henry Tudor and without people believing they were dead he may never have been able to secure the level of support needed to overthrow Richard III.

Margaret Beaufort and Henry Tudor appear to have accepted the weakness of his claim when they arranged the marriage with Elizabeth of York. This was supposed to unite the Houses of York and Lancaster, gaining support from members of the House of York for Henry's invasion and reign. Once he became King, Henry appeared to be concerned to show that he had the right to rule in his own right. Before he organised a wedding, he ensured that his coronation ceremony was completed first. Elizabeth of York would have to wait for her intended marriage and wait even longer for her own coronation. This can be interpreted as Henry trying to demonstrate that his claim was not weak and that he was strong enough to rule by himself.

This marriage, whilst outwardly being used to strengthen the claim of Henry to be King of England and to win him support of people who were unsure of the returned exile was also a major threat to his newly won title.

Elizabeth of York had been declared illegitimate by her uncle Richard when he himself wanted to be king. If Henry were to marry her, he would have to reverse that and legitimise Elizabeth once more. What he couldn't do was restore her legitimacy without restoring it to all her siblings. Elizabeth's sisters posed little threat to Henry Tudor, as Elizabeth of York was recognised as the true heir of the House of York following the rumoured deaths of her brothers. England was still an established patriarchy and the chances of loyal Yorkists supporting a female as the alternative to Henry Tudor was small indeed.

Elizabeth's brothers were another matter. If they were still alive, and declared to be legitimate, they would have a stronger claim to the throne than both Henry Tudor and Elizabeth of York.

When the first major rebellion against Richard III broke out it was in the name of freeing Edward V and restoring him as King of England. It was only once the rumours of their deaths began to spread that the rebels looked for an alternative figurehead, maybe considering the Duke of Buckingham or the Earl of Warwick, before being pointed determinedly in the direction of Henry Tudor by his devoted and formidable mother.

Clearly, Henry Tudor had strong motives for wanting the boys' dead and his actions towards other members of the York line suggest he had the ruthless pragmatism needed to complete a crime as serious as this.

After examining what we know about Henry are there any other signs that could suggest Henry was to blame?

Clements Markham, a clear Ricardian was the first person to directly lay the blame for the deaths of the boys at Henry's door. He claims that they were murdered in 1486.[lxxi] This would suggest that Markham believes that Henry discovered the boys alive when he returned to London and after wrestling with what to do with them, had them killed.

It could also be considered suspicious that there is no record of him looking into what happened to Edward and Richard. There is no record of any search or any enquiry into what happened. This was a perfect opportunity for a new king, unfamiliar with his subjects and country to prove that he had saved them from the tyrant of a man whose ambition had led him to kill his own nephews. Yet, nothing. As they were the most significant threat to his future, surely, he would have been curious to learn of their fate or certainly to prove that the rumours of their deaths were true.

Can we read anything into his challenge on becoming king, to anybody who had a better claim to the throne to come and claim it? Could this have been the bravado of a man who knew that the boys were not going to be able to come and claim their rightful titles or was it the gamble of a man who, having won one battle to become king, feared what threats lay waiting for him in the shadows and wanted to draw them out and defeat them once and for all?

Another area of Henry's life that could suggest his guilt is religion. Henry Tudor was a religious man, which is not a surprise given the importance of religion to his own mother. Yet despite his piety, records suggest that his religious observances increased as he approached death. There are reports of him becoming hysterical and sobbing. The winter of 1508 and Spring of 1509 saw an increase in his devotion and saw him performing penance. This could be taken as a sign that he had something awful weighing on his conscience, such as the murder of two young, innocent boys.

Concern for the fate of his soul following his death is demonstrated by the large amount of masses that he paid to have said for him and suggest a man with a great deal of sin to expunge and a man fearful of what awaited him following his death

Yet, this would again be to speculate. By this time in his life Henry had lost several children, including his heir Prince Arthur and his wife Elizabeth. Henry had been King of England since 1485, responsible for bringing peace and prosperity to his subjects. He had worked hard to make the country solvent and had made ruthless decisions. He had acted with callous pragmatism against his enemies and at the Battle of Bosworth had committed the sin of regicide. His decision to invade and challenge for the title of king had seen an immense amount of bloodshed and death. Whether he killed the two boys or not, certainly Henry would have had a lot weighing on his conscience by the year 1508, as he contemplated his own death to come.

Whilst we cannot know why Henry acted the way he did or why he feared for his soul, we can certainly see that he did have a strong motive for killing the boys and should be considered as a legitimate suspect in this crime. Now we must consider the evidence that suggests that Henry was not guilty of hurting the princes.

Chapter 12 – The Defence of Henry VII

One main piece of evidence that points towards the innocence of Henry VII is the fear he appeared to have that the boys would reappear and pose a threat to the new dynasty he had created.

Henry faced two main threats to his position and the way he dealt with them allows us to speculate as to his role in the deaths of the princes in the Tower.

The first significant threat to Henry, was led in the name of a boy who would become known as Lambert Simnel. This boy did not claim to be one of the princes, instead he was claiming to be Edward, Earl of Warwick, and he received support from his aunt, Margaret of Burgundy, and Richard III's closest ally, Francis Lovell.

With the help of his powerful backers, Lambert Simnel was able to encourage the Irish to give him help and support. When the young pretender arrived in Ireland, he received a magnificent reception. On 24 May 1487, Lambert was crowned King of England, whilst in Dublin.

As before, with the Battle of Bosworth, both Lambert and Henry VII, raised support and supplies, preparing for the inevitable battle to come. That battle did come. On 16 June 1487, Lambert Simnel's forces were challenged by those of the king in what has become known as the Battle of Stoke Field. The battle was another military success for Henry VII. Simnel's forces were defeated, Lovell disappeared and was never heard of again. Simnel was captured.

Although Henry was quick to arrange a force to challenge Simnel, suggesting he was concerned about the threat he posed, the way he dealt with Simnel suggests he was not seriously concerned. Simnel was treated leniently and instead of being imprisoned, he confessed that he had been trained to be a pretender and was set to work in the royal kitchens.

Maybe, another military victory could account for the confidence of Henry at this time or maybe it was the fact that he knew he had the real Earl of Warwick imprisoned in the Tower and knew therefore that this boy was an imposter. On its own this threat tells us little about Henry's role in the disappearance of the boys. However, we can contrast the way he dealt with this to the way he dealt with the next threat, the boy who claimed to be the younger of the Princes in the Tower.

This posed a much bigger problem for Henry. When rebellions against Richard III had broken out, it was in the names of the princes, considered the rightful heirs. Once all hope for the princes had disappeared, rebels had searched for an alternative candidate, and many of the supporters who helped Henry at Bosworth would soon desert him if they believed that the Princes were alive.

History knows this second threat, as the pretender, Perkin Warbeck and he would cause problems for Henry VII throughout the 1490's.

Perkin was claiming to be Richard, Duke of York, the younger of the princes. This had some credibility as there had been rumours that Edward V had been killed and the younger brother had escaped from the country. As nobody knew what had happened to the prince, there was more chance that people would believe that there was something to this claim. The backing he received from world leaders and Henry's inner circle suggests that people did believe him.

Just like Lambert Simnel before him, Perkin Warbeck also had the significant support of Margaret of Burgundy, again the claimed aunt of the boy seeking to overthrow the Tudor King. Warbeck's campaign to shore up support for an invasion of Britain saw him arrive in France, England's constant enemy. He received a magnificent welcome from the King of France and was honoured as Richard, Duke of York.

The response of Henry VII to this crisis suggests he really did fear the threat from Warbeck. In less than six months he had gathered his own invasion force and was ready to attack a less prepared France. The threat worked well for Henry and led to the Peace of Etaples between the two kings. Henry would not attack France, in return, the King of France would have to cease support for Warbeck. Warbeck was sent away from France, with significantly less fanfare than had greeted his arrival.

Forced to regroup, Warbeck, undoubtedly guided by Margaret of Burgundy turned his attention to Scotland. Again, Warbeck appears to have succeeded in convincing the Scots that he was indeed Richard, Duke of York and he was treated accordingly. The King of Scotland even offered the young boy a member of his family as a bride, tying the two countries together once Richard had successfully overthrown Henry VII.

As more and more people began to believe that the boy was who he indeed claimed to be, Henry would be forced to deal with a significant betrayal at home. William Stanley was the brother of the king's stepfather, Thomas Stanley. It was the intervention of William Stanley and his forces that had turned the tide in favour of Henry at the Battle of Bosworth. It must have been difficult for Henry when it was reported that his close ally William Stanley had said he would not fight against Warbeck if it turned out that he was indeed the young Duke.

Henry was left with no choice but to try him for treason and execute him before facing his enemy in battle. Whilst Perkin Warbeck was believed to resemble his supposed father, Edward IV, it appears as though any similarities ended there. Edward IV had been an excellent soldier. Warbeck was not. As soon as battle started, he fled and was easily captured, with his Scottish wife. Henry VII appeared lenient in the way he treated Warbeck, imprisoning him in the Tower, but sparing his life. This leniency would not last. There were reports that Warbeck was plotting with the young Earl of Warwick and had tried to escape. Despite rumours that this was set up by Henry himself, he had Warwick and Warbeck tried and executed for treason. In 1499, the threat posed by Perkin Warbeck was finally extinguished.

The way Henry dealt with Warbeck seems to suggest that he did genuinely fear the boy and the threat he posed to his own position. It could be argued that this proves that Henry VII did not kill the boys. He would only fear someone claiming to be the Duke of York if he hadn't killed them and was unsure of what had happened to them. When Simnel appeared, claiming to be Warwick, Henry seemed more confident in dealing with the threat, allowing the boy to live and to retain his freedom as he knew he couldn't be Warwick. Warwick was securely held in the Tower. There is more urgency to his attempts to neutralise Warbeck that would be unlikely if he were as confident that the latest pretender could also not be who he was claiming to be.

This position is supported by Vergil who states that Henry VII was worried sick about the threat posed to him by Warbeck.[lxxii] The Calendar of State Papers also refers to Henry's dread of being expelled by Richard, Duke of York.[lxxiii]

However, this evidence is not that straightforward and is not as strong as it might seem. Prosecutors may simply state that Henry was so confident in declaring Warbeck an imposter because he was in the best position to know he was an imposter, having killed the real Duke of York.

If people were unsure of what happened to the boys there was always the chance that people would believe him. This may be what Henry feared. Maybe he did not fear the boy himself but the ghost of the boy that was haunting him as people flocked to support the imposter, Perkin Warbeck.

Another piece of evidence that can be used to support claims of Henry's innocence is the way that he treated his mother in law, Elizabeth Woodville. Elizabeth had been a York queen. Although she had been involved in the plotting to make Henry Tudor King, offering her daughter as a bride, Elizabeth seems to have suffered a change of heart and soon released her daughters into Richard III's care and encouraged her son to turn his back on Tudor and return to court.

Yet, Henry Tudor was pledged to marry her daughter and unite the Houses of York and Lancaster. It was important to show the two houses happy in their new settlement. To this end, Elizabeth Woodville appears to have been treated with respect at Henry's court and was awarded estates that would allow her to regain some of her former glory.

This remained the same until around the time that Lambert Simnel started posing problems for Henry VII. Suddenly Elizabeth Woodville was stripped of all her properties and was sent to live a simple life in a nunnery at Bermondsey. Elizabeth found herself separated from her family and removed from the life of luxury she had become used to as Queen. It was reported that when she died, she was so poor that all she could leave her children was blessings.

Based on Elizabeth Woodville's reputation it would be hard to believe that she wound have voluntarily reduced herself to such a state, so far away from the children she had spent so much of her life fighting to protect.

This apparent punishment combined with the timing, so close to Simnel's challenge led to speculation that Elizabeth Woodville had been implicated in the plot to crown the boy claiming to be the Earl of Warwick. David Baldwin goes so far as to say that she was so implicated in treason that it was dangerous to be associated with her.[lxxiv]

This could be used as evidence that Henry did not kill the boys. Maybe he punished Elizabeth Woodville because he feared that she was plotting to remove Henry so that one of the boys could return to the country and claim their right to be king. Simnel was claiming to be the Earl of Warwick which would not benefit Elizabeth Woodville directly, but Henry would not have had sight of either the boys in the Tower or Lambert Simnel. He could not be sure what enemy he was truly facing and if there was any evidence that Elizabeth Woodville had any connections to the plot this would have increased his fear. This would suggest that he did not know what happened to the boys and therefore could not have killed them.

It can, however, also be argued that the relationship between Elizabeth Woodville and Henry Tudor is irrelevant to the issue of whether he is guilty or not. Some of the estates that were confiscated from Elizabeth Woodville were customarily held by the queen and would have ended up being held by her anyway. It could therefore have been a practical decision by a king famed for his frugality to move the estates to his own wife. The only issue with this argument is the timing. Why give the estates to Elizabeth Woodville in the first place if he planned to take them back to give his wife?.Although when he gave the estates to his mother-in-law, he may not have had time to understand the true scale of the financial situation facing the royal court and the country at large.

At the time the estates were confiscated, Henry VII claimed to be angry with Elizabeth Woodville for surrendering her daughters to Richard III and placing them in danger. Again, this could be a legitimate explanation for his actions, yet it would have to be questioned why he felt it right to take that action then, three years after the event, and why if he was so angered by this action, he awarded her the estates in the first place.

Another decision by Henry VII in November 1487, regarding his mother-in-law pours doubt on claims she was being punished for plotting against him. At this time, Henry suggested Elizabeth Woodville as a potential bride for the Scottish King, James III. This would be somewhat reckless if Henry VII feared that Elizabeth was working against him or if he believed that the boys were still alive. If anything, this suggests that he did not consider her a threat to his position. After all, she was the mother of his wife, the Queen, any action she took to hurt Henry, would also hurt Elizabeth of York and the chances of their children carrying on the dynasty they had created.

Whilst conspiracy theories will always continue around the reason why Elizabeth Woodville was sent to Bermondsey and reduced to poverty, there are enough alternative arguments to discredit this evidence of Henry's innocence. His treatment of Elizabeth Woodville is not convincing evidence that Henry VII did not play some part in the murder of her sons.

Another argument to support the claim that Henry VII was innocent was that he never allowed his wife, Elizabeth, to publicly meet Warbeck to confirm that he was not the brother she had been raised with.

At some point the king had custody of both Lambert Simnel and Perkin Warbeck and at no point where they believed to have been in contact with Elizabeth of York. Whilst this is more understandable with Simnel, as he was not claiming to be her brother. She would certainly have spent more time with her cousin, the Earl of Warwick than Henry VII and his inner circle. At some point Henry VII released the Earl of Warwick so he could talk to people and confirm that he was indeed in the custody of Henry. He could have resolved the issue with Simnel simply enough by asking Elizabeth of York to confirm that he was not Warwick. Yet this never appears to have happened.

It is harder still to understand why Warbeck, claiming to be the younger brother of Elizabeth was never publicly put in front of Elizabeth. At an early age, Edward V had moved away from his family to Ludlow to prepare him for his role as Prince of Wales and his contact with Elizabeth would have been limited. This was not the case with Richard. He stayed with his parents and sisters. He went into sanctuary with Elizabeth of York until he was asked to join Edward V in the Tower. She would have been in an excellent position to confirm that the Warbeck boy was indeed an imposter.

One motive for Henry not taking this action is that he was not convinced that Warbeck was an imposter. His actions here only seem understandable if he was worried that something in Elizabeth's reaction would fail to convince people that he was an imposter.

It may be that it was not worth the risk. Whether the boy was an imposter, Elizabeth was under the control of the king and may not have been able to go against him and confirm that the boy in front of her was indeed her brother.

Elizabeth also had a lot to lose if she confirmed the boy was her brother. Richard would have a better claim to the throne than her husband, herself, and her children.

With Elizabeth having everything to lose it should have been a straightforward matter of asking her to confirm that the boy was not her brother. This is the action that would seem reasonable if Henry was one hundred percent certain that the boy was not her brother, one hundred percent sure because he was the one who had had him killed.

One interpretation that can be used to suggest that Henry was innocent is that he was nervous that Elizabeth, overcome with emotion at coming face to face with the brother she had believed to be dead would not be able to hide the truth. Maybe he was still not sure that her allegiance was totally with the Tudor dynasty and would use the chance to side with her estranged brother.

Of course, Henry may have just wanted to appear dismissive of the claims by Warbeck and didn't want to lend any credence to it by getting his wife involved. One thing that we can be certain of is that by staying silent on the matter of Perkin Warbeck, Elizabeth and Henry could be jeopardising everything they worked for as people continued to believe that the boy in the Tower was Richard, Duke of York, a figurehead for rebellion against the Tudor regime.

When considering the evidence or Richard's guilt it was identified that to benefit from their deaths, he would have had to make the deaths public. Surely, the same applied to Henry VII, especially when we consider the problems he faced from Perkin Warbeck.

Henry VII appeared to be haunted by the boys as he faced the threat of imposters appearing, claiming to be the boys and claiming the throne for themselves. This indicates that his failure to confirm the death of the boys suggests his innocence.

His failure to state what had happened to the boys suggests he was as unsure of what had happened to them as everybody else.

Here was the perfect opportunity to arrange a search of the Tower and to then confirm the sad news that the boys had indeed been killed. He could place the blame on Richard III, which would help to portray him as the man who had saved the English from the child-killing tyrant. Yet he never accused Richard implicitly of the crime. The Act of Attainder passed against Richard III makes a passing mention of the shedding of infants' blood but does not reference the young king and his brother as victims of Richard III.

As with Richard, there was no benefit to Henry VII, in killing the boys and then not publicising their deaths, which can be argued as evidence of his innocence and the belief that he feared that the boys were still out there somewhere beyond his reach.

In 1502, James Tyrell was accused of treason and was executed. Thomas More tells us in detail about Tyrell and his confession to killing the boys on the orders of Richard III. Yet nobody except More refers to this confession and nobody else appears to have had sight of it. Surely. If there was a confession to the murder of the boys, which would secure the position of the king it would have been publicised and kept safe. It was also noted that although Tyrell was executed, it was not for the crime of regicide or murder of the boys. One of the accomplices was also set free. This had led some to believe that the confession of Tyrell was a convenience designed to limit support for further imposters and Dighton was set free to spread the story of the boy's deaths.

Yet, this does not explain the lack of information relating to searches of the Tower or other places in London for evidence of what had happened to them.

Henry may not have needed to conduct a search because he knew exactly what had happened to them. His inaction could also be explained by the desire for thoughts of the young boys with stronger claims to the throne to fade and not wanting to stir up the rumours about the boys. It was reported that most people thought the boys were dead so there was no need to raise the subject again as Henry didn't want people thinking too much about who had the best claim to the throne.

Henry Tudor was not in England when the boys are believed to have been murdered so some people believe he cannot possibly have been involved. Yet this does allow for the fact that even from his exile, Henry could have been the person to give the order, as it was claimed Richard III had to James Tyrell. Rebellions against Richard III first broke out in the name of the young princes. Only once rumours swept the country that the boys were dead, did people look to Henry Tudor as an alternative candidate.

It is also noted that at the time nobody blamed Henry VII, or anybody associated with him for the murders. It is only more recently as we begin to revisit the evidence against Richard III that Henry Tudor has been shot to prominence as a main suspect. Whilst this could be an indication that nobody believed he was involved, we also must cautiously consider that most of the chroniclers were writing at a time when Henry VII was their king and they would not have wanted to risk his wrath. We can never be sure how much of what was written was truth and how much was what they believed their king wanted to read or hear.

Whilst nobody was sure what had happened to the boys, Henry Tudor would have faced invading England, beating Richard, only to potentially find himself faced with the two boys who had stronger claims and would significantly destroy the support base he had created.

We also need to consider what Henry would have done, if, on arrival in London he was indeed confronted by the boys, alive and well. Having risked everything would he now make way to restore the York king, Edward V.

Whilst there is not enough evidence to find Henry VII guilty of the murders, it is certain that he had the means, motive and opportunity, with as much, if not more to gain from their deaths than the lead suspect, Richard III.

Chapter 13 – Henry Stafford – Background

Apart from historians, there are probably many people who do not know who the second Duke of Buckingham was or how he fits into this mystery. That is because, although some people believed him to be responsible for the crime, he has not been vilified in the same way as Richard III. Here we will look at the important nobleman who played such a vital role in helping Richard III usurp his young nephews and to hide them away in the Tower.

When Henry Stafford was born in 1454, he was born into one of the most important families in the country. Young Henry could boast of having many links of his own to the throne of England. Yet they were through the claims of daughters from younger sons so despite his ties to royalty, his own regal ambitions would have seemed distant. Whilst nobody would believe that he was ever going to take the title, King of England, as he grew up. he would have been able to console himself with the fact that he was one of the most important noblemen in the country.

The Stafford's had through time, advanced themselves to become one of England's greatest families using prestigious marriages to heiresses who would significantly aid their rise to prominence

By the time the Houses of York and Lancaster faced off against each other at the Battle of Northampton in 1460, Henry had already lost his father and would now, still as a young child, inherit the title of Duke of Buckingham, from his grandfather, Humphrey Stafford who would become another casualty of the Cousin's War.

From the little we know about Humphrey Stafford, the first Duke of Buckingham, it appears as though he was not particularly popular, the combination of a fiery temper and ability to bear a grudge making him enemies he needed to be wary of.

Despite this, he appears to have done what he could to navigate himself and his family through the political tensions that were building. Humphrey Stafford was a Lancastrian and loyal to the king. Yet at the same time he is reported as having tried to reconcile the Duke of York with King Henry VI and Margaret of Anjou. Whilst trying to reduce tensions and keep everyone happy, he ran the risk of having his loyalty questioned. When battle lines were drawn and hopes of reconciliation lost, Humphrey Stafford declared himself for Lancaster. Fighting for King Henry VI, Humphrey Stafford would lose his life.

The death of Humphrey Stafford, so soon after the loss of his own son, thrust his young grandson into the full glare of the new Yorkist king's court. Little Henry Stafford had lost the protection of the family patriarch and would now have his fate decided by the king, who had lost his father and brother at the hands of the Lancastrian forces during the battle for control of the country.

When deciding who would be granted the wardship of the young Buckingham boy, Edward IV certainly made sure he kept the boy where he could be monitored as closely as possible.

Following his marriage to the low born Elizabeth Woodville, Edward was eager to please his new bride. She was given the warship of the young Duke. It was later stated that this was unacceptable to the Duke, to be placed in the care of an upstart, but at the time he had no say in the matter, and this may have been a resentment that lasted long after Elizabeth Woodville's control of him had expired.

The benefit that Elizabeth Woodville got from the wardship of Henry Stafford was that she could benefit from the vast wealth he inherited, until he came of age. However, Elizabeth Woodville was using her influence over the king and her ward to plan for a much longer-term benefit for the Woodville family.

If Henry Stafford felt demeaned when Elizabeth Woodville was given his wardship, we can only begin to imagine how he felt when as a ten-year-old boy, she arranged for him to be married to her equally low born sister, Catherine Woodville. Elizabeth Woodville's family were certainly of humble heritage and she wanted to use the new power she had as queen to advance the fortunes of her siblings and she did this by arranging advantageous marriages for them.

The fact that the marriage was rushed through when the Duke was only ten-years-old, shows that Elizabeth Woodville knew what a prize he would be for her sister, a prize being eyed up by Richard Warwick, possibly for the marriage of one of his own daughters.

Dominic Mancini reported that Stafford was far from happy about the match and claims he was forced into the marriage going so far as to say that he despised the Woodville family.[lxxv] At the same time, this match also made him the brother-in-law of the King of England. The Lancastrian Duke would now find his own prosperity tied to the success of the House of York.

Whatever, Henry Stafford's feelings were, the marriage proved a success in providing him with an heir. His marriage to Catherine Woodville produced three sons and two daughters. As he grew into adulthood, Henry Stafford had every reason to believe that a bright future lay in store for him. Thanks to his inheritance from his grandfather he was incredibly wealthy and held vast amounts of land in several counties, but mainly around the Midlands and Wales. The series of promising marriages that had helped the Stafford family to rise in prominence also led Henry to believe he was entitled to a share of the large Bohun inheritance which was being held by the Crown.

His controversial marriage to Catherine Woodville, as distasteful to him as it may have been, also promised to advance the position of Henry Stafford. He was now related to the new king and at the centre of his court. This offered a unique opportunity for Henry to extend his wealth and power.

The only thing standing in the way of Henry Stafford's further rise to prominence was the king himself. Edward IV appears to have either disliked or distrusted his new brother-in-law. The first issue that caused upset between the two men was Edward's position regarding the Bohun inheritance that Henry Stafford claimed he was entitled to a share of. Henry Stafford claimed that as he was the male heir, most of the inheritance should now be released from the Crown and revert to himself. Edward disagreed. The Bohun inheritance was now part of the Crown and he didn't want to part with it. Edward IV rejected Henry Stafford's claim to the inheritance and the first blow to Henry Stafford's promising future had been struck.

It was not only Henry's financial hopes that Edward IV seemed ready to crush. The great political future expected of such an important nobleman in the country also failed to materialise. The appointments and favours that would be expected to be passed to such an important figure were few and far between.

Edward IV certainly excluded Henry Stafford from his inner circle. Henry Stafford would often be present at festivities, such as the marriage of Anne Mowbray to the young Duke of York. Yet he would often be passed over for areas of responsibility. During the reign of Edward IV, Henry Stafford was very much shown to be an outsider. The grand status he had hoped for appeared to be beyond his reach, until April 1483.

When Edward IV died, he had clearly alienated Henry Stafford who was therefore less inclined to fight for the right of Edward V to rule England. Henry Stafford quickly identified an opportunity to move firmly from the outskirts of the royal court to take centre stage. There is no record of him having any close relationship with Richard III prior to Edward IV's death.

Yet, following the death, he quickly made himself available to Richard and an ally against the rumoured conspiracies of the Woodvilles to deny Richard the Protectorate.

At every step of the journey towards Richard III taking the throne for himself, Stafford was there by his side. It was him actively working to convince leading figures that they should ask Richard to take the throne himself. It was Stafford who was there when Edward V was placed in the custody of Richard III, and it was Stafford who decided he should be sent to the Tower and offered his own men to guard the boy.

Excluded and humiliated by Edward IV, Henry Stafford had taken the initiative upon his death and allied himself with the most important person in the country at the time. His help in usurping the throne had made him invaluable to Richard and he would soon reap the rewards, which would see the Duke of Buckingham taken a lot more seriously, to the point where he became the second most important person in England after King Richard III himself.

Grateful for the help he had received from Henry Stafford, Duke of Buckingham, Richard III was quick to lavish reward after reward on his new ally. Stafford was granted vast lands and authority in Wales that allowed him to act like a sovereign there. He was awarded the titles of Great Chamberlain and Steward of England. On 15 May, Richard named the Duke of Buckingham as Constable of England and some even believe that there was a deal to marry one of Stafford's daughters to Richard's son Edward, the new Prince of Wales.

Henry Stafford, second Duke of Buckingham had left the frustrations of the previous years behind and was now riding high as the most trusted ally of the king and this increased his power and influence at an unprecedented speed. Nobody would underestimate him again as he lapped up the power and wealth that came his way.

History's assessment of the decisions Henry Stafford took in 1483 has not been kind. This has led to the image of an ambitious, ruthless man, bitter at the success of others and envious of all he did not have.

The apparent lack of loyalty to both his own nephew, Edward V and to the man who made him the second most important person in the country are used to portray Stafford as am ambitious schemer.

Stafford, as Duke of Buckingham should have been one of the most important people in Edward IV's inner circle. Yet this was not to be. Instead he was required to attend and take part in festivities and ceremonies, whilst everybody knew he lacked any influence with the king and was regularly passed over for honours and responsibilities. Stafford can only have expected that this would continue if Edward V, who had been isolated in Ludlow, surrounded by Woodville family members and supporters, came to power.

Stafford appears to have wasted no time in identifying the mistrust between the Woodville's and Richard III and was at Richard's side during every step along the way to helping him become the new king and encouraging the people to accept Richard as their ruler. He would have been involved in the plans to arrest Lord Rivers and to try to have him executed, as well as the plans to arrest Lord Hastings and execute him without trial. His ambition had made him the most important person in the country after the king and he appears to have done whatever it took to gain that power. The man who had shown the level of his ambition, using regal images in his coat of arms was not finished.

Not long after the coronation of Richard III, the coronation that Stafford had helped so much to bring about, Stafford was about to change sides again. Stafford turned against Richard III and became involved with the plotting of Margaret Beaufort to overthrow Richard.

Why he did this has been subject to dispute. Those that believe it was down to his ruthless ambition believe that he wanted the throne for himself. He had distant links to the throne, but with Richard III and the princes out of the way, his claim had certainly strengthened. Chroniclers such as Vergil believe that he was not aiming to become king himself and point to the aims of the rebellions to confirm this.

The first rebellion was aimed at freeing the young princes from the Tower and putting Edward V back on the throne where he belonged. This would weaken Stafford's position if he harboured any desire to be king. Yet, if he knew the boys were dead, he could be involved in the rebellion knowing that once the boy's deaths were known they would need a new figurehead to promote as an alternative candidate to support.

Yet, when the rumours of the boys' deaths started to spread, Stafford did not lead the fight to become king but found himself involved in a plot to put a more obscure contender, Henry Tudor on the throne instead. This suggests that Stafford did not want to be king himself and was rebelling against Richard III for noble reasons.

However, Henry Tudor was very much unknown to the English people. He had been in exile since he was a child and Stafford may have believed that this plot could have brought Henry Tudor out into the open, and when he could only attract a small amount of support, Buckingham could use all the power and influence he had gained to challenge Tudor and make himself the new king, having rid himself of all the main obstacles to his own reign.

While we will never know the reason behind his actions people will still argue that Henry Stafford was an ambitious and ruthless man who would do whatever it took to promote his own position. There will also continue to be those that believe that there is a simpler explanation for the behaviour of Henry Stafford.

Maybe Henry Stafford was a political pragmatist who could see which way events were unfolding and made sure that he would find himself on the winning side. Maybe he joined Richard III because he sensed in the country, the ill feeling towards the Woodvilles and the fears people had that Edward V would be manipulated by them. At the death of Edward IV people would have to choose sides and Henry Stafford chose well and made himself invaluable to the winner, Richard III.

As things developed and people started to fear that Richard III had killed the Princes in the Tower, Stafford may have felt the country begin to divide again and knew he would have to analyse the situation and pick the side he believed had the best chance of winning. After assessing the two sides Henry Stafford chose to ally himself with the Tudor plot.
Stafford was not necessarily the ambitious double-dealer he has been portrayed as, maybe he was just a particularly good political strategist who picked the right side to be on at the right time.

Another option is that Stafford was neither ambitious nor politically astute. Maybe he was weak-willed and impressionable. He could have shown himself willing to change sides because he lacked natural ability and would find himself easily manipulated by those around them. Before the rebellion that was named after him, Stafford had been spending a lot of time with his prisoner, Bishop Morton, a known enemy of Richard III, a key ally of Margaret Beaufort, and supporter of her plot to bring Henry Tudor to England to challenge the king. Had Stafford allowed his wily prisoner to manipulate him into turning against the man who had given him so many rewards and made him an important member of his inner circle?

One thing that we can say about Henry Stafford is that whatever his motivations, he was not a popular man. Despite being brother-in-law to the king, he didn't make an impression on him, and Stafford was very much an outsider at the Woodville dominated court. He also appears to have been a tough landlord and was unpopular with his tenants. After his promotions by Richard III, Stafford had significant estates across the country. Despite this, when he tried to call upon his men to support him in his rebellion, he found that he could not muster a lot of support and that his own people were quite willing to turn on him and foil the plans of their own Master.

Regardless of whether Stafford's decision to rebel stemmed from greed, ambition, realism or revulsion at finding out the princes have been killed, what we do know is that he did indeed turn away from and raise his troops against his royal benefactor.

The rebellion would forever be referred to as 'Buckingham's Rebellion' even though Stafford was neither its leader nor its instigator. At some point he appears to have reached agreement with Margaret Beaufort and given his support to the plan that Henry Tudor return to England to challenge Richard III, and when he succeeds he should unite the warring houses through marriage to Elizabeth of York.

Certainly, Henry Stafford appeared to have been committed to the plot by the 24 September, when he wrote to Henry Tudor, offering his support. Henry Stafford would begin to use his considerable wealth and influence to try to assemble a great force to attack Richard III. Richard was furious when he began to be informed that Stafford had changed sides. Richard III summoned Henry Stafford to meet with him. Stafford feigned illness and refused. Stafford was summoned again by Richard. This time he refused and at this point Stafford appears to have been preparing to face the king, but only on the battlefield.

On 10 October 1483, the Duke of Norfolk informed the king that the city of London was under threat of attack from the rebels and John Howard was charged with repulsing the rebels.

Stafford had several issues that would ultimately lead to the failure of the rebellion. Firstly, Thomas Stanley was well known for playing both sides, but as the stepfather of Henry Tudor may have been expected to support the rebellion in the hope of making Tudor the king. There was no love lost though between Stanley and Stafford. If Stanley was willing to risk all for the rebellion, the involvement of Stafford may have led to him changing his allegiance and fighting against the rebellion.

The second factor that hampered Stafford's efforts was his ability to garner support amongst other leading nobleman and his own men. Stafford was not popular and found men were not willing to fight for him. The weather also played a part in making the attack harder and slowing it down, This, and the betrayal of Stafford by his own servants, led to the rebellion being put down easily and without much bloodshed.

Henry Stafford was captured in Shropshire and taken to Salisbury where he asked for an audience with the king. This was refused and on the second November 1483 he was executed.

Early in 1484, Richard III laid out the charges against Henry Stafford in an Act of Attainder. He was charged with inviting Henry Tudor to invade England.

Henry Stafford had, against the odds, risen to the top, second in the country only to the king. Yet within months of achieving more than he could have hoped for, he had tried to raise a force against Richard III and having failed, been executed as a traitor.

Was this the worst of his crimes or do we have reason to believe that he could have been the person responsible for killing the two young boys he had been responsible for guarding, in the Tower of London?

Chapter 14 – The Case Against Henry Stafford

For Henry Stafford to be considered a credible suspect he would need to have a motive to kill the princes. Whilst we cannot be sure why Henry Stafford made the decisions' he did in 1483, there are historians who believe that he wanted the crown for himself. If we accept this as the reasoning behind his decision to join the rebellion against Richard III it would certainly give him a strong motive for wanting the boys out of the way.

When Edward IV died, Henry Stafford was not known to have had a close relationship with Richard, Duke of Gloucester. He quickly formed an alliance, offering any support Richard needed to side-line Edward V. As a reward for this he was given vast wealth and power. Despite this he decided to turn on his ally and benefactor and join in the plot to crown Henry Tudor.

It is possible that for Henry Stafford, being the second most important person in the country was not enough and no matter how much he received from Richard, he still envied the king for the extra power, wealth and status that he was so close to. Stafford would have been aware that he had links to the throne himself and could have planned to work towards the ultimate promotion. Certainly, this was Thomas More's view of Stafford's actions, when he claimed, 'Very truth it is, the duke was a high-minded man, and evil could bear the glory of another; so that I have heard of some that the duke, at such time as the crown was first set upon the protector's head, his eye could not abide the sight thereof, but wried his head another way'.[lxxvi]

Support for the claim that he aimed to make himself king is also supported by the details surrounding the start of the October rebellion. The initial rebellion was aimed at freeing the boys and restoring Edward V. This was not helpful to the aim of making Stafford the undisputed candidate to replace Richard. At this time, the rumours of the boys' disappearance began. This had a dual benefit to Henry Stafford. It removed the princes as figureheads for the rebellion against Richard, whilst also helping to turn public support against Richard as he took the blame for harming his young, innocent nephews. This would have presented Stafford with the perfect opportunity to come to the fore as the person who could save the country from the tyrannical king.

Not everybody believed that Henry Stafford either wanted to or believed he could, become the next King of England. Although Vergil does not claim to know the reason for Stafford turning against Richard III, he did not believe that it was because he sought the Crown for himself.[lxxvii] One piece of evidence that suggests that Stafford did not want to be king was that he joined the plotting of Margaret Beaufort, naming Henry Tudor as Richard III's rival. The fact that he supported another man's claim can be used to claim not only that he did not want to be king, but that he therefore had no motive to kill the boys in the Tower.

This view though does not take account of the political strategizing Stafford had engaged in whilst supporting Richard's claim to the throne. We must accept that it was possible that Henry Stafford was using Margaret Beaufort and her plans for her son, Henry Tudor.

Henry Stafford was as the heart of the royal court, one of the most famous men in the country. Henry Tudor, who had always been considered a threat to the House of York, was a young man, who had been held in exile for fourteen years.

Strategically. Stafford would have been in a stronger position to gain support, troops and money and when the unknown Tudor boy came to England he would only have had limited support, allowing Stafford to easily defeat him and get rid of the threat of Tudor once and for all. At that point he may have underestimated the determination of Margaret Beaufort or his own unpopularity.

It has also been argued that it may have been the murder of the princes that caused Stafford to defect to Tudor. It has been argued that whilst he was happy to argue the illegitimacy of the boys, help to overthrow them and lock them away in the Tower, the news that Richard III had killed the boys was too much for Stafford to bear. When he realised the step, Richard had taken he was horrified and could no longer support him.[lxxviii] If this was accepted as the reason for his moves against Richard it would rule him out as a suspect in this case. There is no evidence to confirm the reason for Stafford's actions.

It is equally possible that he only decided to support Tudor when he realised that he himself did not have the support required to make him a viable candidate. This then would rule Stafford in as a suspect. It was once the rumours that the boys were dead that their support was turned to a new candidate, it may have been after the murder of the two boys that Stafford realised that nobody would support him, the way he had convinced people to support Richard, or the way people were now turning to Tudor. It is also plausible that Henry Stafford didn't have any choice but to rebel. He had shown a talent for picking the winning side, seeing how unpopular Richard was becoming, maybe the political realist in him realised that he had to be on the winning side and retain what he could under Tudor.

There is also the possibility that Stafford's decision to turn against Richard had nothing to do with the princes at all and was a matter of self-preservation. More than two hundred years previously, Simon de Montford had risen to be the second most powerful man in the kingdom at the hands of the King, Henry III. Despite his loyalty and support for Henry, de Montford would witness Henry turn against him to save his own skin. Stafford would also have known that he had a lot of enemies in England and a king ruthless enough to deny his own nephew the crown and indeed his liberty. Maybe Stafford blinked first and took aim at Richard before he would suffer a similar betrayal to that of Simon de Montford.

As we can see, there are many different arguments that can be put forward to explain, Stafford's role in the rebellion against Richard III. Therefore, whilst his own ambition to be king can be given as a motive, this evidence is weakened by all the alternative arguments as to why Henry Stafford rebelled. What we do know is that Henry Stafford was taking a massive gamble with his decision to rebel. He had gained enormous power and wealth under Richard III and he was unlikely to receive the same rewards for supporting Henry Tudor. He was risking an unprecedented fall from grace if the rebellion failed.   We must decide whether he was ruthless or ambitious enough to take the ultimate gamble of killing the boys to further his own desires.

Another motive for Henry Stafford to commit this crime is revenge. Henry Stafford had suffered many slights at the hands of Edward IV and the Woodville family. Stafford's apparent antipathy towards Edward IV and his kin is believed to have started when he was a young boy. Stafford was born into one of the most prominent families in the country.

Edward IV's wife was not. She was a commoner. She was considered far too low born to be a suitable match for the King of England.

When she was granted the wardship of the young Duke of Buckingham, he would have been aware of the great disparity between the status of himself and the woman who would now have complete control over not only himself, but also over his vast wealth which he could expect to be fully exploited until he was old enough to take it back under his control. Although he would grow up to find his financial position had not been weakened by the control of Elizabeth Woodville, the issue of his wardship was something that must have caused some resentment to the man who wanted his regal connections represented in his own coat of arms.

Decisions made during his wardship would be a further source of resentment for Stafford. Elizabeth Woodville ensured her Lancastrian ward was forever tied to the Woodvilles and Edward IV, by marrying him to her sister Catherine. Whilst the issue of his wardship may have been difficult to deal with, this marriage would change his prospects completely. Henry Stafford, with his significant wealth and status was an advantageous match and he would have hoped for a wife that added to the wealth he already had. He may have been a potential match for one of the daughters of the Earl of Warwick, which would have significantly increased his power and influence. Yet he found himself being used by Elizabeth Woodville to secure a stable and prosperous future for her own family.

It has been argued that the marriage was not necessarily as bad as has been portrayed for Stafford as he would have received financial incentives from the king and it did increase his power and influence as now he had another tie to royalty, he was the brother-in-law of the king himself.

This may have been the third cause of resentment towards Edward IV and his family. Technically, Stafford was close to the king, but this proved to be a hollow prize. Edward IV appears to have made his feelings regarding Stafford clear during his reign through the roles offered to him. Stafford attended family and ceremonial occasions, such as the wedding of Anne Mowbray to Richard, Duke of York, but it was clear that he was not trusted or liked. He was not given any positions of responsibility and was clearly not close to the king. Coming from a prominent family, the snub to Stafford's ambitions must have stung.

Clearly, the treatment he received at the hands of the king and his wife must have been difficult for a proud man like Stafford. This makes it easy to believe that he may have claimed that his feelings to the king were hostile and so he was not concerned about his sons and their right to succeed him. This is a far cry from killing the two boys. Could the humiliation that Stafford felt at the hands of Edward IV push him to the point of killing two young boys? People have killed for less.

If there is one thing that has been known to drive people to kill, it must be money. As well as being politically shunned by Edward IV, Henry Stafford also had a big issue with him regarding an inheritance he believed should be passed to him. Stafford believed that as the male heir, he should receive the substantial inheritance of his Bohun relatives. Edward IV disagreed. Edward IV absorbed the inheritance into the crown revenue. Henry Stafford petitioned the king to have the inheritance passed to himself, but to his chagrin, Edward refused. This was another setback at the hands of the king and queen for the Duke of Buckingham, who wasn't being treated with the respect he may have felt he deserved.

It can be argued that this is not a motive for Henry Stafford to kill the boys. Once the boys were declared illegitimate and Richard III was crowned, he began the process of transferring the Bohun inheritance to Stafford. Yet, we still need to consider this, if as we are led to believe, rebellions were about to break out in the name of Edward V. A Woodville dominated boy king would struggle to be convinced that the man who had helped his uncle take his throne deserved to keep the inheritance that his father had previously denied him.

Stafford's money issues would have become more pronounced as he received more rewards from Richard III. The cost of his new extravagant lifestyle would put a squeeze on his cashflow and therefore whatever rewards he was offered by Richard III, they may never have been enough. Buckingham could only solve the issue of living like a king if he indeed had the revenues of the king. For this, he needed Richard III and the two nephews out of the way.

Whatever we think of Henry Stafford, what is clear is that he did have his own motives for wanting the boys out of the way. Certainly, there were several contemporary chroniclers who believed that he was involved in, if not responsible for the disappearance of the boys.

An account of events referred to as Historical Notes of a London Citizen tells us that 'this year King Edward V, late called Prince of Wales and Richard, Duke of York his brother King Edward IV's sons, were put to death in the Tower 'be the vise of the Duke of Buckingham.'[lxxix] Whilst this indicates that there was certainly a belief by some, that the Duke of Buckingham was involved with this crime, there are significant issues with it. The very title of it indicates that we do not know who is making the allegation. There is no indication of how they know this information. This lack of clarity makes it difficult to rely on as a piece of evidence.

The second source, the Dutch Devisie Chronicle, was one of many continental sources to place blame on Stafford.[lxxx] Whilst this was a more official source of information, there are limits to the weight that can be placed on it. Firstly, it was written in the 1500's, long after the events it was reporting had taken place. Maybe this was also a significant time after the character of Henry Stafford as ruthless and ambitious had been widely communicated. There is another issue in consistency. At one point it accuses the Duke of Buckingham of poisoning the boys. Later it goes on to say that he may have only killed the older boy and had the other secretly removed out of the country.

Jean Molinet was another subscriber to the theory that Stafford was behind the murder of the boys.[lxxxi] Molinet states that on the days the boys were murdered, the Duke of Buckingham was in the Tower and wanted the boys out of the way to advance his own claim to the throne. Again, as with the other reports from chroniclers, there are issues regarding timings. Molinet states they were killed in late July. Yet, this is contrary to the reporting of the Croyland Chronicle, which stated that the boys were still alive in August. Although there has been speculation as to the author of the Croyland Chronicle, it has been widely accepted as being the work of somebody who had access to sources close to the royal circle. Therefore, its timing would carry more weight than that of Molinet. If the boys were alive in August this also casts doubt on the claims that the Duke of Buckingham was the one at the Tower who killed him. At the beginning of August, Stafford left London to make his way towards his Welsh holdings. Again, we do not know how they got this information or who their sources were. We also do not know the agenda of a foreign source.

Whether a chronicler is laying the blame at the feet of Richard III or the Duke of Buckingham, there are clearly issues with how much reliance can be placed on them as evidence.

Although they may not be reliable evidence there is an argument that they give us a sense of what the general population believed to have happened. We must remember though that propaganda has been in use for longer than we may care to believe. When rumours circulate and spread, it could be because people believe that is what really happened. On the other hand, when rumours spread and circulate it could be because it serves somebody's purpose. Someone could start the rumour to improve their own position or weaken the position of others.

We see this used to good effect by Henry Stafford himself in 1483. He was happy to see the rumour spread that Edward IV had been pre-contracted to Eleanor Butler, making Edward V illegitimate. Henry Stafford was certainly not present, if and when the precontract occurred. He had no proof of it. Yet it suited his purpose and whether it happened or not, he was happy for this to be believed by the population.

The split of chroniclers blaming either Richard III or Duke of Buckingham give both what we would consider to be reasonable doubt. If there is a chance that both could have done it, it cannot be proved beyond reasonable doubt that it was either one of them.

There are a third group of chroniclers that need to be considered when assessing whether Henry Stafford is guilty. These are the ones that blame both. They believe that Henry Stafford and Richard III were both involved in some way in the murder of the princes.

Commynes, although inconsistent about the death of the boys throughout his account, states, 'King Richard did not last long; nor did the Duke of Buckingham, who had put the children to death.'[lxxxii]

The Ashmolean Manuscripts state that Richard III killed the boys at the prompting of the Duke of Buckingham.[lxxxiii] In addition to the issues of reliability we have previously addressed this leads us to consider another point. If the King of England wanted the boy's dead was Henry Stafford, powerful, but still a subject of the king's authority, in any position to refuse to carry it out.

Alternatively, if it was proposed by Stafford and carried out with the knowledge of the king, surely Richard still carries ultimate responsibility. Either way, the implication that Henry Stafford's involvement was known to the king makes it harder to make a case for guilt against Stafford.

Now that we have considered the evidence of the prosecution against Henry Stafford, we need to examine the evidence that can be put forward in defence of Henry Stafford, second Duke of Buckingham.

Chapter 15 – The Defence of Henry Stafford

Whilst there may be a case to say that Henry Stafford had a reasonable motive to commit this crime, we need to consider whether this is something that he would have been able to achieve.

One argument that has been put forward in his defence is that he did not have the required authority to enter the Tower and so Robert Brackenbury would not have allowed him to enter unless he had a warrant from the king.

Although Brackenbury oversaw the Tower and would exercise authority over it, there are several issues with this argument. The first is that on 15 May 1483, Henry Stafford had been made Constable of England, as reward for the support he had given Richard. In addition to the power he already had, as a close ally of the king and due to his vast wealth, this title was one of the most important titles that could be awarded in the country. This makes it questionable as to whether Brackenbury would have been able to stop Stafford or his men from entering the Tower if this had been Stafford's will.

Another issue is regarding Stafford's purpose for attending the Tower. When Edward V had arrived in London, it was suggested by Stafford that the boy was housed in the Tower of London. A further suggestion from Stafford was that his men were used to guard the boy in the Tower. If it was Stafford's men in the Tower, who had responsibility for looking after the boy, this would give Stafford a legitimate reason to visit and be admitted to the Tower. If a royal warrant was required, this may well have been provided so that he could take responsibility for the safekeeping of Edward V, and later his younger brother Richard.

By forming an alliance with Richard, against the Woodvilles and their supporters, Stafford had enjoyed an unprecedented rise to power. There was nobody in the country with as much power as him, apart from the king. He owned large estates in many counties. This meant that when himself and Richard were believed to be under threat of attack from the Woodvilles, he was able to send a large armed retinue to London, for their protection. If Brackenbury was in any way reluctant to admit Stafford to the Tower, this very public show of strength may have been a deciding factor.

The close relationship Stafford formed quickly with Richard III also makes it unlikely that entry to the Tower would have been refused. He had been by Richard III's side at every step towards making him king and it would not have been unexpected that Richard would want his confidante to have access wherever he needed it.

Whilst it must be accepted that there may have been difficulties in explaining the death or disappearance of the boys to Robert Brackenbury, it also must be accepted that he did indeed have the access to the boys that would have allowed him to commit this crime. His position as Constable of England, close ally of the king and the use of his own men to guard the boys gave him a level of access that would not have been available to many others.

Another factor that must be considered when considering the guilt of Henry Stafford is the fact that following his death on 2 November, after rebelling against the king, Richard III did not blame Stafford for the crime.

This was a time when rumours about the boys were circulating all around the country and causing discontent amongst sections of the population. When Stafford was executed as a traitor, Richard III had the perfect opportunity to confirm the death of the boys, so they could pose no further threat to him, and place the blame on the man who had betrayed his trust.

This appears to support the case that Henry Stafford did not kill the boys. It has been suggested that the only reason for Richard not confirming the death of the boys at the hands of Stafford was because he did not believe the boys were dead. Therefore, Stafford could not be guilty of murdering them. There is another explanation as to why Richard III did not blame Stafford after his death, which does not necessarily assist Stafford's case. Richard and Stafford had been actively working together towards the goal of declaring the boys illegitimate and replacing the boy-king, with his uncle Richard.

There may have been a concern for Richard, that due to the close connection they had together, people would not believe that Stafford had acted alone. The Duke of Buckingham and Richard can be seen as closely plotting to remove Edward V from the throne. There was a risk that if Stafford was blamed for harming the children, there would be a backlash against Richard as people believed that he must have either had knowledge of, or been implicit in, their murder. England was still stunned by the events of the summer of 1483 and without the support of Stafford and his men, he may not have been able to withstand a challenge from opponents wanting to avenge the death of the boys. The silence of Richard III may not have been a sign of Stafford's innocence so much as an act of self-preservation by a new king.

In 1485, Richard III was killed at Bosworth and England once again saw a new monarch crowned. Henry Tudor, or Henry VII as he became, did not have the same close ties to Henry Stafford and was due to be married to the sister of the princes. Surely, if Henry Stafford had murdered the boys or had any involvement in their disappearance, this would have been the time to announce it. Henry VII was portraying himself as the man who had saved the nation from the tyranny of Richard III.

Henry Stafford was the man believed to be responsible for allowing Richard to remove his nephew as king and take the throne himself. Henry VII could only benefit from announcing that the boys were dead, and Henry Stafford was involved in their murders. This would remove the fear of imposters pretending to be the princes and help the country move on from the reign of Richard III, accepting the new Tudor dynasty.

Yet again, there may have been other factors behind the decision to stay silent than innocence on the part of Henry Stafford. Whilst Henry VII did not have the same close connections with Stafford as Richard III did, he did still have an important connection.

Henry Stafford had joined the rebellion aimed at replacing Richard III with Henry Tudor. Uncertainty about when the boys were killed meant that decrying Stafford as their murderer could be as dangerous for Henry VII as it would have been for his predecessor. If Stafford was blamed there may be questions about whom he had hoped to benefit. Henry VII was relatively unknown to the English people and it was the hard work of his mother that convinced people to join his cause. Losing those supporters who may have believed he was involved in any decision to harm the boys could see the Tudor dynasty destroyed as quickly as it was created.

During the 1990's, the Conservative party was led by John Major. During his time in charge there were several scandals involving members of his government. The people involved were quickly identified and named by the tabloid press and they resigned from the government. Yet this was not the end of it. The Major government is still remembered as the government of Sleaze. It was not just the people involved that suffered from the scandal and disgrace. It tainted the rest of the government and saw the Labour Party win a major landslide in 1997, forcing the Conservatives out of power for the first time in eighteen years. If Stafford was involved, this would still have tainted Richard III or Henry Tudor. Silence may have been the lesser of two evils in this matter.

Whilst Richard III and Henry VII may have had fears about being tainted by Stafford's actions, there was one man who was able to lay the blame at Stafford's door if he believed he was the killer. That man was Robert Brackenbury, the Constable of the Tower of London at the time the boys disappeared. As the person with ultimate responsibility for the security of the Tower, he would have been in the best position to know who had been in the Tower the last time the boys were seen. At the time of the murder, Brackenbury could have been intimidated into maintaining his silence by the number of armed guards Stafford had in the Tower and around the city of London. Yet this no longer applied following Stafford's execution. Surely, if Brackenbury believed Stafford guilty of any involvement this would have been the time to make it known.

Brackenbury's silence is harder to understand. He had been responsible for keeping secure a deposed king and his younger brother. Under his care they had disappeared and if not involved in their murder he may well have been suspected of being negligent in allowing this to happen. Wouldn't he have taken the opportunity to clear his own name?

Whilst this can be used to argue that Brackenbury did not blame Stafford because he was innocent, or the boys were still alive there may have been other reasons why Brackenbury refused to blame Stafford. When Stafford died the fate of the boys was still a mystery, there were rumours of their murder, but there were also rumours of their escape out of the country. If Brackenbury confirmed Stafford had killed the boys, he was ultimately confessing to allowing the boys to come to harm on his watch. He would have to explain to the king, how he had let this happen to his nephews and after witnessing the ruthless way Stafford and other opponents were executed, confirming the death of the boys may have been a risk Brackenbury was not willing to take.

There is also the possibility that Brackenbury was aware that Richard III would also be implicated in the crime due to his previous close relations with Stafford. Brackenbury was one of the people who remained loyal to Richard III, fighting to the death for him at Bosworth. This does not sound like the actions of a man who felt threatened by Richard III or believed him to the cold-blooded killer of two young children.

For different reasons, the silence of each of these individuals is not enough in itself to confirm the innocence of Henry Stafford. An argument that may be more convincing is the strength of his motive. It can be argued that although he may have been ambitious and had reasons to dislike the Woodville family, these were not strong enough reasons to commit the crime of killing two children, especially one who was a former king. Whatever we have come to think of Stafford's character, he showed a certain level of political cunning and strategy when choosing to aide and promote Richard III as the new king. Surely, the man who had been so successful in that venture would have been able to evaluate that he would struggle to gain support for his own bid to be king. It doesn't make sense that Stafford would make such a risky move when the odds of achieving his aim were so low. Yet, Stafford is now considered to have been a proud and jealous man. Maybe the success he enjoyed on behalf of Richard III had given him a false sense of confidence or more realistically he saw the tide turn against Richard, in favour of Henry Tudor and he decided to take the sensible option of trying to come out on the winning side.

When the boys were still alive the process of transferring the disputed Bohun inheritance to Stafford had been initiated. There are rumours that he wanted more and was dissatisfied.

Yet he had been dissatisfied throughout the reign of Edward IV and there is no evidence of him acting with this level of ruthlessness during that time. So why would he do it now when he had gained so much? It is true that his costs would have increased with having to keep such a large armed retinue and extravagance suiting his position. None of this would have been improved through the death of the boys. He would then have to take on Richard III and Henry Tudor, so this seems tenuous as a motive for the killing.

A convincing argument in the defence of Henry Stafford must be the lack of evidence against him. It has been acknowledged that European Chroniclers believed and reported that it was the Duke of Buckingham, either by himself, or with the involvement of the king that was responsible for the killing. We have also identified weaknesses with these accounts and who they used as sources of information. We also have conflicting English sources. Both More and Croyland have Stafford turning on Richard III because he had heard what he had done to the boys and wanted no part of it. What is striking though, is that nobody around Henry Stafford or close to the princes ever came out and said that they knew of his involvement. Stafford appears to have been an unpopular landlord and struggled to inspire loyalty and support during the rebellion. It was his own servants that betrayed him leading to his capture. It would be logical to conclude that anybody who had information about Stafford's involvement in the murder would have made it known, certainly after his death. Yet there are no reports of anybody coming forward with evidence of Stafford's involvement. This must be given significant weight when considering whether he was guilty of this crime or not. Whilst we have been able to identify that Stafford had clear motive, means and opportunity to commit this crime, and should have been investigated for involvement, it is clear that there is insufficient evidence to show that he was involved or that he benefitted significantly from its commission.

It will be hard for most of us to imagine a man so desperate for revenge or to help his own cause, resorting to the killing of two young boys. Yet it still happens today. In 2009 an American mum-of-two disappeared. Following the disappearance, her husband was believed to be the main suspect in her disappearance and death, although the police were never able to prove it. The parents of Susan Powell sought custody of her young sons, and they were granted temporary custody whilst the father of the boys was evaluated. In 2012, the boys were driven to their father's house by a social worker. When they got there, the father lured the boys in and locked the social worker out. He attacked the boys and set the house on fire.

The boys and their father died, and the world was shocked, not just that somebody could do this to two innocent young boys, but that it was at the hands of their own father.[lxxxiv] We will never know why he committed this despicable act, but two potential theories were that it was revenge for losing custody of the children, or self-preservation as the boys continued to talk about the night their mum disappeared. Whilst we find the death of young children unimaginable, regrettably it does occur, for different motives, whether it be a parent murdering their children following the loss of custody or as we identified previously the need to secure the right school place for a child.

Chapter 16 – Thomas Stanley – Background

The next person worthy of further investigation in the murky events of 1483 is Thomas Stanley. The Stanley family successfully navigated the Wars of the Roses by feigning loyalty to both sides before declaring support for the winner at the end of the battle. Whilst his strategy had worked well, Stanley would increasingly find himself the subject of a significant conflict of interest. Should he remain loyal to his King, Richard III, or side with his formidable, second wife, Margaret Beaufort and her ambitions for Henry Tudor, Stanley's stepson.

Whilst he would eventually find himself at the heart of the royal family as stepfather to the king, the Stanley family had enjoyed a rapid rise to prominence within the north west of England.

The Stanley family line can be traced back as far as 1125 and they made themselves useful to the king, serving Richard II and Henry VI. A fortunate marriage helped to bolster the influence of the Stanley family. In 1385 John Stanley married Isabel Lathom. A series of tragedies within the Lathom family, within the first five years of marriage, left Isabel Lathom as the only heiress to the extensive Lathom lands,

By the time of Thomas Stanley's birth in 1435, the family had extensive influence, power and lands in Cheshire, Derbyshire, and Lancashire.

Stanley was named after his father, Thomas Stanley, the first Baron Stanley and it was in Lathom, that Isabel Stanley gave birth to the boy who would become Earl Derby, only fifty years later.

Stanley's father had secured a place in the household of Henry VI, becoming a Privy Councillor, and was trusted by the king. This allowed him to introduce Stanley to life in the royal court at an early age Here he would have witnessed first-hand the growing tensions between the House of Lancaster, led by King Henry VI and the House of York, led by Richard, Duke of York. He would also have been aware as the situation escalated that he needed to make sure he was on the winning side in the battles to come. The Stanley family had excelled at promoting their own self-interest and it was up to Thomas Stanley to continue to do so after his father died in 1459.

As well as his fathers' lands and wealth, Thomas Stanley also inherited the title of Baron Stanley and the King of Mann. While Stanley was getting to grips with his substantial inheritance, he would have been monitoring the political developments and making preparation for the inevitable war to come.

Stanley's first marriage would also give him an important choice to make once war finally broke out. Stanley married Eleanor Neville in the chapel at Middleham Castle in 1451. The Neville's were an important family with considerable power and the match was advantageous for Thomas Stanley. Eleanor was the daughter of Richard Neville, the Earl of Salisbury and sister to Richard Neville, the Earl of Warwick. Salisbury and Warwick became key allies of Richard, Duke of York, and sided with him against the king at the beginning of the Wars of the Roses. In an early defeat for York, Salisbury was killed in battle with Richard, Duke of York and Warwick was forced to flee the country, into exile with the son of the Duke of York, Edward, Earl of March, later Edward IV.

Whilst the marriage to Eleanor may have created political problems and difficult decisions regarding the Stanley family loyalty, it was a success in other ways. Eleanor gave birth to eleven children during their marriage. Sadly, many of their children would die at an early age, but Thomas Stanley would see three of his sons grow up to become important men. His eldest son would become Baron Strange, married to a niece of Elizabeth Woodville, Edward would become the first Baron Monteagle and James would become the Bishop of Ely. Producing so many children may have taken its toll on Eleanor as she died in 1472.

The practical Thomas Stanley would not be single for long. On the twelfth of June 1472, Thomas Stanley married the significant heiress, Margaret Beaufort at Knowsley Hall in Lancashire.

At the time of the marriage both Thomas and Margaret had been recently widowed, and it is believed that this was a strategic marriage for both parties rather than a love match. Margaret Beaufort had demonstrated that her true support was with the House of Lancaster and needed protection from Edward IV. Stanley offered her this protection. Despite suspicions over his own level of loyalty to the House of York, Edward IV knew that due to the power of the Stanley's he needed to keep them on side and gave him greater responsibility and showed greater trust in him. This marriage would allow her to demonstrate her loyalty to the House of York. For Stanley, the marriage was also advantageous. He was marrying a wealthy heiress with royal connections. Thomas Stanley had children from his first marriage and Margaret was devoted to her own son Henry, and no children were born from this marriage. As a practical marriage, it seems to have worked. Margaret was accepted back into the heart of the York regime and seemed to win back the trust of Edward IV.

Stanley also seems to have saved the life of his wife when she was caught plotting against Richard III. Richard was aware of the need to keep the Stanley family on his side and so was forced to administer a lenient punishment to Margaret, giving control of all her estates to her husband, Thomas Stanley.

The nature of this marriage once Henry VII became king also shows that this was a political match. With the king's approval they very much began to lead more separate lives. Margaret was given the right to act as though she were a single woman, with respect to her estates. Although they spent time together, Margaret now spent most of her time with her son, desperate to make up for the fourteen years he was away in exile.

Thomas Stanley navigated the political twists and turns of the war tearing England apart better than most. He managed situations well enough that he never needed to lead his men into any of the battles that broke out throughout the Wars of the Roses. Despite failing to send troops out to support either side, he managed to maintain good favour with the eventual winners. Although they wanted his support, they realised that his power base in the north west meant that whoever was to rule England needed the Stanley's on their side.

To help ease himself back into favour Stanley would gather his forces and make slow progress towards the battle. This allowed him to claim that he would have fought for the victor, he just hadn't made it in time. This tactic was first used in the first major battle to break out once he inherited his father's titles.

This battle was one of the first battles in a war that would last until the beginning of the Tudor dynasty in 1485. The Battle of Blore Heath was fought in Staffordshire in September 1459. The Yorkist forces were led by the Earl of Salisbury, Stanley's father-in-law. Despite this the king's forces hoped that Stanley would declare for them and strengthen their forces significantly.

Stanley made the appearance of preparing for battle and gathered his troops and supplies and started to make his journey to Staffordshire. Stanley, however, was in no rush. His brother William had rushed to join the king's forces, but Thomas Stanley progressed slowly towards the field of battle. He had no intention of joining the battle. Once he arrived at the battlefield, he watched for three days, observing the turns the battle took, evaluating who had the upper hand. On this occasion the win went to York. Stanley's response to his father-in-law was to send him his congratulations and to apologise for not being able to arrive in time to be of assistance. No doubt offering the same apology to Margaret of Anjou and the king. He had not burnt any bridges with Lancaster either, as his brother had acted on their side.

This became a form of insurance policy used by the Stanley's. Thomas would appear to be supporting one side, whilst his brother William would look as though helping the other. Either way the battle went, the Stanley's were on the winning side. It would be a decade later in 1469, that Thomas Stanley would find his loyalties tested. His brother-in-law, the Earl of Warwick had become increasingly disgruntled by his reducing influence over Edward IV and the rapid rise of the Woodville family. When he decided to rebel against the king, he wanted his sister's husband to join him. Yet, Stanley was cautious. At this point he decided not to join Warwick, and gained the trust of Edward IV when the rebellion was over.

In 1470 when Warwick rebelled again, the circumstances were different, and Stanley now decided to join his brother-in-law. Warwick changed tactics and tried to restore King Henry VI to the throne. This was more popular in the country than Stanley had expected and resulted in Edward IV being forced to flee the country and Henry VI on the throne, once more. Given this turn of events, Stanley felt safe in joining with Warwick. He met him in the Midlands and was by Warwick's side when they arrived in the city of London. A state procession to Westminster Abbey was held so that they could say thanks and prayers for the restoration and Stanley was a prominent member of the procession.

Edward IV though, had lost the battle and not the war. In exile he gathered a force and invaded England. Once in England he quickly defeated Warwick, took Henry VI and his wife prisoner, and was declared the rightful king once again. Stanley had a problem. He had been a proud ally of the briefly restored regime and now it was over. Stanley backed away from his alliance with Warwick, staying away from the key battles that would see Warwick and the Prince of Wales killed. In return, Stanley received no punishment for his actions and began to win the trust of the York king.

In the year 1483 it would be a wholly different family dynamic that would make Stanley choose where his loyalty lay. After the usurpation by Richard III, rebellion was brewing. Initially this was in the name of the princes, yet when rumours of their deaths started to spread this quickly changed in favour of a new contender, Henry Tudor, Stanley's stepson.

Margaret Beaufort was a major force in gathering support and money for her son and his campaign. This was despite the risk to herself. She may have expected her husband to share her desire to see Henry Tudor crowned. This would have meant changing his policy of caution and neutrality. As the Buckingham Rebellion developed, it may have been expected that Stanley would join them. It is possible that he may have done if Henry Stafford had not got involved. There was no evidence that Stanley was involved. This may have been because of his dislike of Stafford or it may have been his natural inclination to avoid coming to the attention of the king for the wrong reasons.

In August 1485, as two sides prepared to face each other, at the Battle of Bosworth, both sides would have been anxiously awaiting news of Thomas Stanley. Would he join his forces with the king and fight by his side or was he ready to declare for his stepson?

Here, Stanley had everything to lose. If he backed his wife and Henry Tudor and they lost he could lose everything including his life, and the great future he planned for his children. Richard III was holding his eldest son as a hostage to ensure the cooperation of Thomas Stanley. Yet if he sided with Richard III and he lost he would find himself at the mercy of his wife and stepson, who would now hold ultimate power. Here, more than ever, he had to make the right choice.

We will never know what negotiations he entered with each side or what he agreed to. As the battle progressed it became clear to both sides that Stanley was not willing to commit to either side, and as at Blore Heath he watched and waited. It was a last-minute intervention from William Stanley that saw Richard III struck down and won the day for Henry Tudor. It was not the level of support he had hoped for, but he still owed his life and title to the Stanley's who would now expect to be rewarded appropriately.

Keeping Thomas Stanley on side was a challenge that both Edward IV and Richard III had been forced to contend with. The Stanley family's policy of neutrality and making sure they were on the winning side meant that they could never fully be trusted, and both kings lived with the knowledge that they could be betrayed by Stanley.

Both kings also knew that they needed his support to be able to continue to rule and so they had to find a way to come to some form of understanding. Edward IV managed this effectively. Despite his fears of betrayal Edward IV began to show more trust to Thomas Stanley and he was frequently at court, later with his wife Margaret Beaufort.

The relationship was complicated by Stanley's brief defection to join the restoration of Henry VI. Rather than hinder his influence with the king, he would see his position elevated as he was appointed Steward of the King's Household. In 1482 the families became closer as Stanley's son George was given permission to marry Joan le Strange, the niece of Elizabeth Woodville. George would become Baron Strange and Edward had ensured that the fates of the two families were now dependant on each other.

Thomas Stanley genuinely appears to have gained the trust of Edward IV as Stanley was named as an executor of his will and made the guardian of Elizabeth of York after his death. The relationship between Richard III and Thomas Stanley was more complicated due to disputes they had engaged in before Richard became king. Thomas Stanley had become embroiled in a bitter despite over ownership of Hornby Castle. Stanley resented the support that Richard was giving to the Harrington family. Stanley did not like the influence that Richard was developing in the north of the country and the decision to replace Lord Stanley as the Duchy's chief steward in Lancashire.

The two were forced to work together on an invasion of Scotland in 1483. At times, the objective of the mission was in danger of being overshadowed by strong arguments between the two leaders.

So, when Richard III became king there were already tensions between the two men. Now they would have to deal with added complications of Stanley's objections to Richard taking the throne in the place of Edward V and Stanley's marriage to the mother of Henry Tudor, his main rival. Stanley had been imprisoned briefly at the same time as Hastings had been arrested and executed.

Despite these issues an uneasy truce appears to have been reached. Richard knew he needed the support of Stanley and offered him rewards in return for his support. Richard III made Stanley Constable of England and he was invested with the Order of the Garter. For their part, Stanley and his wife were happy to accept all rewards offered to them, but the extent to which Stanley supported Richard and the level of support he gave to his stepson at Margaret Beaufort's request is unknown.

Certainly, at Bosworth, Stanley appeared more concerned with being seen to support the victor without offering them any support. At the end of the battle, when Tudor was declared King Henry VII, Stanley would be happy to accept any new rewards that would come his way in exchange for his support as he had before.

Despite the lack of support for Henry Tudor at the Battle of Bosworth, rich rewards were quickly offered to the king's stepfather. On 24 October he was created Earl of Derby, as well as being awarded substantial grants of property to add to his already vast portfolio.

Stanley finally seemed ready to commit to a king. Realising that any threat to Henry VII was a threat to the power and influence he himself had received Stanley did not hesitate to move to the Battle of Stoke Field to stop the rebellion that had arisen in the name of Lambert Simnel who was claiming to be Edward, Earl of Warwick and the true heir to the throne of England. Stanley knew that nobody else would offer the same inducements as Henry Tudor.

As powerful as they had become, the Stanley's were not immune to the wrath of the king. When Henry VII was faced with a new challenger, Perkin Warbeck, William Stanley said that he would refuse to fight against him if it was proved that he was the real Duke of York. William Stanley was charged with treason. He was found guilty and executed. Nothing could save him.

This hit Thomas Stanley hard and he retired to Lathom with Margaret Beaufort to deal with his grief. To demonstrate that this incident did not in any way change the relationship between them, Henry VII went to Lathom to visit the couple and comfort his mother.

Thomas Stanley remained in favour with the king and kept all of the rewards he had received from King Henry VII, but he was now getting older and as Margaret was spending more time close to her son, Stanley chose to spend more time on his estates in Lancashire until his own death on 29 July 1504. His policy of making sure he appeared to be on the winning side served him well. He survived all the bloody Battles that made up the Wars of the Roses. He died quietly on his estates as one of the most important men in the country.

Chapter 17 – The Case Against Thomas Stanley

We know that Thomas Stanley was a key figure in 1483, who went on to benefit from the disappearance of the princes. We now need to consider whether this advancement, or any alternative reason gave Stanley the requisite motive to carry out this crime or whether his significant gains were purely a mixture of good luck combined with astute political strategy.

Certainly, the Stanley family, most especially Thomas were ambitious. This had seen them pursue a policy of playing both sides so they were always close enough to the victor to reap any rewards that might be on offer.

Taking steps to have his stepson crowned as King of England would offer Stanley the ultimate opportunity for self-advancement. The Stanley's would have the closest connection they could have hoped for with the royal family. Whether or not he was trying to help Henry Tudor, he would always be under suspicion, due to his marriage and the continued plotting of his wife. This time Thomas Stanley was not a neutral bystander deciding which side to support, he was at the heart of events and he may have had to act to prevent what may have seemed an inevitable fall from grace. Previous kings had known they needed the support of the Stanley family to remain in power, but his closeness to Richard's main rival may have made him more of a risk and he could end up being summarily executed like Lord Hastings had been.
The only real guarantee of a prosperous future may have lay with Henry Tudor and removing the princes removed a significant hurdle to Tudor's success.

Yet, this would be a major gamble for Stanley. Even if the princes were removed, and Henry Tudor defeated Richard III, there were several other figures who could have become a new candidate for the Yorkists, especially the young Earl of Warwick. This would have meant that he had killed two young boys for no good reason. There was also the risk that he would be implicated in the deaths, which would jeopardise everything he already had.

It also must be remembered that Thomas Stanley had received prominent titles and rewards from both Edward IV and Richard III for his support. He played a key role in Richard III's coronation and had more power and influence than most in the Kingdom. Whilst the success of Henry Tudor would raise his status further, it would be little reward compared to the risk involved in being accused of harming the princes.

The behaviour of Thomas Stanley during the Buckingham Rebellion and at Bosworth, cast doubt that Thomas Stanley would kill the boys to further his own ambition. Stanley would not join the rebellion in 1483. The failure of the rebellion almost led to the capture of Henry Tudor. He also seemed indifferent to the outcome of the Battle of Bosworth, no doubt pledging support to both sides, but not allowing his troops to take part in the battle itself. This behaviour appears inconsistent with that of a person who has killed two young children, to help crown his stepson and secure significant advantages for the Stanley family.

When considering this as a motive for Stanley we also need to remember that he was already related to the royal family. His son had married Elizabeth Woodville's niece, a cousin to the young Edward V. Fighting for Edward V, along with his current ties to the royal family could also have proved rewarding for Thomas Stanley. Certainly, the young king was a safer bet than the unknow exile, Henry Tudor.

Stanley's marriage could also provide a motive to commit this crime. When Stanley married Margaret Beaufort, it was not believed to have been a love match, or a match to provide Stanley with an heir. It was a strategic match. Beaufort was a wealthy heiress. Removing all obstacles to Henry Tudor becoming king would allow him to wring as much as possible out of his marital agreement as was possible.

Virtually from the moment Richard III became king, Margaret Beaufort appears to have been plotting against him and working towards the advancement of her own son. Whilst she continued her intriguing, it was going to become harder for Stanley himself to avoid suspicion from Richard III. This was especially the case after the failure of the Buckingham Rebellion. Margaret Beaufort was one of many named in an Act of Attainder and was lucky to escape execution for her role in the failed rebellion. It was because of the power of the Stanley family that Richard III acted so leniently. What he did do, was give Thomas Stanley control of his wife and her properties. He was expected to keep her under close supervision, which would stop her having the required contact with the outside world to continue contacting her son and raising support on his behalf.

Despite these conditions, Margaret Beaufort was allowed to continue her support of Tudor and to contact those who could aid him. She was under the control of Stanley, and if she had been caught they were both in grave danger, This could lead us to conclude that Stanley had realised that he had no option but to commit to the cause of his stepson.

Whilst Margaret Beaufort was certainly a powerful woman of her time, there were limits on the power of women in these times and she may have needed her husband to have the required access to the boys and to commit the act without drawing too much suspicion to themselves.

Certainly, we must accept that his connections to Henry Tudor through his marriage would have been a factor Stanley would have had to consider as events progressed. This does not mean that he was fully committed to the Tudor cause and would have committed such a ruthless, risky act on his behalf.

We have already considered that his behaviour during both the Buckingham Rebellion and the Battle of Bosworth suggest that Stanley was following the long-term Stanley policy of waiting to see who would be victorious before declaring himself for either side. This does not make sense if there was a risk Richard would win and could then find out that he was responsible for the murder of his nephews.

It also must be considered that Stanley's previous marriage had also presented him with a dilemma, in earlier battles. When his father-in-law, Lord Salisbury had gone into battle for the Duke of York he had expected the support of Stanley as his daughter's husband and was forced to carry on without the backing of the significant Stanley force. In the same battle his own brother fought for Lancaster, and this was not enough for Thomas Stanley to get involved. If those family ties had not been enough to bring him into the Wars of the Roses, then a marriage of political and financial strength to Margaret Beaufort is also unlikely to have galvanised Stanley into action.

There is also the fact that Stanley was not prepared to fight for Richard III at Bosworth to save his own son. As Richard III awaited the imminent invasion from Tudor, Stanley asked his permission to retire to his estates. Richard III was suspicious of Stanley's desire to distance himself from the king at such an important time and insisted that his eldest son was kept at court to ensure the future assistance of Thomas Stanley.

As Richard III's troops made their way towards Bosworth, Lord Strange was taken with them, a kind of hostage to force Stanley to bring his troops to his aid. Stanley was sent a summons and said he could not attend. When Richard III sent a reminder to Stanley that he had his son under his control he was sent the reply, "Tell King Richard to act as it so pleaseth him – the Lord of the Isle of Man has other sons alive.'[lxxxv]

If Stanley was unwilling to commit himself to a side to save his own son and heir, or to act upon previous marital connections, it is hard to conclude that his marriage to Margaret Beaufort would have compelled him, not only to get involved, but to murder two young boys, and expose himself to immense risk of execution, especially as Richard III was the firm favourite going into the battle with Henry Tudor.

As with the other suspects we must consider whether revenge could have been a motive for Thomas Stanley to kill the boys. The father of the boys was Edward IV and there had been issues between the two men. Edward IV would have been aware that Stanley had not sent his troops out to support him in his battle to become king. Worse than that, during the short-lived restoration of the reign of Henry VI, Stanley had shown support for Warwick and was prominent in the celebrations that followed.

Whilst King, Edward IV, amply rewarded his younger brother, Richard for his loyalty, giving him the basis of a substantial power base in the north. The Stanley's were one of the most powerful family's here and may have felt as though their power and influence was being diluted as Richard's was growing.

The relationship between Stanley and Edward IV had the potential to be difficult, with Stanley removed from political importance. Yet, Edward IV seemed to accept that he needed to keep Stanley onside and despite his lack of overt support, Stanley found himself in good favour with the York king. He was regularly at court and was offered new titles and lands by Edward IV. This makes it hard to believe that he would want revenge for his treatment by Edward IV. Stanley made such an impression on Edward IV that he was made guardian of Edward's eldest daughter Elizabeth, on his death and was believed to be keen to ensure that Edward V succeeded his father. This commitment to the sons of Edward IV, may explain why Richard III had Stanley arrested at the council meeting on the thirteenth of June 1483.

Whilst it is hard to believe that Stanley may have committed this act out of revenge against Edward IV, there was another king involved who had a much more troubled relationship with Stanley. Richard III and Thomas Stanley had a history of disputes and tension. So, whilst we may not accept that Stanley had the motive of revenge, in relation to Edward IV, he may have sought revenge upon his long-time rival, Richard III.

The relationship between Richard III and Thomas Stanley was completely different. The tensions within their relationship mean that we must consider whether Stanley could have been motivated to kill the nephews out of revenge for his treatment at the hands of the new king.

Richard and Stanley's men had come to blows during Stanley's legal battle with the Harrington family. As part of his plan to become king, Richard III had orchestrated the arrest of those he believed he would oppose his plans. Stanley was one of those arrested and was injured in the process. Although Stanley was released a short time later and escaped the summary execution handed out to Lord Hastings, the arrest showed the mistrust that existed on both sides.

The rumours of the boy's deaths had two significant benefits for Stanley, his wife, and his stepson. Rumours that Richard III was responsible for the deaths of his young nephews helped to turn people against him. This helped Margaret Beaufort convince people to join her son's cause and create a force that could pose a real threat to Richard III's forces. This would place Stanley at the centre of power in England.
Killing the boys and allowing Richard to take the blame and consequences for something he did not do would be an ultimate act of revenge, whilst also making Stanley, the stepfather of the new King of England.

Revenge could explain why Stanley deviated from his long-held strategy of avoiding taking sides. Yet we must consider that following the death of the boys, he did not appear to take sides. He appeared to accept the rewards offered to him and Margaret Beaufort when Richard III became king. He refused to side against Richard during the Buckingham Rebellion, believed to have been led by Margaret Beaufort, his own wife.

Even at Bosworth, we see the cautious Stanley, waiting to see which way momentum would sway before committing to either side. Despite his somewhat dysfunctional relationship with Richard III, all the behaviour we observe from Stanley does not suggest that he had decided which side to favour. All his behaviour in inconsistent with him killing the boys out of revenge against Richard III

During the Wars of the Roses, people's motivations could have been based on a loyalty to either the House of Lancaster or the House of York. Most prominent families could be described as Yorkist or Lancastrian. This is difficult in the case of Thomas Stanley as we cannot be sure whether he had any allegiance to a particular house.

We know that publicly he strived to keep on the right side of whoever the victor may prove to be. This could just have been a strategy to further their own ends, whilst privately he was hoping for one side to prosper. Today, the Civil Service, the machinery of government, is made up of individuals who all have their own personal views on which party should run the country and more recently, whether we should remain a part of the European Union. These views are required to be kept private, as regardless of which side wins the day, all civil servants are required to serve that government to the best of their ability. This is not so different to the approach of Stanley, who would serve whichever king won the day.

As we cannot identify who Stanley genuinely supported during these battles, we cannot argue that he would be motivated to act out of loyalty to the House of Lancaster. Although Stanley was expected to support the forces of Henry VI and Margaret of Anjou at the Battle of Blore Heath, to their disappointment he did not. He also seems to have served Edward IV loyally, as he was made an executor of his will and guardian of his oldest daughter.

Clearly, Thomas Stanley benefitted more than most from the death of the boys in the long-term, giving him a motive, no matter how tenuous. Having considered whether there is any evidence to point to his guilt, we must now consider the evidence in defence of Thomas Stanley.

Chapter 18 – The Defence of Thomas Stanley

We have seen that Thomas Stanley benefitted significantly from the disappearance of the two boys. Whilst this may have given him a motive, we must consider whether the chances of success in the plot to make Henry Tudor king would be enough to induce Thomas Stanley to take the risk involved with killing them.

The general belief is that the boys disappeared in July 1483. At this point Richard had become king and Henry Tudor was still an unknown quantity, biding his time in exile. Whilst Stanley may have been sympathetic to the intriguing of his wife, the chances of her schemes succeeding must have seemed remote. This requires us to believe that Thomas Stanley killed the boys at a time when their uncle was still in charge of the country, unopposed and may seek to avenge the death of his nephews.

Stanley was a major power in England and whoever ruled the country knew that they needed their support to continue to rule in peace. It is possible that Stanley knew more about the plans for Henry Tudor's invasion than we believe. If he had agreed either to not fight on the side of Richard III or to join forces with Henry Tudor, this could have swayed the balance of the battle. Maybe Stanley believed that Richard III would not retain power long enough to discover the identity of the murderer, or to clear his own name.

Whilst his behaviour in the Buckingham Rebellion suggests that Stanley hadn't chosen what side to take in the forthcoming battle, his decision to leave court and return to his estates in Lathom is suspicious. Richard III was preparing for an invasion by somebody asserting their own right to be King of England and he needed his men around him. Richard III most certainly saw the move as dubious, taking Stanley's son as a prisoner to ensure his loyalty.

There is some evidence that Stanley was involved in helping Henry Tudor prepare for his invasion. When Richard III was trying to secure the extradition of Henry Tudor, Margaret Beaufort was informed of the plan and was able to get word to Henry Tudor, enabling him to escape from the guards that were to transfer him into Richard's custody. Thomas Stanley would have known about Richard III's plans and was in the best place to warn his wife of what was due to occur.

Another indicator that Stanley had turned against Richard is the behaviour of his wife, Margaret Beaufort. She was believed to have been one of the leading figures in the Buckingham Rebellion. When the rebellion failed, she was attainted and punished quite leniently. Richard, keen to keep Stanley on good terms, released Beaufort into the care of Stanley. Her estates were transferred over to him and he was to keep her secluded, unable to continue communicating with the outside world and the supporters of her son.

Stanley had always been cautious when dealing with the political tensions around him, not wanting to earn disapproval or punishment from those already in power, or those who were about to take it. Stanley would not have wanted to risk being accused of treason and losing everything he had. Despite this, he does not appear to have kept Margaret Beaufort excluded from contact with others, allowing her to continue advising her son, raise money for his upcoming invasion and canvas nobles for their support. This was a risk to both of their lives and seems inconsistent with a man who had strived to appear politically neutral for decades.

Historian, Ralph Griffiths credits Thomas Stanley, as being one of the advisors that suggested Henry Tudor should start referring to himself as King of England before the invasion.[lxxxvi] Again, this was a risky course of action for Stanley to take, as it was difficult to know who to trust and word could have easily gotten back to Richard III.

Elizabeth Norton, a biographer of Margaret Beaufort, confidently asserts that by the middle of 1485, Stanley had committed himself to the cause of Henry Tudor.[lxxxvii] This indicates that Stanley was helping, but the date of 1485 is significantly later than the date when the boys were last seen and does not support the case that he was involved with their disappearance.

Clearly, there is evidence to suggest that Thomas Stanley may have been supportive of his young stepson and may have aided his attempts to seize control. It is true that murdering the boys would have carried considerable risk for Stanley, but if he was aiding Henry Tudor, we can see that he was already engaging in acts that were dangerous to his life and therefore his involvement remains a possibility.

It can be argued that the death of William Stanley points to the innocence of his brother, Thomas. William Stanley was believed to have said that he would not fight against Warbeck if it was proved that he was indeed the younger of the missing princes. For this he was tried and executed for treason.
This suggests that the Stanley brothers were unaware of what had become of the boys. Surely, if Thomas Stanley committed the crime he would have turned to his brother for help, the one person he would have trusted to keep his dark secret. If Thomas Stanley did kill the boys, William Stanley was best placed to know that they were dead. He would therefore not have had to risk his life by declaring that he would refuse to fight for Henry.

It is possible that having carried out this deed, Stanley did not feel as though it was safe to share the burden of that secret with anyone, even his brother. However, as rumours started to circulate that Warbeck was the son of Edward IV, there would have been conversations between the brothers, where William may have confided his fears, and Thomas Stanley sought to reassure his younger brother that it could not be Richard, Duke of York.

A further argument that can be used in defence of Thomas Stanley is that he would not have had the means and opportunity to commit this crime. It is believed that he would not have had the required access to the boys to carry out this crime. He was Constable of England, but he was awarded this title after the failure of the Buckingham Rebellion, in October 1483. If he had been Constable of England, he would have been able to access the Tower with ease.

The issue with this is the timing. He was made Constable in October 1483, months after the boys were last seen, and certainly the rumours of the boys' deaths had been circulating since the previous July. When evaluating the importance of this evidence two things must be considered.

The first is that although there is speculation about when the boys died, nobody has ever been able to confirm this. As well as rumours of their deaths, rumours circulated about different ways they were killed and even that they were smuggled out of the country to safety. The rumours are unreliable. Whilst they may not have been seen from July, it may have been that Richard III wanted people to forget about the innocent young nephew he had cast aside to obtain power.

The second issue regards the power of Thomas Stanley at the time the boys are believed to have died. He may not have been Constable until October, but after his June arrest at the hands of Richard III, he had made peace with Richard and was a trusted member of his inner circle, and one of the most important nobles in the country. The Tower of London had another Constable, Robert Brackenbury and it has been argued that he would have been able to refuse entry to Stanley. Given the power of the Stanley family it is open to speculation as to how far Brackenbury would have been able to resist Stanley or his wife if they wanted to gain access to the Tower. Therefore, it cannot be clearly shown that Stanley was without the requisite means and opportunity with which to carry out this crime.

Thomas Stanley was famous for never leading his troops into battle during the Wars of the Roses. There was one battle where Stanley appears to have realised that he had to act or lose everything he had. After the death of Richard III, his supporters began plotting to remove Henry Tudor and replace him with the boy they claimed to be Edward, Earl of Warwick. Stanley did not show his usual hesitation regarding involvement in this particular battle.[lxxxviii] As stepfather to the king, he may have realised that if Henry Tudor was defeated by the new, rival candidate, he would be punished for his support of and closeness to him.

Stanley being worried that this boy could become king, suggests he did not kill the boys in the Tower as he appears to have been worried about the threat they posed to the new regime. A problem with this is who the boy we now refer to as Lambert Simnel was claiming to be. He was not claiming to be one of the missing boys, he was claiming to be an entirely different nephew of Richard III, Edward, Earl of Warwick. There is not necessarily a link between Stanley's progress towards the Battle of Stoke Field and the missing boys.

In recent years, new theories have developed around who Lambert Simnel was really claiming to be. Some historians have pointed towards Henry VII's treatment of his mother in law, Elizabeth Woodville. They claim she was being punished for taking part in the Simnel plot. This would make no sense if Elizabeth Woodville was removing her daughter as Queen, only to replace her with the son of Clarence, who she blamed for the death of her father. The inference is that Elizabeth Woodville's involvement points to the possibility that Lambert Simnel was one of her missing son's. If rumours were spreading at the time that it could have been one of the boys then, Stanley's lack of hesitation to head to battle is more suggestive of innocence in relation to the princes' disappearance.

An interesting point to consider with Stanley, is the fact that nobody has ever blamed him for the deaths. With regards to the contemporary sources we have, that is not surprising, as they were written during the reign of the Tudor's and nobody would have been wanting to incur the wrath of the royal family by insinuating that a close member of the family was involved with such a crime. This is especially true as it was ultimately Henry himself who benefitted the most from the disappearance.

For many decades it was widely believed that the disappearance and death of the boys could only have been brought about by one man, Richard III. Whilst people speculated about the details of the case, the culprit appeared to be universally acknowledged.

As time has passed historians have tried to restore Richard III's reputation and this has led, not just to a defence of Richard III, but also to other people being suspected of involvement. Margaret Beaufort has been accused of poisoning the boys, less important figures such as John Howard and Sir James Tyrell have been implicated in the suffocation and burial of the boys. A crucial tactic in criminal trials is to introduce other suspects, to achieve the goal of reasonable doubt. This has recently been used in this case as Ricardians look for someone else who could have committed the crime. Yet, despite the desire to solve the mystery and find a new suspect, and his proximity to Henry Tudor, nobody has blamed Thomas Stanley and surely this is something that has to be considered when assessing whether he could be guilty of this crime.

It is unlikely that Stanley could have committed a crime like this without anybody helping him, or somebody knowing or whispering about his involvement. Yet this major figure of the Tudor regime, who reaped the rewards offered by his stepson has yet to be recognised as a potential suspect.

Following on from this point is the lack of any evidence against Thomas Stanley. We can show that he had a motive for wanting the boys out of the way and it is possible he had the access to commit the crime. That is where it ends. We have speculated about the level of support he gave Henry Tudor and whether he was under pressure from his wife, but that is all that we have, speculation. Based on the evidence we have it is unlikely that the Crown Prosecution Service would agree to charges being filed and the case being taken to court. At the same time, it is unlikely that the police would feel confident in ruling him out as a suspect in the investigation.

One of the motives we considered for Stanley was that of ambition and greed as he was amply rewarded by Henry VII. The killing of children for financial gain or to gain power is not as hard to imagine as we may think.

In New York in 2013, Karl Karlsen was found guilty of murdering his own son so he could claim the $700 000 insurance policy. Whilst this was a crime that, to most of us, was shocking enough, it turned out that this was not his first kill. Whilst he was serving his prison sentence for the murder of his son, police began to investigate the unexplained death of his wife back in 1991. On completion of the investigation, Karlsen was charged with murdering his wife so he could claim $200 000 life insurance.[lxxxix]

If a parent can kill their own child and wife purely to receive an insurance pay out we have to believe that back in medieval England, an important noble such as Thomas Stanley could have killed two young boys with no real connection to him to become stepfather to the King of England.

Chapter 19 – Anne Neville

Anne Neville had a short, but dramatic life. Despite this, little has been written or discovered about the women who would be Queen of England, as wife of one of history's most notorious kings.

As the women who became the queen when the boys were declared illegitimate, Anne must be one of the figures considered in a full examination of what could have happened to them.

Anne Neville was born in Warwick on the eleventh of June 1456. She was born into a family at the heart of the political intriguing that would tear the country apart for the rest of her life.

Her father was Richard Neville, Earl of Warwick and her grandfather was the Earl of Salisbury. They were related to the Duke of York through his marriage to Cecily Neville and proved to be loyal allies in his battle to challenge the unlimited authority of Margaret of Anjou, as her husband the king failed to provide effective leadership.

Richard Neville had secured a very advantageous marriage to the heiress, Anne Beauchamp, which allowed him to develop his own power base in the Midlands. Anne was born into a very noble family with every advantage they could wish for. At the time of her birth, and as she was growing up, her parents would have expected to make equally advantageous marriages for Anne and her older sister Isabel.

Things looked even more promising for the Neville family, when Richard Neville was made Captain of Calais. Before the age of one, Anne probably found her family packing up ready to accompany her father to Calais. It is believed Anne and Isabel travelled with their parents to Calais.

When the battle between the House of York and House of Lancaster broke into violence, Anne witnessed her father choose to fight against the king and support the Duke of York. From an early age, Anne would find herself the victim of Fortune's wheel. Whilst waiting for news, probably at Middleham, Anne would have received news of her father, who had been beaten and forced to leave the country. It would not be long before she heard the news that her father and Edward, Earl of March, had returned to England with their own forces and had swept to power following bloody battles that led to Edward, becoming, Edward IV.

Richard Neville was now one of the chief advisors to the new king and would become known as the 'Kingmaker'. As the reign of Edward IV began, Anne and her parents would have been expecting that a grand marriage was awaiting. The Neville's were at the heart of the new royal family. Edward IV showed his trust in Neville, by sending his younger brother Richard to live with him to complete his education. This may have led to Anne and Richard spending time together as children and there is debate over whether they developed a close friendship.

Anne would soon realise the fickle nature of Fortune, as she spun her wheel once again. Whilst her father, Richard Neville was negotiating a marriage alliance that would secure England's future, Edward IV surprised everybody by announcing that he was already married to Elizabeth Woodville, a widow with two sons. As Edward tried to please his wife, by marrying her siblings off to distinguished nobles and started to take advice from her father and brother, Richard Neville felt himself exerting less influence over the Edward, and found the chances of prestigious marriages for his daughters slipping away. This was worsened by Edward's refusal to allow the marriage of Anne's older sister, Isabel, to his own younger brother, George, Duke of Clarence.

As Neville's discontent grew, he began to raise rebellion throughout England. He defied the king and had Isabel secretly married to George. Neville's first attempt at rebellion, led to Neville capturing Edward and trying to control him. He soon realised that he could not control the king. Edward was released and Neville was forgiven. Elizabeth Woodville would never forgive George, Duke of Clarence, or Neville as they had executed her father, Earl Rivers.

Despite the truce, tensions again began to build, and Neville once again found himself fighting against the king. This time he was not so successful, and Neville was forced to flee by boat, with his wife, daughters and new son-in-law, George. On this trip, where Anne would have been aware of the bleak prospects for her own future, she would be at Isabel's side as she gave birth to a still born baby aboard the ship they were fleeing on.

Once they landed in France, Neville would make an alliance with the queen he had fought against years before, Margaret of Anjou. This alliance would force Anne to leave the House of York and her childhood behind as the alliance was sealed with her own marriage to Prince Edward, Margaret of Anjou's son.

Despite becoming Princess of Wales, through a marriage alliance with the House of Lancaster, and ultimately gaining the title of Queen of England through marriage to Richard III, of the House of York, very little information about her was recorded during her lifetime and in the ongoing debate about what happened to the Princes in the Tower.

One of the few sources we have when trying to identify what Anne Neville was like is the Neville family chronicler, John Rous. Rous describes Anne as 'seemly amiable and in conditions full commendable and right virtuous and according to the interpretation of her name, full gracious.'[xc] Obviously, we must consider that Rous would have aimed to please the Neville family with his descriptions of them, but this gives us a starting point for trying to understand who Anne Neville was.

The contemporary account of the Croyland Chronicle tells us that she had a similar complexion to that of her niece, Elizabeth of York.[xci] We do have images of Elizabeth, so this also gives us the beginnings of a description of the little-known Queen of England.

Despite being Princess of Wales, wife of Richard III and ultimately Queen of England, Anne Neville does not appear very often in written documents from the period of her life. She clearly was popular in the north, as Warwick's daughter, which allowed Richard III to gain their trust and support.
As a young woman in fifteenth century England we can assume that Anne would have taken her religion seriously. Anne maintained strong connections with her local church, was a regular visitor with her husband, to York Minster and even became a lay sister during her short life.

Growing up in a grand household, with her father once the most trusted advisor of the King of England would have prepared Anne for a grand future and she would have been raised to be proud of her Neville and Beauchamp lineage. Maybe this explains why, despite the controversy caused by her husband's actions, she stood by his side as they were crowned together, accepting the title of queen.

Whatever her feelings where, as she was crowned Queen of England, she could not have been anything but proud when she saw her son, Edward invested as Prince of Wales, next in line to be king.
From television dramas and books, Anne appears very much to be a weak young woman, unable to stand up for herself and having no choice but to accept what decisions were made on her behalf. This portrayal of Anne suited the narrative of the Tudor's and their supporters. Anne was forced to marry the tyrannical Richard III and had no choice but to be his queen.

Yet, this was a woman who Richard III trusted. He was often away from their estates and left the running of them to his wife. In 1475, she deputised for Richard at York.[xcii] This may have involved arbitrating various disputes and corresponding with important figures in York. This indicates a woman who was capable and strong, able to make important decisions and argue her cause, a woman who would have insisted on some say in the decisions that affected her and Edward, her son.

Whilst it is hard to understand who Anne Neville was, we do know that her life was changed when her father fought Edward and was forced to form an alliance with his former enemy, Margaret of Anjou. Anne was no longer for the House of York; she was now the very future of the House of Lancaster. Warwick's alliance with Margaret of Anjou was to be sealed by the marriage of Prince Edward to Anne Neville. Clearly Margaret of Anjou did not fully trust Warwick as she insisted that the marriage did not take place until after Warwick had secured control of England and restored the authority of King Henry VI. Some accounts claim that Margaret of Anjou was reluctant to wed her son to Anne, and even that she was expecting a marriage to be concluded between her son and Edward IV's eldest daughter, Elizabeth.

Despite any reservations Margaret may have had, the match was made and Anne Neville found herself about to become the daughter-in-law of the women she had always viewed as the enemy, and wife to a young man rumoured to have a love for violence.

On 25 July 1470, the couple were formally betrothed in Angers Cathedral. Anne remained in France waiting for news of her father's victory, so her marriage could be completed. Warwick found success quicker than had been anticipated and his swift progress through England forced Edward IV and his younger brother Richard to flee England for their safety.

As Warwick arranged for Henry VI to be restored and the pair celebrated the victory together, publicly, Margaret of Anjou appears to have become more convinced of Warwick's sincerity. On the 28 November, a papal dispensation arrived which would allow the marriage of Anne and Edward to proceed. Anne officially became wife of Prince Edward in Amboise on 13 December 1470 and arrangements for their journey to England began in earnest.

When Margaret of Anjou and Anne Neville landed in Weymouth in April 1471, they expected to be able to progress to London to be reconciled with King Henry VI. What they received was the unexpected news that Edward IV had launched his own attack and Warwick had lost his life in the Battle of Barnet. Edward was now back in control of the country, with Henry VI a captive in the Tower of London once again.

Prince Edward left his mother and new wife at Cerne Abbey whilst he led the queen's forces out to face the full force of Edward IV's army at Tewkesbury. Anne had seen herself and her family forced to flee their home and face ruin as exiles in France, only to rise once again, as she became Princess of Wales and the future Queen of England. On news of Warwick's death, Anne's mother had fled to seek sanctuary and left Anne with Margaret of Anjou. At Cerne Abbey the two women would wait for the latest spin of Fortune's wheel to end.

When they received the news that Prince Edward had lost his life at the Battle of Tewkesbury, they knew that Fortune had not favoured them this time. Margaret had lost her only son and any hope of being Queen of England again. At the age of 14 Anne was a widow, alone and at the mercy of the York king.

Anne and Margaret were captured and on 11 May, they appeared before Edward IV in Coventry. Anne was released into the custody of her brother-in-law, George, Duke of Clarence, and her sister Isabel. Whilst the reunion with her sister would have offered some comfort to Anne after her recent traumas, she must have despaired about her future. She was only 14 and yet to have a family. Now she was in the custody of the Duke of Clarence, who knew that as long as he controlled Anne, he had control of her lands too, Clarence was not going to let go of Anne or his control over her inheritance easily.

The desire of Clarence to keep control of Anne's wealth appeared more obvious once he believed that his younger brother Richard wanted to take Anne Neville for his wife. There are stories of Clarence trying to prevent Richard from meeting with Anne, who was forced to escape and seek sanctuary whilst awaiting rescue from her new suitor. Whether Anne was deliberately kept hidden from Richard is unknown, but we do know that the division of the sisters' inheritance led to a bitter row between the two brothers, which even the king could not fully resolve.

The reasons behind Richard's pursuit of Anne Neville is also subject to significant debate. The ferocity over the division of the Neville girls' estates has added some credence to the arguments that Richard wanted the wealth that would come from the marriage. Marrying a Neville was fundamental in enabling Richard to establish a major power base in the north of England, as he replaced Warwick as the head of a branch of the Neville family.

The reports of the Milanese Ambassador suggest that it was a strategic match on Richard's part when he states, 'Richard by force has taken to wife a daughter of the late Earl of Warwick.'[xciii] Rous, who would have met both Richard and Anne described the marriage as being unhappy, also suggesting that it was not a love match.

One of the first people to try to promote a more positive impression of Richard III was George Buck who believed that Richard and Anne were married because they loved each other. Buck claimed that Richard refused to take part in the killing of Prince Edward at Tewkesbury because it may upset Anne, who he cared deeply for.[xciv] We know that Richard was sent to live in the Warwick household to complete his education. What we don't know is the full extent of the contact the young Anne and Richard had with each other and how close their relationship was at that time.

Whilst it is possible that they may have spent time together when they were young, the lack of evidence means we just don't know what the nature of their relationship was. Even after their marriage there is little evidence about the state of their life together. It is possible to identify that they spent a lot of time together and obviously she stood by him when he cast his nephews aside. If we accept that Richard III was as ruthless as he has been portrayed, we must believe that Anne would have had little say in these decisions.

The marriage did produce an heir for Richard. Their only child, Edward, was born at Middleham, sometime between 1473 and 1477. The desperate grief shared by Richard and Anne when they heard that their beloved son had died gives us the slightest glimpse of a close couple, leaning on each other for support in the face of tragedy. Despite this, like so many things surrounding Richard III, the reasons for his marriage and the strength of that marriage remain a mystery, unlikely to be resolved.

Whatever the motivation for or state of Richard and Anne's marriage, what we can be certain of is that on 6 July 1483, the date of Richard's coronation, Anne was right by his side; they were crowned King and Queen of England together. This occasion is one of the few examples where we have a record of Anne's actions.

It is believed that she arrived in London at the beginning of June, weeks after the date when her nephew's own coronation had been planned for. This could suggest that she was aware of her husbands' plans and knew she did not need to travel for a coronation that would never take place. Alternatively, she could have been following direction from Richard.

Details of Anne's movements and actions begin on 3 July 1483 when she exchanged gifts of cloth with Richard, before travelling to the Royal Lodgings in the Tower of London, to await the day she would be crowned as Queen of England. On the day of the coronation, Anne appeared in the procession to the ceremony, wearing her hair loose and dressed in white cloth of gold, following behind her husband. [xcv]

As was custom following a coronation, the new king and queen embarked on a progress across the country, showing themselves and their power to their new subjects. Once they arrived in Greenwich, Anne and Richard were separated and would meet up again in the middle of August, in Warwick, as they prepared to journey to York.

Whilst we know that Anne and Richard celebrated their first Christmas as king and queen, grandly together, once again Anne appears to disappear into the shadows. In 1484 there was a second progress where her only son was invested as the Prince of Wales, in front of his proud mother. This pride and moment of joy for Anne Neville would not last long. As Richard and Anne stopped at Nottingham as part of their progress, they were to receive the heart-breaking news that their son had died unexpectedly, plunging them into deep despair and grief.

The death of her son appears to have been the beginning of the end for Anne Neville, as her suffering continued to increase. By Christmas 1484 it was clear that Anne Neville was ill and was deteriorating.

The daughters of Edward IV emerged from sanctuary and although Anne appears to have developed a close relationship with Elizabeth of York, she would not have been able to ignore the rumours that Richard sought to marry his young niece when Anne died or the speculation as to what was causing her worsening illness. John Rous believes that Richard poisoned his wife so he could marry again and have the new heir he needed to secure his legacy.[xcvi] Vergil appears to also have believed this was a possibility, claiming 'whether she was despatched by sorrowfulness or poison.'[xcvii] Commynes and Hall also reported that some people believed she had died of natural causes whilst others pointed the finger at her husband.

Whatever the cause, Anne Neville succumbed to the illness on 16 March 1485 and was interred in Westminster Abbey nine days later. Anne Neville was 28 years old when she died and according to Agostino Barbarigo had 'led so religious and catholic a life and was so adorned with goodness, prudence, and excellent morality, as to leave a name immortal.'[xcviii] Whoever Anne Neville was, one thing that cannot be denied is that her short life was full of struggle, adversity, and disastrous twists of fate.

Chapter 20 – The Case Against Anne Neville

Despite being Queen of England, little is known about Anne Neville, compared to her predecessors. This lack of recognition or scrutiny could explain why she has never been mentioned in connection with the disappearance of the boys. Yet, Anne Neville must have been as aware of the threat the boys posed to her family as Richard himself.

One of the lessons we can see repeated throughout history is that mothers' will risk everything for their children. Like Isabella of France, Margaret of Anjou and Margaret Beaufort, Anne Neville had a son that she would have wanted to protect. Anne's desire to protect her son could give her a motive for murdering the princes. Edward was her only son and was now the heir to the throne. She had watched on proudly at Edward's investiture, as he was crowned Prince of Wales. A rebellion in the name of Edward V could see her son fall from Prince of Wales to nothing, as she had lost everything when she was the Princess of Wales at the hands of Edward IV. To be sure of her son's future the two major obstacles residing in the Tower needed to be removed.

As noted, when considering the evidence against Richard III, Anne also had to consider the financial future of her son. The complex nature of the way the Neville estates had been split meant that they only kept a share of it whilst George Neville was alive and had a male heir.

George Neville had been in the custody of Richard III but died in May 1483. If Edward V had taken the throne, he could have deprived them of that share of the inheritance. This would be a big loss for the family, especially the heir. When Richard became king, he solved the problem, as he was the person who would decide what happened to the inheritance. This solved the problem as long as Richard remained king, If, as had happened during the previous decades, one king was deposed, only to take power again in the future, the family could face financial insecurity. Anne Neville would surely have believed that if Edward V regained the throne, he would take everything away from the man who had declared himself and his brother illegitimate and kept them prisoner in the Tower of London.

Anne Neville may have also had another reason for believing that she needed to protect her son from the reach of the Woodville family. The relationship between the Neville's and the Woodville's had been fraught from the moment Edward announced he had married Elizabeth. The Woodvilles were blamed by many for the death of George, Duke of Clarence. Anne may have feared that history would repeat itself if a Woodville gained control of the country.

Although Isabel and Clarence's children were not harmed, they were removed from the line of succession, as the children of a traitor and it was Anne that took the children in and took care of them. She will have known that the children were not killed, but also aware that Clarence had not taken such a drastic step as declaring Woodville's children bastards and crowning himself as king. The Wars of the Roses could see her son Edward killed as her first husband, another Edward, Prince of Wales had been.

The bad blood between the Neville's and Woodvilles also suggests that Anne may have been after revenge and that also gives her a motive to hurt the boys. Anne Neville may have blamed Elizabeth Woodville and her ambitious family for causing the breach between her father and the king. It was the marriage between Edward IV and Elizabeth Woodville that initially caused tensions between the two men. These increased as Edward and Elizabeth sought out prosperous matches for her many family members. Warwick had great plans in mind for his daughters, and with each marriage arranged to benefit a Woodville, the eligible bachelors available became few and far between. Warwick may have seen the Duke of Buckingham as a suitable match for one of his daughters, only to see him married to Elizabeth Woodville's sister.

As well as fearing for Anne and Isabel's futures, Warwick himself began to feel excluded. Edward IV was becoming less reliant on his advice and support as he promoted Woodville family members to his council of advisors. This ultimately led to the Neville's having to pack as much stuff as they could, before fleeing on a boat. Refused entry to Calais, Isabel was forced to endure a difficult labour on board the ship before giving birth to a still born child. Anne was only young, but she was a witness to the despair of her family and her older sister.

The breach between the two families would not only result in the Neville's losing everything they owned but also for Anne, eventually the loss of both her parents. After joining forces with Margaret of Anjou, Warwick was killed at the Battle of Barnet. Anne Neville would receive this news as she arrived back in England, ready to be received as the new Princess of Wales. On hearing the news, Anne's mother would flee to seek sanctuary, leaving Anne with her new mother-in-law and husband, fearful of what her future would now hold. Although Anne would reunite with her mother at Middleham, the relationship appears to have been strained with Anne supposedly helping to keep her mother locked away.

Despite the issues Anne Neville had with Elizabeth Woodville, it was to her that she appealed during the dispute over her inheritance. Anne Neville may well have expected to receive support from Elizabeth Woodville, given that her battle was with George, Duke of Clarence, who was no friend of the Woodville family. Despite that ongoing feud, Anne Neville did not receive the support from Elizabeth Woodville that she had requested.

Anne Neville had lost so much, at what she rightly or wrongly believed to be, the hands of the Woodvilles. She had suffered, she had lost people close to her and there was one family to blame. During the debates over what happened to the princes, much has been made of the fact that they were the sons of Edward IV. Yet, they were also the children of Elizabeth, the matriarch of one of the most unpopular families in England. By taking the boys away, Elizabeth Woodville would suffer, may feel as though she was losing all that mattered to her. Revenge is as much a motive for Anne Neville as it was for anybody else involved.

Whilst Anne Neville may have been portrayed as weak previously, it cannot be forgotten that she was also the daughter of the 'Kingmaker', one of the most ambitious men in England. Anne was proud of her Neville lineage, as she signed her books Anne Warwick.

Anne had grown up witnessing first-hand the dynastic plans of Warwick. She had observed the way he changed sides when his power and influence were at risk. Her father had started a war with Edward IV, allied with his previous enemy, killing on the battlefield those he had previously fought alongside.

Anne may have been aware of the risks he took to take him as close as possible to the crown. Like Warwick, Anne had come close to being an actual member of the royal family. She had returned to England as Princess of Wales, only to be stripped of her title as quickly as she had been given it. Maybe Anne's experience left her with a taste for the ultimate power. When she became queen, there was a fear that history might repeat itself and herself and her son would lose their royal status. Given the opportunity to secure her family's future she may have looked at what Warwick would have done it that position.

When Anne Neville was reunited with her mother, the family dynamic certainly appears to have changed. If we believe that Anne was as responsible as her husband for keeping her mother locked up, deprived of any rights to her inheritance, then we can see that there may have been a ruthless side to her that she inherited from her father and the events she witnessed.

After all the suffering and twists of fate that Anne Neville suffered in her short life, she may have wished to take control of her own destiny once and for all. She had grown up in a noble household with expectations of a great future and a prosperous marriage. As her family were forced to flee the country, she would have known that fortune had turned against her again and now her family had lost everything. She was forced to wait to see if she would indeed be married to Prince Edward before fortune took away her hopes for the future once again with the deaths of her father and husband.

We do not know what Anne's views were as she heard about the events unfolding in the capital but we do know that she was happy to become Queen of England and was there, observing proudly as her son was named Edward, Prince of Wales. This suggests that Anne was supportive of the ruthless determination of her husband to take control of their future. Just one more spin of the wheel of fortune could see positions reversed and Edward V ruling England, with Anne, Richard and the young Edward, prisoners in the Tower. Whilst nobody could claim to be able to control the fickle and random nature of Fortune, they could try to limit the damage she could wreak, be removing potential candidates. With the two boys out of contention there were few people in England that could garner the required level of support to pose a real threat to the new royal family.

The turbulent life of this determined young woman also could provide Anne with a motive to kill the boys and take control of her own fate once and for all.

Anne Neville could also have realised that the issues of the boys needed to be resolved out of loyalty to her husband. There has been significant debate about the nature of their marriage and how close they were when Richard was sent to live with Warwick. Whether they entered the marriage out of love like Edward and Elizabeth or for financial reasons, there is reason to believe that they were closer than many other noble couples of the era. They had certainly known each other and spent time in each other's company as children.

Ricardians may also choose to see Richard as Anne's saviour. If Anne was unhappy at her match with Edward of Lancaster, it was Richard who played a role in his death at the Battle of Tewkesbury. He is also presented as the man who saved her from the financial exploitation of her brother in law, Clarence. They both benefitted from the marriage and together they formed a powerful union.

They spent a lot of time together and appear to have supported each other through the initial stages of grief, following the news of their only child's sudden death. Back in the fifteenth century it was her duty to support her husband, even if that support was contrary to her moral code. Cecily Neville had stood by her husband as he launched his own schemes to replace Henry VI and was believed to have supported Clarence in his bid to remove Edward IV, aware that it could ultimately lead to two of her sons facing each other in battle, with only one returning.

Richard was known for his loyalty to his brother and would have been aware that the boys he was seeking to destroy were his own nephews. Anne did not need to battle such demons. They were her nephews through marriage, a marriage to the family she blamed for the destruction of her own family.

Whilst Anne remains a mystery in many ways, we can see that she did benefit hugely from the rumoured deaths of the boys and that there was no love lost between her family and the boys' parents. Anne clearly had the required motive to remove the boys. The next chapter will consider the evidence to be used in her defence.

Chapter 21 – The Defence of Anne Neville

As with the other figures to have been suspected it is important that arguments in the defence of Anne Neville are given due consideration.

The first argument that must be made when evaluating whether Anne Neville is a viable suspect in this mystery is that she was their aunty. The boys themselves were the cousins of her very own son. Today we may find it hard to believe that a woman could have taken such action, yet alone against family members. We must remember that Anne Neville lived in a quite different time to ourselves, where mothers would do whatever it took to provide for and protect their sons. Anne had witnessed and could have been influenced by the way both Margaret of Anjou and Margaret Beaufort fought to secure the best possible future for their sons.

Family relationships at this time were vastly different to what we experience now. Parents sent their children out to battle, to fight for or against the king. Margaret of Anjou sent her only son, still a teenager out to fight for his right to be the King of England. Cecily Neville had waited anxiously for news of first, Edmund and then Edward, as they fought for the House of York. The death of children was much more of a reality than we can possibly understand. The chances of a child living to adulthood were significantly lower back then. As cold as it sounds, families in the fifteenth century were not strangers to this kind of loss. Children were used as insurance. When Eleanor of Aquitaine, considered one of the strongest Queens of England, decided to flee the country and plot against her husband, King Henry II, she ensured her favourite son was safely by her side, whilst her other sons would be left to face the wrath of their father and possibly pay the price for their betrayal.

Relationships during the fifteenth century were vastly different to the type of relationships families enjoy today. Firstly, the eldest prince, Edward would have been a stranger to Richard, Anne Neville, and their son Edward. The young prince had been sent to live in Ludlow with his own household, surrounded by members or supporters of the Woodville family. The younger prince had remained in London but would still have had little contact with his uncle Richard and especially his wife Anne, who mostly remained on their estates, away from the capital. So, although it is true that Anne Neville was related to the boys, we also have to remember that the relationship between the boys and Anne Neville would probably not have been strong enough to overcome the tensions between the two families.

Although we may find it hard to believe that an aunty could be responsible for the death of her young nephews, it is something that still happens in modern culture. In California, as recently as 2018, a woman was found guilty of the torture and murder of her niece and nephew. She had assumed custody of the two young children when their mother died, and their father was in jail. The children were aged three and six when they were suffered torture at the hands of their aunty before finally being killed. The two children were found after being dumped in a storage unit and it is believed that their ordeal was a punishment for an older sibling stealing a bagel as they were starving.[xcix]

The distressing case of the two children who suffered at the hands of their own aunt is obviously an extreme case, but it does highlight that close relatives are capable of extreme actions in certain circumstances. These children suffered and died, possibly over the theft of a bagel. The Princes in the Tower were a threat to the survival of Anne, Richard and their son and took place in a more violent, more desperate time.

Therefore, although it can be argued that Anne Neville could not have committed this crime due to her relationship with the boys, it is certainly still a possibility and aunts have killed their nephews and nieces for a lot less.

In defence of Anne Neville we also must consider the relationship she appeared to enjoy with Elizabeth of York, her niece, and sister of the missing boys. When Elizabeth Woodville agreed that her daughters could be released from sanctuary, Richard promised that he would keep her daughters safe. Elizabeth was invited to court and is believed to have spent a lot of time with Anne Neville, and they are described as behaving as sisters. At Christmas there were reports of the two swapping dresses and appearing terribly similar.

There is no evidence that Elizabeth of York was mistreated or unhappy when in the household of the queen. This is even though there were clearly reasons for the two women to be wary of each other. Firstly, the women would find their roles reversed. Whilst Edward IV had been king, Elizabeth of York had been his eldest child and it was hoped that as a Princess of England, she would make a very prestigious marriage. During these times, Elizabeth clearly enjoyed a higher status than Anne Neville. Now Elizabeth of York had lost her status and was dependent on the goodwill of her uncle Richard and his wife Anne Neville.

Anne Neville would also have been aware that after the disappearance of the Princes, Elizabeth was considered by many in the country to be the legitimate heir to the throne. Elizabeth of York was clearly as much of a threat to her family as the boys had been, yet she would outlive Anne, Richard, and their son Edward.

As well as posing a threat to her family by nature of her birth, Elizabeth was also linked with the plots to replace Richard III with Henry Tudor. The plan had been formed that to strengthen Tudor's claim he would be married to Elizabeth of York. Anne's true role may have been to monitor the activities, correspondence, and visitors of the young Elizabeth. Was Anne Neville Elizabeth's 'sister' or was she her guard?

The final tension in the relationship between the two women revolved around the affections of Richard. When Elizabeth of York arrived at court, rumours began to circulate that Richard had feelings for his niece. Things deteriorated when Anne and Richard received the news that their only son had died suddenly, and Anne herself fell into ill health. Richard found himself without an heir to secure his legacy and without a wife capable of delivering him one. This led to rumours that Richard wanted Anne Neville to die so that he could marry Elizabeth and that he may have been responsible for her deteriorating health.

Despite these threats that Elizabeth of York posed to Anne Neville, her husband, and her son, she never caused any harm to her. Elizabeth of York survived her time with Anne Neville and after marrying Henry Tudor, would become Anne's successor as Queen of England. It could therefore be argued that it makes no sense for Anne Neville to have killed the boys but to have allowed Elizabeth of York to continue to play an important part in the plot to kill her husband.

Before accepting this as evidence of Anne Neville's innocence we also must accept that there may have been other reasons why after killing the boys, Anne Neville did not take any action against their older sister. By the time Elizabeth of York had left sanctuary and joined the king and queen at court, rumours had already spread throughout the country that the boys had been killed, and probably at the hands of Richard III. Richard had given his word to Elizabeth Woodville that the girls would be safe. With these rumours already swirling it would have been very suspicious if something had then happened to Elizabeth.

Whilst Richard III had managed to keep control of the country after the disappearance of the boys, the disappearance of Elizabeth of York may have turned the country against him. So, although Anne Neville clearly had easier access to Elizabeth of York and she remained safe, this cannot exonerate Anne Neville

Of course, it was not just Elizabeth of York who was entrusted into the care of Anne Neville, her four sisters also joined the royal household. As with their older sister, the younger girls appear to have been welcomed into Anne Neville's care and there was evidence that Richard was trying to find them good marriages. All five of the Woodville girls, all potential rivals to Richard's rule would outlive Anne Neville.

At this point in England, there had never been a woman on the throne so maybe Anne Neville did not see them as much of a threat as she had the boys. Yet she would have been aware of the danger a powerful marriage could have done to the future of her son, as plans were already being made for Elizabeth of York to marry Henry Tudor. Ambitious nobles in England may have sought the marriage of one of the daughters so that they could rule themselves. Despite this danger, no harm came to them whilst they were in the care of Anne Neville.

Anne Neville also took responsibility for other children in her short life. Her only sister Isabel had died not long after giving birth to her second living child and the erratic behaviour of her widower, George, Duke of Clarence had seen him executed for treason, leaving the two children as orphans. It is possible that shortly after this Anne took in the children to look after them. Whilst this was an aunt taking responsibility for her orphaned niece and nephew, again the children posed a threat to the reign of Richard III.

Their father had been the Duke of Clarence, the brother of Edward IV. More importantly he had been Edward IV's eldest brother. Therefore, after Edward IV's children were declared illegitimate, the line of succession would pass to Clarence and his children.

Technically, these two children had a stronger claim to the throne. Before the death of Edward IV this would probably not have been an issue for Anne Neville and her husband. Once Richard became king it would be a factor that neither could ignore. The children were in the care of Anne Neville after their coronation and yet, they also never came to any harm. Her nephew, Edward, Earl of Warwick was knighted in the September and passed into the keeping of another of Richard's nephews who was given responsibility for the Council of the North.

A prosecutor could argue that these children were no threat to Anne, unlike the princes, as Clarence had been executed for treason and his children were attainted which was also a barrier to them taking the throne. However, the attainder could be overturned as easily as the illegitimacy of Edward's children could, so if they were alive, they still posed a threat to the new king and queen.

It is possible that Anne Neville had a different relationship with these children as they were the children of her only sister. Yet, the relationship between the two sisters had soured as Clarence and Richard clashed over the division of the sisters' inheritance so they were not as close as they had previously been. Isabel had died shortly after giving birth to Margaret who may have spent a lot of time in the care of her aunt.

As with other suspects, there is no tangible evidence that can connect Anne Neville to this crime. There is truly little of Anne Neville's life that has been recorded, which could suggest that there was little to note in her life. Surely, if people believed that Anne had been involved there would be some record of it in the chronicles from the time, or in later accounts, where writers have sought to find an alternative candidate for the crime.

Yet we know that there was a lot of drama in Anne Neville's life. She had been Princess of Wales through Price Edward, only to see him killed in battle and then married the man responsible for her being a widow. She had to have had some involvement in or accepted the actions of Richard III in becoming king. Clearly, despite everything that had happened to her she somehow managed to stay under the radar. The low profile of Anne Neville could suggest she played no part in this mystery, but it could also explain why she has never been considered a suspect. People just didn't appear to consider Anne Neville worthy of mention regardless of her actions. This could help her blend in and further her ambitions unnoticed. With regards to whether Anne would have had the means and opportunity to commit the crime, you would think that it would be hard for a queen to carry out this crime without help and without being noticed. We have already seen however that Anne seemed able to blend into the shadows despite being at the centre of events.

In his work on Richard III, Sean Cunningham describes the imprisonment of the boys at the hands of their uncle and claims that they were still receiving visitors, specifically naming the Duchess of Gloucester, Anne Neville.[c] She stayed in the Tower before her coronation and as queen had access and opportunity to be admitted to the Tower. It is reasonable to consider that Anne Neville would have had the requisite motive, means and opportunity to commit the crime and her possible involvement could not be ruled out.

Already we can see that there were several people who would benefit from the death of the boys, and whilst Anne Neville is one of them, her true motive could be quite different from the others. Yes, Anne Neville was a mother with her son's future to protect who had seen her own fortunes fluctuate wildly and with devastating results. There was an extra dimension to Anne Neville's relationship with the Woodville family. The Woodvilles were blamed for causing the breach in the relationship between Richard Neville and Edward IV which had seen friends face each other on the battlefield, with Neville ultimately losing his life. The Woodvilles blamed Richard Neville for the death of Elizabeth Woodville's father, Earl Rivers. The hatred between the two families had seem plenty of blood spilled. Could this have been the factor that tipped Anne Neville to seek vengeance against two young children.

In New York in 2012 a 55-year-old nanny was found guilty of killing two of the young children in her care. Yoselyn Ortega fatally stabbed a two-year-old boy and six-year-old girl. Ortega had been the family nanny with responsibility for the three children of the Krim's.[ci] At the trial Ortega and her family claimed that the killing was a result of mental illness and cited a history of hearing voices. However, this was not accepted, and she was found guilty of murder. Whilst the defence claimed mental illness was to blame, the prosecutors had a different motive. Ortega is believed to have complained about her workload and conditions and they argued that she killed the children in spite. She may also have resented the wealth of the family compared to the childhood she had been able to provide to her own child.

Whilst we will never know the true explanation for Ortega's actions or the motive of whoever moved the princes, it is clear that spite and vengeance, even today can reasonably be put before a jury, to explain a motive for murder. Anne had lost everything due to the Woodville's and at the same time she was required to defer to the higher status of Elizabeth Woodville, until the roles were reversed.

Chapter 22 – John Howard – Background

John Howard, Duke of Norfolk is another key nobleman from the fifteenth century who has suffered from the campaign to rehabilitate Richard III. As historians have searched for answers to the mystery of what happened to the boys, they have looked to create reasonable doubt by stating that others such as Margaret Beaufort may have been responsible. John Howard is one of those figures who has been dragged into the pool of possible suspects as the battle to clear Richard III has raged on.

John Howard was another key figure who could claim to descend from royalty. His father Robert Howard who was a minor gentleman, had married Lady Margaret Mowbray, the daughter of Thomas Mowbray. This meant that John Howard was a descendent of Edward I. John Howard would remain close to his Mowbray relatives, serving them loyally in years to come.

It is believed that Howard was born in 1422. Compared to the status of the other figures considered in this book, Howard's beginnings would have been significantly more humble, yet he would still have had a comfortable life as he grew into adulthood. His status as a gentleman meant that he was allowed to serve on government commissions of the peace and of array, although for many years it appears as though he was overlooked by Edward IV. John Howard would have to wait patiently for the recognition he felt due to him at the hands of the royal family.

In 1443, Howard turned his attention to building a family when he decided to marry. Like his father before him, John Howard also sought a suitable marriage for himself. Howard's first wife Katherine Molines was a baron's daughter and the couple set up home at Tendring Hall.

Together they would see the arrival of six children. The eldest son was Thomas Howard who would become the Earl of Surrey. The youngest child was a daughter Jane who was born in the 1450's. The marriage between Howard and Katherine appears to have been a successful one, producing an heir for Howard, until the death of Katherine in 1465. Following the death of his wife, and with five children to take care of, Howard was quick to arrange a second marriage. In 1467, Howard married Margaret Chedworth. The marriage to Margaret also produced another child for Howard, a daughter, Katherine.

Whilst we may not know much about the early life of John Howard, his long career at the side of the Yorkist kings offer us a glimpse into what type of man John Howard turned out to be.

John Howard rose from the position of gentleman to become one of the closest and most rewarded allies of the King of England. He had one thousand men he could call upon to fight on his behalf at one time and created his own power base in East Anglia. Whilst his connections to the Mowbray family may have helped him to achieve this, he must have been able to exude enough power and charisma to get people to follow him.

If that wasn't enough, he may have been able to use his violent temper to encourage people he was in the right. Howard is recorded as showing this vicious temper on more than one occasion and even ended up earning himself a short stint in prison when one violent outburst went too far. When he wanted to become a parliamentary candidate the reaction to his nomination being opposed was recorded as 'Howard was wode as a wilde bullock.'[cii]

These characteristics combined with a sense of his own importance create a negative impression of John Howard, but there was another side to Howard.

During the many years serving the York royal family two important aspects of John Howard are made clear. The first is that he was clearly a capable fighter and leader. He fought for Edward IV at Towton, where he was knighted for his service, and at other important battles like Barnet and Tewkesbury. He was also a leading figure in the development of the English navy. He was responsible for commissioning and outfitting vessels for Edward IV and displayed a reputation for his innovative nature.[ciii] He also appears to have had strong political skills, working as a diplomat for Edward IV and clearly working with Richard on his plan to remove Edward V and crown himself.

The second feature of John Howard's character is his loyalty. As he was growing up, Howard was close to the Mowbray side of the family and served his uncle and cousin. Howard also demonstrated significant loyalty to the House of York. He had fought for Edward IV and helped him when he was facing rebellion from Warwick and his own brother Clarence. This loyalty continued when Richard III became king. Howard played a vital role in helping to quash the Buckingham Rebellion and would die in battle, fighting alongside Richard III.

Howard also appears to have taken his religion seriously. He is recorded as having taken pilgrimages and having patronage of certain churches. When he finally received the Dukedom of Norfolk that had previously been denied him, the celebration he held seemed to have a certain religious motivation. Despite his perceived pious nature, he appears to have turned a blind eye to the sexual exploits of his men and his own son.[civ] There is also some evidence that Howard was a charitable man. He helped to pay for the education of young men at Cambridge as well as giving money to the clergy.

Records of the Howard's also show that there was a happier side to Howard who appeared to get enjoyment from music, hunting and literature. There are records of payments for repairs of musical instruments, for minstrels and the performance of plays. His house contained a house organ and a chapel organ. Howard was also a patron of the theatre. Howard was a man who worked hard to improve his position in life and took his duties to his country, king, and family seriously. His success allowed him to pursue the interests he enjoyed.

The loyalty of John Howard to Edward IV seems unsurprising given the rewards he earnt during his service to the king. Further to being knighted at Towton, Howard would later receive a baronage and have the honour of being included in the party that accompanied the king's sister, Margaret to her wedding in Burgundy. Howard would find himself the recipient of many prominent positions, being appointed the Constable of Norwich Castle in 1461 and being named Treasurer of the Household in 1468.

Howard was also rewarded with the tenure of many manors and was granted custody of Colchester Castle in 1461. Clearly Howard was enjoying success at the hands of Edward IV and therefore his unwavering loyalty makes sense.

There was one decision of Edward IV that could have caused a major fracture in the relationship between the two men. This related to the issue of the Mowbray inheritance. Howard was due a substantial share of the inheritance and should have become John Howard, Duke of Norfolk. Instead, Edward IV used his power to circumvent the inheritance laws. Howard saw little of the inheritance pass to himself and was powerless as the king passed his entitlement to his young son, Prince Richard.

Clearly John Howard was well rewarded at the hands of Edward IV, but he had come from a more humble background than some of those nobles surrounding the king and the Mowbray inheritance would have significantly increased the power and influence of the Howard family. The failure to secure the Dukedom of Norfolk must have been a bitter blow to the loyal Howard.

The decision to keep the inheritance for his own family angered many lords who believed that it was wrong to deny Howard his expectations, mainly out of concern that the king's decision to disregard the laws of inheritance would have implications for their own families in the future. Despite the anger of various lords, there is no record of any grievance being made by Howard himself, a man famous for his temper. His continued loyalty and support for the then king, despite the decisions made against him speak to the character of Howard and suggest that loyalty was an important feature of his character, rather than something that was bought by the rewards he was offered.

The loyalty of all key nobles was to be tested during the limited reign of Edward V. Concerns over increasing the power of the Woodvilles caused people to turn to Richard as an alternative leader, even though they had been key supporters of Edward IV. Howard was one of those who would support Richard to become king and would reap the rewards. Thomas More believes that Howard was involved from the beginning with the plot to install Richard as King.[cv] Howard and Richard had known each other for a long time and Howard had previously worked in the household of Richard's mother and possible conspirator, Cecily Neville. As well as potentially helping Richard to seize the throne, Howard played a vital role in helping him to keep it. It was Howard who was responsible for defeating those involved with the Buckingham rebellion and Howard would travel with Richard to the Battle of Bosworth where he would die fighting for the king.

It did not take long for Howard to start receiving the rewards for his service to Richard III. Even before his coronation on 6 July, Richard III rewarded Howard with the ultimate prize. Richard III ensured that the inheritance he had been due was taken away from Prince Richard and John Howard finally became the Duke of Norfolk. Following this, Howard continued to be rewarded for his support for the new king. Howard would see himself named as Marshall and Admiral of England and especially following the fall of The Duke of Buckingham would become one of the most powerful nobles in England. Crucially he would be named as Constable of the Tower of London, home of the young princes. His eldest son Thomas would also prosper, becoming Earl of Surrey.

John Howard continued to support Richard III for the duration of his short reign. John Howard was trusted to help deal with rebellions such as the one that led to the downfall of Buckingham. Howard was also responsible for investigating and quashing any treasonous behaviour that threatened the stability of the new royal family.

John Howard would have been one of the people that Richard III relied on as he began to hear the rumours that Henry Tudor was gathering support and preparing to invade and challenge for the Crown. Howard had proven himself to be an effective military leader and so will have been involved in the plans made by the king for the defence of the realm.

Following the initial invasion of Henry Tudor, as he marched through Wales to face battle, Norfolk worked to muster his men and moved to Leicester with the king's forces. Norfolk was given command of the vanguard in the Battle of Bosworth and following fierce fighting he was killed fighting alongside the man he believed should be king. His son survived and would go on to initially make peace with the new Tudor dynasty.

Chapter 23 – The Case For and Against John Howard

Questions began to be asked regarding the involvement of John Howard in the disappearance of the princes, fundamentally due to the issue of the Mowbray inheritance. This was the inheritance which should have benefitted Howard and saw him take the title, Duke of Norfolk. Edward IV, as king, had chosen to circumvent the inheritance laws to his own benefit and passed the land and titles to his own son, Prince Richard, the younger of the Princes in the Tower.

Once Richard III became king this grievance was one of the first things he dealt with. He removed the inheritance from Prince Richard and at last, John Howard received his share of the inheritance. On 28 May he formally became John Howard, Duke of Norfolk.

It has been argued that the issue of the inheritance gave Howard the required motive to kill the boy. This way he could ensure that he would get what was entitled to him. Also, this was only the beginning, in terms of rewards that Howard would receive at the hands of the new king. This led to suspicion that Howard was being rewarded for more than his mere support during Richard III's usurpation. Maybe Howard was being rewarded for killing two birds with one stone. He removed the obstacle to his own problem as well as removing potential threats to Richard's reign.

The flaw in the argument that Howard killed the boys to get his inheritance is that to regain this, he only had to kill one of the boys. The inheritance had been passed to the younger boy, there was no reason for him to kill the older boy. It would have also been a lot less suspicious if just one of the boys had died. Child mortality was significantly higher in the fifteenth century and his death could have been easily explained away. It is much more difficult for people to believe that both boys became ill and died at the same time. Despite it being easier to cover up the death of one boy, Howard may have feared retribution at the hands of the older boy, if a rebellion in his name ever saw him restored as King Edward V.

Howard had clearly supported Richard III and had now taken the inheritance of the younger nephew. Howard would stand to lose everything if Edward V ever won back the throne. Another issue to consider regarding the issue of Howard killing the boys to receive his inheritance is the date of when he was awarded it. Howard became Duke of Norfolk on 28 June. There are reports of the boys being seen, after this date, into July. The fact that he received his inheritance before the boys disappeared, discredits the argument that he killed them to achieve it. Howard didn't need the young prince to be dead to claim his inheritance. The boy had been declared illegitimate and therefore may not have been considered worthy of the titles that had been passed to him by his late father. They had lost their status and everything that went with it.

Another motive that could be applicable to Howard is revenge. Clearly, he had been denied his inheritance. Whilst this was the decision of Edward IV, it was widely believed that Elizabeth Woodville was the driving force behind the decision to award Howard's inheritance to her own son. Whilst Woodville was securing the future of her own son, she was doing so at the expense of Howard and his own children. Whilst there is no record of Howard complaining to the king about this decision, it was a decision that would have huge implications for Howard and his desire to progress and improve his own position.

Howard's inheritance was symbolic of a more significant problem. The Woodville's were not an influential family and Elizabeth Woodville had a large family. As soon as she became queen, she used her influence to promote the interests of her family at the expense of the noble families, who had fought bravely for the king and now expected their rewards. We have seen how the Duke of Buckingham was forced to marry one of Elizabeth Woodville's sisters. As the Woodville family sought out the best prospects for their family members, the chances for Howard to secure a prestigious match for his sons diminished.

This wasn't the only area were the Woodville's sought to dominate. As Edward IV settled into marriage with his new bride, he started to turn away from the advisors and nobles he had previously trusted and sought advice from. His council would come to be made up of Woodville relatives such as his father-in-law and Elizabeth's older brother.

Howard was, like Warwick, of an older generation than Edward IV, and had fought loyally for the House of York. In return they would have expected to have their voices heard and respected. They would expect to increase their own power and influence through their closeness to the king. Yet they found themselves being excluded more and more, even Cecily Neville, the king's mother, was losing her influence over Edward.

This exclusion from the heart of power also affected Howard and his determination to make the Howard's, one of the great noble families in fifteenth century England.

The combination of the loss of inheritance and influence could have made nobles at the time bitter. As the close ally of the new king, Richard III, Howard found himself in the ultimate position to avenge himself against the humiliations that had been heaped upon him. Having suffered at the hands of the Woodville's he would have known that he would suffer under the rule of a boy king, dominated by his maternal family. As well as removing that threat, Howard would be close at hand to see the suffering of the woman he blamed for the wrongs against him.

Given that it can be argued that Howard did have some form of motive for involvement in the killings we will go on to consider whether he had the means and opportunity to commit the crime.

It has been suggested that Howard would have easily had the opportunity to commit this crime as he was Constable of the Tower, guaranteeing him access to the boys. As Constable he would have been able to arrange for his men to enter the Tower whenever he needed. However, Howard was never fully in control of the Tower as Constable. He only held the second reversion of the title and so would not have had the level of authority imagined.

Although this suggests that there were limits on his ability to arrange access to the Tower, it must be remembered that he was one of the closest allies of the king. Although the Constable had control over the Tower, it is not clear whether he would have dared refuse access to one of the most powerful nobles in the country at the time. It is also possible that his work on behalf of Richard III required him to have access to the Tower or for his men to enter.

When Edward V was escorted to the Tower, he was initially kept by himself. His younger brother was in sanctuary with their mother, Elizabeth Woodville. Howard played a significant role in arguing for the younger boy to be released from sanctuary and removed to the Tower to join his brother, initially on the basis that he could attend Edward's coronation.

Once Richard III agreed that Elizabeth Woodville should be asked to release the boy, Howard was one of the delegation sent to persuade her. Once the boy was released from his mother's care, it was Howard who escorted him to the Tower. Howard had been allowed close access to the younger brother straight after his release and had given assurances to his mother that no harm would come to him. This gave him a ready excuse to visit the boys, claiming to check on their safety and wellbeing.

During the negotiations to release the boy, Elizabeth Woodville stated that she was worried that some harm would come to him and even that he was ill and needed to stay with his mother. Howard would have heard this and knew that it could be claimed that the boy had been ill when he had arrived at the Tower and had died shortly after, not before passing his illness to his older brother who would also succumb to it. Howard had access to the boys and an excuse that could be used to explain away the deaths.

Yet, if Howard was responsible for the deaths, he chose not to use the rumours of their illness to his advantage and everybody close to the king kept silent about the fate of the boys, either because they didn't know or because they thought they would be blamed.

Given the level of rewards Howard received it could be argued that this was what caused him to be loyal to Richard during and following his plotting to become king. Yet, this is to forget that Howard was in his sixties when he played a ceremonial role in Richard III's Coronation.

Howard had proved to be a loyal supporter of the House of York through his many years of service.

He had started off serving Richard, Duke of York and Cecily Neville. He had fought for Edward IV to take the throne from the Lancastrian, King Henry VI. He had fought alongside Edward IV despite the withholding of his inheritance. His record of loyalty did not appear to be motivated by the desire for money and influence, as he was not as rewarded as others under Edward IV. We cannot know whether Howard supported the decision to depose Edward V, whether he foresaw the problems a young king, dominated by his mother could cause for the country. Given his loyal service to York it can be believed that he would have served Richard III as the new king anyway without the inducement of the many rewards he was offered.

When Henry Tudor started to mount a credible challenge to Richard III, many people fled to join his growing invasion force. If Howard was motivated by money and the need to secure his inheritance, he may have followed the path of others like Buckingham and negotiated a deal with Tudor in return for his support. There is no reason to believe he considered deserting his king, rallying to destroy the rebellions breaking out in the name of Edward V and later Henry Tudor.

One of the first people to try to rehabilitate the image of Richard III, George Buck refers to a letter he claims was written by Elizabeth of York to John Howard. He states that this letter was urging the Duke of Norfolk to intervene on her behalf with the king. Would Elizabeth of York have turned to Howard for support, if she herself or her mother, Elizabeth Woodville believed that he had been in involved with the disappearance of her brothers? Her reliance on Howard could point to a belief in his innocence.

Alternatively, it must be considered that Elizabeth of York and Elizabeth Woodville were short of options and of influential friends willing to be seen to help them. It may have been out of necessity that the women felt they had to silence any doubts they had about Howard. He was one of the closest allies of the king and also had connections to Elizabeth's grandmother, Cecily Neville.

Doubts have also been cast on the existence and contents of the letter. This in itself is not enough to suggest that Howard was not involved with the disappearance.

The decision to name John Howard as a suspect in the disappearance is quite a new phenomenon, a result of the desire to believe that Richard III could not be guilty of this heinous crime. Certainly, he benefitted from the downfall of the young boys, and so, all historians have offered us is, what can only be considered a weak motive at best. There is no evidence to connect him to the death of the boys. Rumours swirled around the country regarding the disappearance of the boys and yet nobody named Howard.

Howard had become incredibly rich and powerful because of his relationship with Richard III. This rise in prominence would have caused resentment around the nobility, people would have wanted him to fall from favour. Despite this, nobody felt the need or desire to name Howard as being involved with the mystery.

Of course, as one of the most powerful men in the country, who could easily gather a force to fight for him, there is a possibility that people were scared of Howard, especially given his famous temper. Yet, this doesn't make much sense when people were quite happy to spread the rumour that it was the king himself or The Duke of Buckingham, men whose power exceeded even that of John Howard, that had caused harm to the boys.

This lack of evidence leaves John Howard as merely a person of interest in this case. Whilst it can be argued to some extent that he had a motive, there is no evidence to condemn him, nor to clear him.

It may be hard for us to imagine someone killing two young children merely for an inheritance, but times were very different in the fifteenth century. People killed for less in a time when family honour, power and legacy were everything to some people.

Even now, an inheritance can lead to the death of children. In 2003, in Nigeria Edmund Adiele, was allegedly beaten up by his brothers resulting in his death. The argument had started over Edmund's house. Fifteen years later, his widow returned home from church to find the body of her 17-year-old son. She heard that her son had been beaten to death by the children of his uncle. Again, it was about an inheritance, the house that had been the subject of the first dispute fifteen years earlier.[cvi] Children have murdered their parents to receive their inheritances, brothers have turned against brothers, time and time again, proving that blood ties and loyalty can mean nothing when money is involved.

Chapter 24 – Francis Lovell – Background

One of the less well-known figures covered here has to be Francis Lovell. Francis Lovell is considered to have been a close and loyal friend of Richard III. His desire to stay out of the spotlight and fade into the background means that we know a lot less about him than we do of others.

It is believed that Francis was born in Oxfordshire in 1456. He was born into an old, established and very wealthy family, probably at the manor house of Minster Lovell. His parents were John Lovell and Joan Beaumont. Francis entered the world with a twin sister and may have been named after St Francis of Assisi.

Francis could look forward to a comfortable life, being the heir to five baronies and would have been raised in luxury surroundings, not wanting for anything. As with many families, the twists and turns of the various battles, in the Wars of the Roses would determine their fate. John Lovell had been a committed supporter of the House of Lancaster and would fight for King Henry VI.

This decision would have a significant impact on John and Francis Lovell. Finding himself on the losing side, Lovell found himself at the mercy of Edward IV. Whilst he was lucky enough to escape with his life, there was still a high price to pay. Lovell was stripped of all his land and possessions. The wealthy Lovells, used to having whatever they needed, found themselves reliant on the kindness and charity of others.[cvii] Francis Lovell was only a young child, so whilst he may not have understood the political changes that were sweeping the country, he may have been aware that something was wrong.

The life of Francis and his two sisters would be sent into turmoil yet again, when Francis was still only nine years old. Unexpectedly, on 9 January 1463, John Lovell died. Although this would lead to significant change for Francis, the fact that he arranged to have prayers said for his grandfather but not his father, suggests the relationship between father and son was not close. As was the law then, the death of John Lovell would see Francis become a ward of the king. It was up to the king to decide who should benefit from controlling Francis, his choice of wife, and his estates. Initially, the king didn't award it to anyone, but possibly in an attempt to ease the rising tensions between himself and Warwick, Francis was sent to complete his education under the one-time close friend of Edward IV.

During him time with Warwick he would have met important people, leaned how to manage his estates, how to fight and this was probably where he first became acquainted with Richard, Duke of Gloucester.

Francis would find himself dragged back into conflict with the king when Warwick began to rebel. Having been found a suitable wife by Warwick, Francis would go to live with his wife's family. Having survived Warwick's rebellion, better times were destined for Francis. On the death of his grandmother, Lady Sudeley, Francis received a substantial inheritance, making him one of the wealthiest barons in England.

Before his failed rebellion against Edward IV, Warwick did use his power over Francis to arrange a marriage for him. The bride he chose for Francis was in fact, one of his own nieces, Anne Fitzhugh. The Fitzhugh's were also a very wealthy family. Like Francis, Anne also had two sisters, but she also had five brothers. This was the family that would welcome Francis after the death of Warwick.

The marriage appears to have been beneficial to Francis emotionally as well as financially. The limited evidence we have suggests that they were a close couple, who would have been disappointed that they were unable to produce any children. It was believed that Francis sought guidance from his wife, valuing and trusting her opinions. Francis made generous provision for Anne on his death[cviii] and their marriage would last until he disappeared, presumed dead, after the Battle of Stoke Field.

There is limited evidence still available to give us much insight into the character of the man who would become one of the closest friends of one of England's most notorious king's. The letters that he sent during his lifetime give us the most important glimpse into what Francis the man was like. The tone of his letters indicate that he was a polite man. His writing is concise and to the point. There was no room for sentimentality in his words, indicating that he may have had a more reserved nature.[cix] The very fact that we do not know much about Francis also indicates that he didn't like to the be the centre of attention and was happy to stay on the sidelines as other key figures fought to receive the attention of the king.

There is no record of Francis Lovell publicly losing his temper and he may have been a calm figure who managed to manouvre the political game-playing without making too many enemies. At the same time, the treatment of his father paints him as a man who was slow to forgive slights against him. Francis made no effort to mark the memory of his father after his death or even to say prayers for him.[cx] This could have indicated that he just wasn't very pious, although this would be unlikely in deeply religious England in the fifteenth century, if he had not taken the time and trouble to have prayers said for his grandfather. The failure to mark his father's memory therefore appears to be a sign of contempt for his parents.

Typical of the time, Francis appears to have taken his religion seriously and enjoyed taking part in hunting trips.

The relationship between the new, York king Edward IV and young Francis certainly got off to a rocky start. Francis would have been aware that his family were staunch Lancastrians and that his father had fought against Edward IV and had been stripped of all his possessions. After the death of his father, Francis' fate was determined by Edward IV who ultimately sent him to live with his close friend and advisor, Warwick. This was a decision that would send the young ward on another collision course with the king.

When Warwick and Clarence decided to rebel, as Warwick's ward, Francis was required to support him in his attacks. Again, Francis would find himself on the losing side and at risk of punishment from Edward IV. Luckily, Edward forgave Francis who was still considered a minor and sent him to live with the Duke and Duchess of Suffolk.

Following the king's marriage to Elizabeth Woodville, there was another issue that could have caused tension between Francis and Edward. After the death of Edward IV, it was alleged that Edward had previously been married to a lady called Eleanor Talbot. A woman who also had a family connection to Francis. If the story of the secret first marriage was true, Francis may have posed a serious threat to the king's sons.

Despite these issues, Francis appeared to develop a close relationship with Edward IV. In January 1483, Edward IV raised Francis Lovell from a Baron to a viscount. Only one other person became a viscount in the whole of Edward's reign, which suggests Francis Lovell was a trusted, valued supporter of the king and the House of York. The decision to make Francis a viscount may also have been influenced by the close friendship that had developed between Francis and the king's brother, Richard, Duke of Gloucester, although it is unlikely, that this alone would have caused Edward IV to act as he did.

It is possible that the close friendship between the future Richard III and Francis Lovell began when they were both living in the household of Richard Neville and would have received a similar education.

Whenever the relationship began, it was a relationship that endured the usurpation and even the death of Richard III. Although Francis had become a viscount under Edward IV, it was his close friend that would ensure that he was well rewarded. Before he became king, as Lord Protector, Richard began to show his favour to Francis, naming him as Chief Butler and Constable of Wallingford Castle.

Richard appears to have trusted Francis completely and this loyalty continued to be rewarded once Richard became king. Francis played a key role in the coronation ceremony, carrying one of the swords of state. During the short reign of Richard III, Francis Lovell became a Knight of the Garter, Privy Councillor and the Speaker of Parliament. He aided Richard III in defeating the rebels in the Buckingham Rebellion and helped Richard as he prepared for the invasion to come from Henry Tudor.

There is some confusion about where Francis Lovell was during the infamous Battle of Bosworth. Some accounts have Francis Lovell fighting alongside his long-time friend and he is listed as one of the people that died in the fighting.[cxi]

Other accounts indicate that Francis was sent to the south coast to try to repel the Tudor invasion. It is believed that the Duke of Howard sent him to Milford where they believed that Tudor was going to land. However, Tudor actually landed at Milford Haven in Wales. Francis was now miles away from the battle and unable to stop the invasion force from heading towards the king's forces. Whilst it is possible that on hearing that Tudor had landed and was progressing through Wales, Francis Lovell headed straight to Leicester to join the king's army, what is not possible is that Francis Lovell died fighting by the side of Richard III.

Francis Lovell was one of the few close allies of Richard III that outlived him. Wherever he was when the battle was decided and the Tudor dynasty began, Francis headed to Colchester, specifically St John's Abbey. This was where he would seek sanctuary whilst regrouping and planning how he would avenge the death of his friends and allies. Whilst not famed for his military prowess, the threat of Francis Lovell lurking in the shadows, would haunt Henry Tudor as he adjusted to life in England and life as a king.

The new Tudor king was probably disappointed when he found that Richard III's closest friend had escaped and had sought sanctuary but may have underestimated how much Lovell would want to avenge his friend's death.

It was about five days after the Battle of Bosworth that Francis Lovell arrived at St John's Abbey. Whilst he should have been able to consider himself safe after claiming sanctuary, he would have been aware that Edward IV had ignored the laws of sanctuary after the Battle of Tewkesbury. He would have to hope that the religious devotion of his mother would prevent Henry VII from doing the same whilst he planned his next move.

He stayed in sanctuary until the spring of 1486, when he is believed to have escaped and disappeared. Although Henry VII could not locate him, he would have been aware that he would be trying to get to Flanders, to the court of Margaret of Burgundy, sister of the late Richard III.

Francis made it safely to Flanders and helped Margaret to plan an invasion, aimed at placing Lambert Simnel on the throne of England. Claiming that he was the Earl of Warwick, and therefore the rightful heir, they gathered an invasion force and prepared to challenge Henry VII.

All the plans to have Simnel recognised as the Earl of Warwick culminated in an invasion of England on 4 June 1487. Simnel, Lovell and their troops landed at Furness Falls and on 16 June they met up with Henry's army and the Battle of Stoke Field yielded another victory for Henry VII. Simnel was captured and was forced to go and work in the royal kitchens. Nobody knows what happened to Lovell. There was no evidence he was killed in the battle, but he was never heard of again.

One rumour of what happened was that he tried to cross the river Trent and unable to do it, drowned.[cxii] Another rumour was that he fled back to MInster Lovell, his family home, where he hid in a vault. Credence was given to this rumour when in 1708, workmen at Minster Lovell entered a sealed room. At a table they found the full skeletal remains of a human being.[cxiii] Upon exposure to the air, the skeleton turned to a pile of dust, so we will never know whether these were the remains of the elusive Francis Lovell or not.

Whilst we cannot be sure of what happened to Francis Lovell after the Battle of Stoke Field, we can be sure that he was committed to the House of York and his closest friend, Richard III.

Chapter 25 – The Case For and Against Francis Lovell

Francis Lovell was one of the closest friends of the man who has been considered the main suspect in this case. Lovell would have been one of the few people that Richard III trusted and confided in. This relationship with Richard III means that we must consider whether Francis Lovell could have been involved in the events leading to the disappearance of the princes.

When looking at Lovell as a suspect, his determination to destroy Henry VII, after Richard III's death shows the lengths he was willing to go to on behalf of his loyalty to Richard III and the House of York.

Whilst there is debate about whether he was at Bosworth, fighting for his close friend, he certainly carried on the battle, long after Henry VII was declared king. Lovell sought sanctuary whilst he planned his next move. He used his time to plan a way to escape England, to the safety of Flanders, where he could continue to work on a way to overthrow the new Tudor king.

Whether or not he believed that Lambert Simnel was actually the Earl of Warwick, he played an active role, with Margaret, the sister of Richard III, to convince leaders around the world that the boy was the rightful heir to the throne. He travelled with Simnel to Ireland where he was crowned King of England. Lovell was also by Simnel's side when he confronted the king's forces at the Battle of Stoke Field. Again, Lovell was on the losing side and again he appears to have escaped, but the evidence confirms that he was there, fighting to bring down the man who had caused the destruction of his friend at Bosworth. Lovell showed that he would fight against an anointed king, this could lead us to conclude that he felt strongly enough about the cause to have been involved in the death of another king. Edward V.

As with many other key figures of the period, greed and acquisitiveness may have been a motivating factor for Francis Lovell. Lovell had been born into a very wealthy family but had witnessed the sudden changes in his family's fortune, when his father was stripped of all of his land and possessions. The luxurious lifestyle he was used to was for a short period, not something his family could take for granted, as they relied on the charity of those around them until they had their fortune restored. This period of his childhood could help to explain why as an adult Lovell would be considered greedy and fought hard to get as much as he could.

Under Edward IV, Lovell did not appear to be especially favoured, although he was one of only two people raised to the title of viscount. Lovell could not have expected to gain much more under the rule of the young Edward V. Alternatively, the rule of his close friend could pave the way for more substantial rewards. Richard III certainly gave substantial rewards to those closest to him, Howard, Stafford and Lovell. This increasing prosperity made the boys a threat to Lovell. The restoration of Edward V would see Lovell lose not just what he had gained under the reign of Richard III, but ultimately everything as the young king would pursue all those that helped Richard III take his place on the throne. Lovell, as much as anybody benefitted from the boys' disappearance. The real question is whether he was a lucky bystander or whether he actively took control of his fate.

There is a connection between Edward IV and Francis Lovell that could be used in the prosecution or defence of Francis Lovell. The princes had been declared illegitimate on the basis that Edward IV had been pre-contracted to another woman before Elizabeth Woodville. The other woman referred to is believed to be Eleanor Talbot. Lovell had a familial connection to the Talbot family. His connection to the family could mean that he was one of the few people at the heart of the royal court who knew whether there had indeed been a pre-contract between Eleanor and Edward IV.

This connection appears to work against Lovell. as if he was aware that the story was a fabrication and that the princes had not been illegitimate at all, he knew the danger they posed to Richard III and his circle of favourites. If the rumours were false, he would have known that the boys needed to disappear. He would have been unable to share the information with anyone for fear that the news got out that the boys were legitimate and support for Richard slumped dramatically.

If, on the other hand, through his connection with the Talbot family he knew that there was indeed a pre-contract, he may feel more secure. He may have been confident that the boys were illegitimate and if necessary, he would know people who would have been able to swear to its existence. Confident in the knowledge that the boys had no claim to the throne, he would not have needed an alternative solution to secure Richard III's, and ultimately, his own position.

Religion is also another common factor that must be considered. Francis Lovell is considered to have been a pious man who took religion seriously, which as we have previously seen, can be used to argue towards innocence. Nobody who took their religion seriously could take the step of shedding the blood of innocent children. The defence may seek to argue that his pious nature is evidence that he could not have committed this crime.

We have also seen though, that religion can be used to justify acts of violence. It can be seen as God's will when one army, brutally defeats another. Visions and voices can also be interpreted in a way that leads people to believe that a certain course of action needs to be taken.

The treatment of his fathers' soul also suggests that there were limits to the religious devotion of Lovell. The fact that he had prayers said for his grandfather demonstrates that he believed this to be an important act, carried out after death.

Yet, Lovell took no such action for the sake of his fathers' soul, following his death. No prayers were said for John Lovell and no care was taken to erect a suitable memorial in the years that followed. Whilst this suggests that there was a serious issue that blighted the relationship between father and son, it could also suggest that there were limits to the strength of Lovell's religious commitment. Whilst he is seen as observing religious traditions at times, clearly, if he feels strongly enough, he is willing to forgo religious convention.

Another argument to be used in the defence of Lovell is that he was not considered to be a key player in the tumultuous fifteenth century politics. He served the York dynasty well but seems to have been more concerned with securing his own financial situation rather than the power games playing out in London. Lovell is considered to have been someone who preferred to remain on the sidelines, away from attention. The jump from somebody looking after their own interests to killing a young prince is significant. This low profile of Lovell makes it easy to forget that he received his education at the hands of Warwick, who had actively plotted against the king he had previously fought to Crown. Warwick had deceived, killed relatives of Elizabeth Woodville and formed an alliance with his previous foe.

Lovell had seen up close the lengths people were prepared to go to when they saw their own position at risk, saw their own plans thwarted by the ambitions of others and ultimately observed the way Warwick was proactive in trying to improve the position of himself and his family.

Lovell's low political profile during the reign of Edward IV also raises questions as to whether he would have the means and opportunity to commit the crime. The boys were locked in the Tower of London under the guard of Stafford and Richard III's men. He would also have had to get past the Constable. Other figures had the contacts and influence required to allow them to access the Tower if they needed to, Lovell was a close friend of the king, but this in itself would not have been enough to gain access.

It is likely that Lovell would have been introduced to important figures during the time he was under the guidance of Warwick, but that was a number of years previously, and those too closely associated with Warwick would have lost the influence they had following Warwick's failed attempt to restore Henry VI as King of England.

There is also no evidence that he had anything to fear from the Woodville family. He had not been shown as much favour as others by Edward IV and this would probably continue with the rule of his son. There is no record of any disputes between the Woodville family and Francis Lovell. Whilst others stood to lose substantially if the Woodvilles increased their influence, Lovell did not have that fear. Helping Richard III take the place of Edward V was a gamble for Lovell. If Richard III failed and Lovell was found to have been involved, he would have lost all the land and money he had worked so hard to maximise. In the brutal reality of life during the Wars of the Roses, he was risking his life.

Whilst there is nothing to suggest that Lovell personally had any disputes with the Woodville family, he was in danger of being tainted by association with two people in particular. Back in 1469/70, Lovell as a minor, and a ward of Warwick, had no choice but to support Warwick as he launched his campaign against Edward IV and his Woodville relatives.

Warwick had also taken advantage of his control of Lovell to marry him to his own niece, so he would forever be connected to the Warwick family. Lovell was a man who could be slow to forgive others. The lack of recognition by Edward IV may also indicate that the Woodvilles never forgot his support for the man who had killed their father.

Lovell was also a close friend of Richard, Duke of Gloucester. The Woodvilles were already being blamed for causing the execution of Richard's brother, George, Duke of Clarence. As soon as Edward IV died, they were trying to gain support for limiting the control Richard would have as Protector until Edward V was old enough to rule in his own right.

In the twelfth century, Henry II had a close friend that he decided to promote. Against the wishes of the church he appointed Thomas Beckett as the Archbishop of Canterbury, to assist him in his desire to reform the church and limit its power. Henry II didn't bank on Beckett finding God and, rather than helping to reform the church, he resisted Henry's attempts and resigned as his Chancellor. The best of friends were now enemies, to the point that when Henry decided to have his son crowned, the Archbishop of Canterbury who should have been performing the ceremony was not even invited. Beckett responded by excommunicating those that had taken part in the ceremony. This put Henry II into a rage. During one of his raging outbursts he is believed to have rhetorically asked out loud who would rid him of this troublesome priest. A small number of knights that were present, took this not as an angry rant, but as a direct order. They headed to Canterbury where they murdered Becket. Although Henry's words were taken out of context he was still blamed for the murder.

Those close to Richard III, such as Francis Lovell, may also have been witness to the despair he felt as rebellions broke out in the name of the young princes. He may have misinterpreted his words as he bemoaned the presence of his nephews. Whilst those on the outside of the political game playing arena may not have had the strongest of motives, loyalty to the man who had raised them to some of the most prominent nobles in the land may have been enough for them, as it had been for the knights close to Henry II.

Chapter 26 – Sir James Tyrell

Thomas More is the only person who claims to offer us a definitive account of what happened to the boys. In his account he claims that the man who was responsible for murdering the boys was Sir James Tyrell, therefore he must be considered as a suspect in a full investigation of the evidence.

Sir James Tyrell is believed to have been born around 1445 and was the eldest son of William Tyrell. The Tyrell family lived in Gipping, Suffolk, a place that would become significant in theories that the boys survived and were sent away inro hiding.

Sir James had certainly come to the attention of the House of York by the age of seven when he became a ward of Cecily Neville. Their association at this time appears to have been brief as Cecily Neville sold the wardship back to Tyrell's mother.

In 1469 James was married to Anne Arundel and together they became parents to three sons and one daughter. Tyrell was clearly a loyal supporter of Edward IV during his acrimonious dispute with Warwick and Clarence, as he was actually knighted by Edward IV following his efforts fighting on his behalf at the Battle of Tewkesbury, not as More claims, by Richard III, following the murder of the princes.

Following the Battle of Tewkesbury, Tyrell appears to have entered the service of Richard, Duke of Gloucester and was certainly trusted with important errands on behalf of Gloucester. It was Tyrell who was tasked with escorting Richard's mother-in-law, Anne Beauchamp from her self-imposed sanctuary at Beaulieu to Middleham, to be reunited with her youngest daughter.

Later, as King Richard III, he would task Tyrell with another important journey. Following the betrayal of Buckingham and his failed rebellion, it was Tyrell that Richard turned to ensure that Buckingham was safely escorted to Salisbury where he would face execution. Certainly, we can conclude that if Richard needed a sensitive task completing, Tyrell would be considered a suitable candidate.

As with others close to the king, Tyrell received vast rewards for his service and loyalty to Richard III. After attending the coronation of Richard III, Tyrell would see a variety of titles added to his knighthood. Richard III named Tyrell his Master of the Horse and Master of the King's Henchman. He would become a Commissioner of Array for Wales and Steward of the Duchy of Cornwall for life.

One of the last appointments Tyrell would receive at the hands of Richard III was Commander of the Castle of Guisnes in January 1485. Tyrell's ambitious and unscrupulous nature meant that when Richard III was killed, he was able to quickly come to terms with the new king, Henry VII. This arrangement with Henry VII allowed him to keep his post of Commander of Guisnes Castle where he would remain peacefully until 1501.

At this time, Edmund de la Pole was leading the Yorkist charge against Henry VII and received support from Tyrell. This led to the arrest of Tyrell who was charged with treason. He was found guilty and was executed in May 1502. It was during his arrest for this crime that More tells us he confessed to the murder of the princes.

The main piece of evidence pointing to the guilt of Tyrell must be the account provided by Thomas More, who describes the events below:
'I shall rehearse you the dolorous end of those babes, not after that way that I have so heard by such men and by such means as methinketh it were hard but it should be true
Sir Robert Brackenbury, constable of the Tower was asked to kill the boys 'who plainly answered that he would never put them to death

'Sir," quod his page, "there lieth one on your pallet without, that, I dare well say, to do your grace pleasure the thing were right hard that he would refuse" meaning this by Sir James Tyrell

The man had a high heart and sore longed upward, not rising yet so fast as he had hoped, being hindered and kept under by the means of Sir Richard Ratcliffe and Sir William Catesby

Wherefore on the morrow he sent him to Brackenbury with a letter by which he was commanded to deliver Sir James all the keys of the Tower for one night, to the end he might there accomplish the king's pleasure in such thing as he had given him commandment

Which, upon the sight of them, caused those murderers to bury them at the stair-foot, meetly deep in the ground, under a great heap of stones

Very truth it is, and well known, that at such time as Sir James Tyrell was in the Tower for treason committed against the most famous prince King Henry the Seventh, both Dighton and he were examined, and confessed the murder in manner above written; but whither the bodies were removed, they could nothing tell.' [cxiv]

More's account appears to condemn Tyrell, He tells us that there was a confession and gives us the details of Tyrell's involvement. Although Vergil does not make any reference to a confession or give us the same details as Thomas More, he does also confirm that it was Tyrell that was responsible for this crime.

However, as discussed earlier, there are issues with the account of Thomas More. Apart from inaccuracies in the piece of work and his failure to name any of his sources there are issues with his account of the murder itself. The first issue relates to the knighthood that Tyrell received. More's account tells us that Tyrell was knighted for committing the murder, by Richard III. Yet, we know that cannot be true, as Tyrell was knighted years earlier, in 1471, by Edward IV for his support during the Battle of Tewkesbury. If we know that this element of his account is untrue surely we must question the credibility of the rest.

Another issue relates to the confession he refers to by Tyrell. There is no record of this confession, of what he confessed to, who he confessed to and how, when on a charge of treason, he was prompted to confess to the murder of the two boys.

The confession would be vitally important to the Tudor dynasty. Henry VII was married to Elizabeth of York and so Henry needed to reverse the declaration that she and her brothers were illegitimate. This meant that the boys were then a real threat to Henry VII. If he had a confession that the boys had been murdered, why has nobody seen it, why has a copy not been held safely to secure the Tudor dynasty. Nobody else makes any reference to this confession and there is no record of it having been publicly displayed. Horace Walpole certainly was not convinced of the existence of any confession, referring to it as a 'pretended confession.'[cxv]

It can also be argued that Sir James was well rewarded by Richard III and this could be for his role in the murder. The flaw in this argument is that Richard III was generous to all those who were loyal to him during and following his usurpation. Tyrell had begun to receive rewards for his loyalty back in 1471 by Edward IV. Tyrell was clearly a trusted ally of Richard, tasked with sensitive and important tasks such as collecting his mother-in-law and escorting Buckingham to the place of his execution. This also calls into the question the claim of More that somebody had to point out to Richard who James Tyrell was and that he might be suitable to complete the task. Richard III was aware of who James Tyrell was and if he wanted someone to complete the task of killing the boys' he would have known that Tyrell was one of his men who could be considered.

We also do not know under what conditions Tyrell confessed. Torture was a commonly used tactic to encourage people to confess to crimes, especially on those believed to have been involved in treason. If there was a confession and it was obtained through torture, we would also have to treat this with a significant amount of caution. People would confess to crimes they had not committed in the belief that the pain they were enduring would stop.

As well as having no credible record of a confession, we certainly cannot guarantee that any confession he made was made of his own free will.
We must also remember that Tyrell also prospered under Henry VII, being reappointed as Commander of Guisnes Castle.

David Starkey has previously claimed that Henry VII and Elizabeth of York were present at the trial of Tyrell, suggesting that this was because he was the man responsible for the deaths of Elizabeth's brothers.[cxvi] However, the couple resided at the Tower of London, where it was believed that the trial was conducted. This was not the case, with the trial of Tyrell taking place at the Guildhall. Even if the couple had attended the trial, it seems disingenuous to claim that this was because of the murder of the boys, when he was on trial for treason, for threatening the reign of Henry and Elizabeth, which could also have prompted them to attend.

Records indicate that Tyrell was sent to London in 1483 and this could have given him the opportunity to commit the crime. Yet there were many reasons why somebody loyal to Richard III would be sent to London as news was received of rebellions being planned. The fact that he was in London certainly does not seem enough to confirm his involvement.

The most significant argument that must be made in favour of Tyrell's innocence has to be the fact that he was never charged with the crime. He was arrested for the support he gave to those plotting against the king. This is what he was charged with and why he was executed. If he confessed to the murders of the princes, these charges were never publicly laid against him. Despite the claim that he confessed to murdering the boys, one of whom could have been considered a king, they only executed him for helping Edmund de la Pole.

Surely if Elizabeth of York received news that the person who killed her brothers had confessed, she would want the news to be public and for him to be punished accordingly. Also, Henry VII had faced significant threats from two pretenders, one of whom was claiming to be the younger of the princes. It was in the best interest of the Tudor's to promote the death of the boys and to be seen to be dealing harshly with those responsible.

One of the people that Tyrell allegedly employed to help him complete the task of murdering the boys was a man called Dighton. Despite the confession implicating Dighton, he was also not punished for his role in the crimes, which is more disturbing, as Tyrell was to be executed any way. Dighton was not punished in any way. He was released, possibly to spread the rumour that the boys were dead.

Another point to consider regarding whether Tyrell is guilty is his motive. According to More, the reason he killed the boys was because he was asked to by the king. Given the supremacy of king's in the fifteenth century, if indeed Richard had ordered Tyrell to kill the boys, he would not have been in any position to refuse the order. This is equally true if you believe that Tyrell killed the boys in 1486, when Henry VII was king and issued Tyrell with two pardons.

In the case of R v Howe [1987] AC 417, the two defendants, Howe and Bannister were driven, with their victim to an isolated area, where they assaulted and killed the victim. They also killed a second victim and tried to murder a third. Their defence to their charges was that they had committed these crimes because they feared for their own lives if they did not do as directed. The court held that duress is not a defence to murder, even if you are acting to protect your own life or the lives of family members.

Therefore, although there is a lack of evidence linking Tyrell to this crime, if he did act on the orders of either King Richard III or King Henry VII, today he would still be considered responsible for the crime, regardless of any threat he feared from failing to carry out the act.

Chapter 27 – Elizabeth of York – Background

The last suspect we will examine has to be considered as one of the most important women of all time. She was the daughter of King Edward IV and the sister of Edward V, during his brief reign. She was the niece of Richard III and married his successor King Henry VII. After helping her husband to create the Tudor dynasty, she gave birth to the boy who would become Henry VIII, making her the grandmother of Edward VI, Queen Mary and Queen Elizabeth I. She is the ancestor of every English monarch since 1509. The current Queen, HRH Queen Elizabeth II is descended from Elizabeth of York.

The matriarch of the British royal family was born in Westminster on 11 February 1466, the daughter of Edward IV and Elizabeth Woodville. Two days later she was christened, with both her grandmothers, Cecily Neville and Jacquetta Woodville acting as godparents, alongside the Earl of Warwick.

As a princess she would have been raised in a stately household ruled by her governess, Margaret, Lady Berners, with a nurse and wet-nurse. She is believed to have been named after her mother and despite her many siblings, was considered the favourite of her father, the king.

Elizabeth appears to have inherited the good looks of both her parents, with her long blonde hair and fair complexion. She is described as being tall, stately with delicate features.[cxvii] The traditional view of Elizabeth's character is that she was the complete opposite of her much-disliked mother.

This trait combined with her piety is thought to have endeared her to the English people, and certainly it appears as though she deferred to and was possibly dominated by her husband, Henry VII, and her formidable mother-in-law Margaret Beaufort, during their reign together.

This view of Elizabeth was not universally accepted, with the Croyland Chronicle claiming she was not as placid as she was reported to be.[cxviii] The evidence of the letter she supposedly wrote to John Howard, the Ballad of Lady Bessie, and claims that she was distraught that she would never be queen, allow room for the view that like her mother, Elizabeth did indeed have an ambitious nature. Unlike her mother, Elizabeth was popular among the people. This may have been down to her personality and the way she dealt with those around her. It could also be because of the charity she showed to those less fortunate than herself. She looked after her servants financially, even when she was forced to live on a tight budget.[cxix]

Elizabeth was born a princess and was raised in preparation for a grand marriage alliance. This meant that she received an education fit for a future queen. She could speak French and some Spanish. She was skilled in embroidery, singing and dancing. Her love of music is demonstrated in the records of her having her own minstrels and two clavichords. As with many young girls of high status she enjoyed watching archery and jousting and took part in hunting trips.

As soon as she was born it was believed that a great marriage awaited the Princess Elizabeth, but by the age of four years old, the offer of marriage to Elizabeth was being used as a tool by her father to placate those whose support he needed to guarantee.

Elizabeth was first betrothed to George Neville on 5 January 1470. In anticipation of the match, George Neville was made the Duke of Bedford. Yet, whether Edward IV ever intended for this marriage to take place is doubtful. Tension between Warwick and Edward IV had seen Warwick begin to plot against the king.

The decision to marry Elizabeth of York to George Neville can be seen as a cynical attempt to keep the Neville family loyal to Edward IV, rather than side with their kin, Warwick. Elizabeth of York was only a young child and Edward IV and Elizabeth Woodville would have known that a lot could change in the intervening years, before Elizabeth was old enough for the marriage to be completed. When the threat from the Neville family was over, a more prestigious marriage could be arranged.

The next match arranged for Elizabeth was to the son of the King of France. Edward IV had raised money and supplies so he could invade his erstwhile enemy, the King of France. Hardly had the invasion force landed when Edward IV lost all interest in the planned invasion. The King of France entered into negotiations and in August 1475 the Treaty of Picquigny was agreed between the two kings. The King of France offered a favourable settlement to Edward IV and his leading nobles and the agreement was celebrated by both sides. The Treaty also provided for the marriage between the king's son, the Dauphin and Elizabeth of York. Elizabeth of York would remain in England until the time was right for the marriage when she would be called over to France. Edward IV and Elizabeth Woodville appeared delighted with the match and insisted that Elizabeth was addressed as Madame le Dauphine, whilst also dressing in the French style.[cxx]

The excitement of the match began to turn to anxiety as time passed and still no preparations were being made for the marriage or for Elizabeth to travel to France, and Edward IV continued to push the French king. Ultimately, the treaty broke down and the pension payments to Edward IV stopped.

Nobles in both France and England believed it was unlikely the marriage would ever take place and things deteriorated even further when news reached Edward IV that Louis XI had been trying to arrange another marriage for his son.

On 23 December 1482, the worst fears of Edward IV were confirmed when the Treaty of Arras was sealed, confirming the forthcoming marriage of the Dauphin to Margaret of Burgundy.

As 1483 approached, Edward IV's plans for a great marriage for his daughter were in ruins, and he may have seriously considered marrying Elizabeth to Henry Tudor, as part of the negotiations with Margaret Beaufort to allow him to return to England as the Earl of Richmond. If this was an option the king was considering, it was a planned marriage he would never live to see as he died before the agreement with Margaret Beaufort could be completed.

Despite being a member of the Royal Family, Elizabeth of York would find herself fleeing to the safety of sanctuary on two occasions. In September 1470, Warwick had formed an alliance with Margaret of Anjou and had successfully invaded England. The swift success of Warwick may have caught Edward IV by surprise as he found himself outmanouvred and forced into exile with his brother Richard.

Elizabeth Woodville took her daughters and sought sanctuary, believing Warwick would harm them all. At this time Elizabeth Woodville was heavily pregnant, and in contrast with the ceremony surrounding the births of her other children, Elizabeth Woodville was forced to give birth to her first son, Edward, in basic conditions, still in sanctuary. The future King Edward V was christened in the Abbot's House in the presence of the young Elizabeth.

Despite the desperation they felt as they waited for news, they still had hope that Edward IV would fight to restore himself as king and rescue them from their new living conditions, which he did. He was reunited with his family, where he met his son and heir and moved his family to the safety of his mother's residence whilst he returned to the field of battle to extinguish the threat of Warwick forever.

The second time the family entered sanctuary they would not have that hope of being rescued as they had in 1470, as Edward IV was dead, and the new king could be on the throne for decades to come. She would have heard the rumours regarding whether her brother would ever become king and witnessed her mother having to hand over her younger brother Richard.

Perhaps it was the realisation of how different the situation was this time that led Elizabeth Woodville to reach an agreement with Richard III. It was agreed that her daughters would leave sanctuary once Richard III gave his word that no harm would come to them and he would seek advantageous marriages for all the girls.

Elizabeth of York may have spent some time at Derby House under the care of Thomas Stanley, but at some point, the girls entered the household of their aunt, Anne Neville. This must have been bitter-sweet as they now had their freedom, but they were now required to defer to Anne Neville who had previously been of a lower rank than themselves.

The sisters appeared to have been welcomed by Anne Neville and certainly Elizabeth was seen wearing similar clothes to the queen and appeared to have been treated well by her aunt.

Elizabeth settled in so well to Richard III's court that rumours began to circulate that Richard wanted to marry her, despite her being his niece. Elizabeth is believed to have written a letter to the Duke of Norfolk asking him to intervene with the king to bring this marriage about. The rumours coincided with a significant decline in the health of Anne Neville and more rumours began to swirl that Richard was helping to bring about Anne's death so he could proceed with his plan to marry Elizabeth.

Those close to Richard III are believed to have warned him that the people, especially in the North, where he had significant support would not accept this marriage and he was forced to publicly deny that he had any intention to do so. Any plans that Richard III and Elizabeth of York had to marry ended on 22 August 1485, when Henry Tudor defeated Richard III and became King Henry VII of England.

To win support for his invasion and challenge to Richard III's rule, Henry Tudor had committed to marrying Elizabeth of York, now considered the legitimate heir to the House of York and one of his first acts was to secure the custody of his future wife.

Having become king, Henry had to wait for a papal dispensation to allow his marriage to Elizabeth to proceed as they were too closely related. The dispensation was finally received in January 1486, allowing the uniting of the Houses of York and Lancaster to take place on 18 January. The match was popular with the people who desired a period of stability after the turbulence of the Wars of the Roses.

On 20 September 1486, Elizabeth and Henry appeared to have secured the future of the Tudor dynasty, when Elizabeth gave birth to an heir whom they named Arthur. The union would produce more children with Henry, Margaret and Mary surviving into adulthood.

Although the people had supported the marriage between the two houses initially, supporters of Elizabeth became concerned as no plans were made for Elizabeth's coronation. Aware of the unease this was causing and confident that he had established the right to rule in his own right, Henry arranged for the coronation to take place on 25 November 1487, nearly two years after they had been married.

As Queen, Elizabeth appears to have played a passive role, making no public attempt to interfere in the political affairs of England, as her husband dealt with rebellions in the names of Lambert SImnel and Perkin Warbeck. Elizabeth also had to deal with her strong mother-in-law, Margaret Beaufort who was a constant presence in the couple's life.

Together the couple faced tragedy when their eldest son, Arthur, shortly after his marriage to Catherine of Aragon, died, plunging them into grief. At this point it appears that they tried to deal with their grief by producing another heir as Elizabeth was soon pregnant again as she approached her thirty seventh birthday. The pregnancy appears to have ended with a premature birth on 2 February 1503. Elizabeth didn't recover from the birth and died on 11 February, her birthday and was laid to rest at Westminster Abbey.

As with most royal marriages at the time, clearly this was a strategic match used to gain support for Henry Tudor and to unite the two warring factions. Despite the tense start to the relationship, they remained married and spent a lot of time together up until the death of Elizabeth. Despite the apparent success of the marriage there is debate about whether it was a happy union.

The letters from Henry VII to Elizabeth appear to show affection and tenderness and Henry was completely grief stricken when his wife died. He withdrew from public and his mother had to move in to look after him. After her death Henry paid for her to have an extravagant funeral, costing more than that of her father and their son, Arthur. The death of Arthur also appears to show a united couple who supported each other. Henry was overcome with grief and Elizabeth had to rush to comfort him. After seeing to Henry's grief, Elizabeth retired to her own chamber where she broke down. This time it was Henry who rushed to comfort his wife

In his biography of Henry VII, Francis Bacon states that the state of the marriage was poor, and that Henry VII was not a good husband to Elizabeth. He believes this is because Henry did not want to marry Elizabeth at all and had wanted to marry Anne of Brittany.[cxxi]

Whatever the personal nature of the relationship, it cannot be denied that the couple successfully created the Tudor dynasty, bringing stability to England at last and bearing an heir who would become King Henry VIII and continue where they left off.

Chapter 28 – The Case For and Against Elizabeth of York

Elizabeth of York was never meant to be a suspect in this book. During all my research it had never been mentioned and nothing had led me to believe that she was a viable suspect. A chance discussion during a visit to the Battlefield Heritage Centre informed me that the latest person to be linked to the potential murders was Elizabeth. This led me to carry out more research on Elizabeth to identify whether there was any evidence that she was capable of such a diabolical act and whether she would have had any opportunity to carry out this act.

The obvious motive for Elizabeth of York to carry out this act is her own desire to be queen. From her birth, Elizabeth was being raised to be a future queen. After the Treaty of Picquigny she believed she was going to marry the Dauphin of France and would ultimately become the Queen of France. Elizabeth saw her dreams of being queen of her own court ruined when the King of France arranged a different marriage for his son. The chances of her being queen were further destroyed when she was forced to flee into sanctuary, whilst her uncle Richard lobbied for support to replace Edward V as King of England. Elizabeth must have believed that she had no future.
The reports of the letter Elizabeth allegedly wrote to the Duke of Norfolk also suggests that she was ambitious and was impatient to become queen. If the letter is genuine, it alludes to Elizabeth being angry that Anne Neville was taking so long to die. If she was callous enough to wish death upon her aunt, could she have acted against her own brothers?

She was also handed the perfect opportunity when the rumours that the boys were dead began to circulate and that Richard was to blame. This gave her the chance to take control of her destiny and seize the opportunity to make herself queen. Sarah Gristwood describes Elizabeth as desperate to find her place in the world.[cxxii] The rumours of her brother's death gave her this opportunity.

The problem with this argument is that once Elizabeth became Queen, she did not appear to play an active role in the political affairs of the country. To the contrary, following her marriage to King Henry VII, Elizabeth appears to have been a passive wife and daughter in law. Other reports of Elizabeth's character suggest she was nothing like her mother, who tried to influence the decisions of Edward IV during their marriage. Elizabeth's reign as queen may not be an accurate representation of her character. Henry had invaded England, killed the king, her uncle and his first act was to secure the custody of the woman whose status as heir to the Yorkist line would give him the support he needed to rule England. He did this with the full support and advice of his determined mother Margaret Beaufort. Given the strong personalities at play and Henry's control, it may not have been Elizabeth's decision to leave the running of the country to her husband.

At the same time as Henry VII was dealing with the threat posed from Lambert Simnel, he also chose to deprive his mother-in-law, Elizabeth Woodville of her lands and wealth. The timing of this punishment has led to speculation that maybe she had been involved in the plot. Against this it was argued that Elizabeth Woodville being involved in the plot would not make sense as Elizabeth Woodville would be removing her own daughter from power. Involvement in a plot against Henry and Elizabeth would be more credible if it was in fact Elizabeth of York, determined to secure the crown for herself, that made the rumours of the boys' deaths a reality. Elizabeth Woodville had other daughters who could marry Henry's replacement.

The inclusion of Elizabeth of York as a potential suspect also raises questions about her failure to publicly confront Perkin Warbeck. She could have easily met with Perkin Warbeck and confirmed that he was not her younger brother, ending support for more rebellions in his name. Yet, she remained silent. Maybe Elizabeth of York didn't feel the need to confront him because she knew the truth, he could not possibly be her brother, Richard, as she was one of the few people who knew he was dead. If she was involved in their death, the last thing she would have wanted would be to have to confront the truth directly.

When looking at Sir James Tyrell, questions were raised about the confession he made and why it was never made public and why he was never put on trial for the crime. The story of this confession may have been a propaganda tool, to use the death of Tyrell to confirm the death of the boys and put the threat of pretenders to bed once and for all. A confession would be an important document used to secure the legitimacy of the Tudor dynasty and there would have to be an exceptional reason why it was not made public, not kept safe for posterity. Unless of course it implicated either Henry VII or Elizabeth of York.

Confirmation that this act had been committed by either monarch could turn the country against them. Whilst the secrecy used could have been to protect Henry VII, we also know that Henry VII genuinely seemed worried about the threat from Perkin Warbeck, maybe believing he could have been the younger prince. Yet, little is known of how Elizabeth of York responded to the threat, apart from her never meeting the 'Pretender' to confirm for herself whether this could be her missing brother. If she did not know he was dead, surely she would have wanted to make sure that the young man being sent to the Tower was not the brother she had witnessed her mother having to hand over to Richard III's men whilst she was in sanctuary.

One of the few things that we know about this period was that there was an agreement that Henry Tudor would marry Elizabeth of York. The plotting is generally believed to have been conducted by Margaret Beaufort and Elizabeth Woodville, through Beaufort's physician, Lewis Caerleon. Caerleon had access to both Elizabeth of York and Elizabeth Woodville whilst they were in sanctuary. Ten years after Elizabeth of York became queen, the intermediary in the plot, Caerleon was in the service of Elizabeth of York, not Margaret Beaufort. Obviously, we cannot rule out that a domineering Beaufort forced Elizabeth to take Caerleon on, but it does show a strong connection between the two.

'The Ballad of Lady Bessie' believed to be about Elizabeth of York seems to indicate she was the instigator of the plot to replace Richard III. This, as the alleged letter to the Duke of Norfolk, paint Elizabeth as a ruthlessly ambitious woman, desperate to be queen.

Thomas Stanley, stepfather of Henry Tudor also claimed that Edward IV had asked him to act as guardian of Elizabeth of York on his deathbed. There is nothing to corroborate this claim by Stanley. When she emerged from sanctuary, it has been recorded that she went to stay at Derby House, where she would have been able to establish contact with Margaret Beaufort and Thomas Stanley.

One difficulty with claiming that Elizabeth of York could have been responsible for the death of her brothers is whether she would have had the means and opportunity. Once Elizabeth Woodville knew that Richard III had custody of her eldest son and had arrested her brother, Anthony Rivers, she moved with her daughters to sanctuary. Elizabeth of York would remain there with her sisters until their mother reached an agreement with Richard III and they were allowed to leave. The obvious issue here is that the rumours the boys were dead began in July 1483 and there were no records of the boys being seen after this time. Elizabeth of York was in sanctuary until March 1484. Surely, this rules her out of involvement.

The version of Elizabeth we see in the Ballad of Lady Bessie and the apparent letter to the Duke of Norfolk, is a determined woman who desperately pleads with powerful people to help her bring about her wishes. In one she is imploring Lord Stanley to assist her to become queen, in the other John Howard. If this interpretation of Elizabeth is to be believed, then it is not incredible that a third person was asked to help her to become queen.

Also, although the rumours of the boys' deaths started in July 1483 we do not know when they disappeared. It was claimed that the boys were moved further within the Tower when the king began to receive news of rebellions breaking out in their name. They could have been moved for their safety, and obviously for that of the king, Richard III. Some historians have gone so far as to claim that the boys were still alive in 1486. This makes it possible that Elizabeth had time to arrange the murder once she emerged from sanctuary, possibly during her stay at Derby House.

The final question we have to ask with regard to Elizabeth of York is whether a young woman like Elizabeth could have been involved in anything that would lead to deliberate harm coming to her younger brothers. Bernard Andre describes Elizabeth as having an unbounded love for her brothers and sisters.[cxxiii] This doesn't sound like a woman who would plot to kill them.

We must consider though that familial relationships in the fifteenth century were very different to what we have now. Elizabeth and her siblings would have grown up knowing that grand marriages would be planned for them, planned marriages which could see them moving away from each other, living in different countries, possibly never seeing each other again, or infrequently at best.

Children received very different educations based on their gender. Whilst men were taught the art of warfare and diplomacy, women were left to tackle embroidery and music. This would mean that the children would not spend that much time together. Elizabeth would have had a distant relationship with the elder of her brothers. As he was now the heir, having taken Elizabeth's title on his birth, he was sent as a young child to Ludlow, as Prince of Wales, where he had his own household and would not have spent much time with his siblings following this move. The relationship between siblings was different then, in a time when infant mortality was incredibly high and children became accustomed to losing their siblings through illness.

Whilst we may find it difficult to believe that a sister could have brought about the destruction of her own brothers back then, unfortunately it still happens today.

In April 2016, a 14-year-old boy, Lucas Markham knocked on the bedroom window of his girlfriend of the same age, Kim Edwards. This was the signal for her to let him in to the house quietly so that nobody else knew he was there. In the house, in Spalding, Lincolnshire, they carried out the plan they had devised together, Markham took a kitchen knife and stabbed the mother of Edwards' to death. At this point Edwards claims she had reservations about continuing but, Markham took his knife and killed her 13-year-old sister. After the murders the teenage couple stayed in the house with the bodies of their victims where they shared a bath, had sex and watched a vampire film. The prosecution claimed that although Markham was the one who had committed the murders, it was Edwards who had helped to plan it. They claimed that Kim Edwards did not like her mother and resented her sister's close relationship with her. Edwards and Markham were both found guilty and became infamous as possibly Britain's youngest double murderers.[cxxiv]

Whilst we may not like to think that sisters could turn on brothers, in a world where reason gives way to obsessive ambition, the game of thrones tears families apart and creates the most unusual suspects.

Chapter 29 – There Was No Murder

Previously historians have told us that there is no doubt that the princes were murdered and almost certainly by their uncle Richard III. The only thing I believe we can say about this mystery for certain is that we do not know what happened and are unlikely ever to know.

There is no evidence to confirm what happened to the boys in the Tower so to fully complete an investigation into this matter, evidence of whether they survived and escaped from the Tower must be considered.

The point about the murders not being established is demonstrated by Francis Bacon who stated that there were rumours that at least one of the boys was alive.[cxxv] Horace Walpole was one of the first to make the point when he confirmed that these rumours showed that the murders of the boys were not universally accepted.[cxxvi]

If the rumours that Richard III killed the boys are accepted as some of the most powerful circumstantial evidence against him then rumours that one of the boys was still alive also have to be used to argue that there is a possibility that the boys were not murdered.

The fate of William Stanley also serves to demonstrate that powerful members of Henry VII's allies were not certain that the boys had been murdered. When Henry VII was facing the threat of Perkin Warbeck, Stanley had confirmed that if it turned out to be the real Richard, Duke of York he would not be able to oppose him in battle. The Stanley family had always been close to the ruling monarch and would have been aware of the rumours that they had been killed at the hands of their uncle. Yet, he clearly had not been convinced that the rumours were true, as he was willing to refrain from fighting for the king, who was his brother's stepson.

Historians Matthew Lewis[cxxvii] and V B Lamb[cxxviii] claim that it is significant that there is no record of any funeral masses ever having been said for the souls of the dead boys. In the fifteenth century, people believed that after death most people would not make it straight to heaven. To make is straight to heaven you would have to be completely perfect and free from sin. Most people could not meet this and so before being received into Heaven they would be stuck in purgatory, 'a place or state of suffering inhabited by the souls of sinners who are expiating their sins before going to heaven.' The relatives of those that had died believed that by having masses said for their souls they would speed their journey through purgatory. The more masses that were said, the faster the journey. The powerful, noble families would pay priests to constantly say masses for their own souls and the souls of their loved ones.

Edward V and his younger brother Richard had many wealthy and influential relatives who surely would have wanted to ease their journey through purgatory and lessen their suffering. This is especially significant given it was believed that they had been murdered and already suffered significantly before reaching purgatory.

Ordering masses to be said for somebody that you knew to be alive was considered a deadly insult so it was unlikely, if the boys were alive that anybody would go to the extreme of ordering masses for the boys.

Lewis and Lamb believe that this lack of funeral masses could imply that the boys were not murdered. John Ashdown-Hill, a late historian, heavily involved in the Richard III Society, believed however that there is actually a record of a funeral mass being said for a king called Edward in Rome on 23 September 1483. He believes that this could relate to Edward V, arguing that if the boys died on 22 July, this mass coincides with the two-month anniversary of their death.[cxxix] Whilst it is accepted as possible that this does indeed relate to Edward V, it was still only five months since the death of his father, another King Edward.

Another point relied on by Lewis and Lamb to allow for the possibility that the boys survived is the fact that the alleged pretender Perkin Warbeck was rumoured to bear a striking resemblance to his claimed father, Edward IV. If Warbeck looked like Edward IV, this makes it possible that they were related. There are two issues with relying on this as evidence that the boys were not murdered. The first is that it is wholly possible that Perkin Warbeck was related to Edward IV. Edward IV was an infamous womaniser. Perkin Warbeck could have been an illegitimate, unknown relation of the late king, which would move us no closer to solving the mystery of what happened to the two recognised sons of Edward IV.

The other issue is interpretation. There were also people who reported to Henry VII that Warbeck looked nothing like Edward IV. Sometimes people see what they want to see. People wanted to believe that the boys survived, wanted to believe that Perkin Warbeck was the younger prince, returning to England to make his claim as heir to the English throne. This may have led people to believe they saw a resemblance to Edward IV. People can look at things and see them differently.

A famous example of this is the 'white and gold' dress. An image posted on social media caused a national debate over the colour. Whilst some people looked at the picture of the dress and thought it was white and gold, others looked at it and thought it was blue and black. People may genuinely have thought he was the image of Edward IV and others may have genuinely believed he was not.

There are two people close to the princes whose actions could give us an insight into whether Lambert Simnel could have been one of the Princes in the Tower. The first we shall consider is their mother, Elizabeth Woodville.

Elizabeth Woodville had feared the intentions of Richard III and had been powerless to stop him declaring her sons illegitimate and replacing her eldest son as King of England.

She is believed to have plotted with Margaret Beaufort to support plans for Henry Tudor to invade England. She would have known that rumours were circulating that her boys were dead and that the finger was being pointed firmly in Richard III's direction. So, why in 1484 she reached an agreement with Richard III which saw her daughters released from sanctuary and welcomed into the household of his wife has been subject to fierce debate.

Another controversial aspect of Elizabeth's life was the decision of her son-in-law, Henry VII to strip her of all her possessions and for her to retire to a convent in Bermondsey. It has been claimed that either she did this of her own free will or that Henry VII was punishing her for her decision to place her daughters into the care of Richard III. Together, the two events could be linked to show that Elizabeth Woodville did not believe her sons were dead. She may have allowed her daughters to be released from their life in sanctuary because she knew her sons were safe, and Richard had caused them no harm.

The punishment by Henry VII coincided with Lambert Simnel challenging Henry VII's right to be king. Simnel was claiming to be the Earl of Warwick, but he had been captured by Henry VII straight after Bosworth and was being held in the Tower. Horace Walpole was sure that Elizabeth Woodville genuinely believed her youngest son was alive.[cxxx] If she was involved in the Lambert Simnel plot, it would only make sense if she had reason to believe that Lambert Simnel could be the younger son she was forced to hand over to Thomas Bourchier, whilst she remained in her sanctuary.

The problem with this theory is that it is hard to understand why she would have engaged in the plot to crown Henry Tudor if she knew that her son was alive and could claim the throne again in his own right. Obviously, Elizabeth was in sanctuary, closely monitored by Richard III's men. She had limited access to visitors and news and may have initially believed that her sons were gone. It may have been when she received proof that at least one of her sons was living that she agreed to release her daughters and encourage her eldest son to turn against Henry Tudor and return to England. Of course, we also know that it is possible that the person plotting to make Henry Tudor king may have been his intended bride, Elizabeth of York and not Elizabeth Woodville as previously believed.

The second person whose actions could imply that Lambert Simnel was of greater importance than has been generally accepted is John de la Pole, the first Earl of Lincoln. Lincoln was another nephew of Richard III that had a strong claim to the throne yet managed to outlive him. He was the son of Richard's sister, Elizabeth. After the Battle of Bosworth, he initially reconciled with the Tudor regime. Yet, two years later he would be one of the leaders of the Simnel rebellion. He would die at the Battle of Stoke Field in 1487, fighting for the right of Lambert Simnel to become king.

The curious thing about this is why Lincoln would risk everything for an imposter. As a nephew of Richard III, he also had a strong claim to the throne in his own right. Edward, Earl of Warwick's claim was weakened by the fact that his father had been attainted for treason, technically making him ineligible to claim the throne. Lincoln had no charges of bastardy and treason attached to his claim, making it the strongest claim to be the Yorkist heir, after only two other people: the two princes.

If Simnel was just a pretender, it makes no sense for Lincoln to lose everything fighting his cause. Whilst people were in doubt as to whether Simnel was a pretender they may have been unlikely to turn against the king and join them. Yet, there was no doubt with Lincoln. If Lincoln had chosen to fight for his own right to challenge Henry VII, he may well have gained more support than Simnel did. Lincoln's actions only really make sense if Simnel had a superior royal lineage to himself.

Matthew Lewis in his blog tells us about a theory by Jack Leslau. Jack Leslau, an art enthusiast believes that the boys survived after being smuggled out of the Tower and argues that the truth lies in a portrait of Thomas More and his family, by Hans Holbein. In 1527 Holbein was commissioned by More to paint the portrait. He produced an initial sketch before using that to help him complete the final painting. Leslau argues that the many differences between the sketch and the painting are a form of code left by Holbein to signify that the younger of the princes was present in the picture. One of the figures in the painting was Dr John Clements, who had married More's adopted daughter. This is the figure that Leslau believes is in fact Richard, Duke of York.

In the picture Leslau argues that Clements is standing slightly higher than the other people captured in the image and is standing under fleur-de-lys, the symbol of French royalty. Leslau claims there are limited records of Dr John Clements' childhood and cites over eighty changes between the sketch and the painting which point to the existence of Richard, Duke of York. Whilst we may never know whether Leslau is right about this code he certainly was able to argue his case well. In 1995 he was granted permission to investigate a hidden tomb in Mecklen Cathedral, having argued that Richard, Duke of York lived under a false identity and was buried in Belgium. He also believes that Edward V survived and is buried in Chelsea. This is a theory he clearly feels passionate about having dedicated years of his life and thousands of pounds to it.[cxxxi]

One issue with it is that More was the one person who was certain enough about the death of the boys, giving a full account of the details of their demise and citing the infamous confession by James Tyrell. It could be argued that he would not have written this if he knew the boy was alive, yet this may have been an attempt to protect the identity of the boy. His account may have been designed to convince people the boys were dead so they would stop looking for them and they could live safely. Certainly, there were other errors with More's work that lead us to question whether the details he provided of the murder were genuine.

The last issue to consider that could lead us to believe that there was in fact no murder committed by any of the suspects relates to details recorded at the time. Clements Markham claims that in the orders for King Richard's household there is mention of children who were so important they were to be served before every other noble. He believes that this could only relate to the two princes.[cxxxii] Yet it could be suggested that having been declared illegitimate they may not have continued to warrant that level of deference.

The Harleian Manuscript 433 refers to 'Edward Bastard' which has been interpreted both as referring to Edward V, after he was declared illegitimate or an illegitimate son of Richard III. If it relates to Edward V, this is important as there is an entry referring to 'Lord Bastard in March 1485. This equally could relate to the younger boy, Richard, leading us to believe there is a possibility that the boys were still alive nearly two years after Richard III is believed to have had them murdered.

Clearly there is information and events that can be interpreted as demonstrating that the boys outlived their uncle, but we need to consider whether these arguments are convincing.

Chapter 30 – There Was No Murder – Rebuttal

There are always going to be people who refuse to accept even the possibility that the boys survived, citing the lack of definitive proof. Yet, despite any sort of evidence to confirm they were murdered, they will happily conclude how they died, when they died and by whose command.

Having examined the evidence against each of the suspects all we have is speculation. Whether it be stories of rumours circulating round the country or an analysis of what people gained from their death, there is nothing compelling to inform us one way or the other. So, if mere speculation is enough for people to condemn Richard III for over 500 years, surely it is enough to make us accept that it is at least possible that they survived.

For some, the fact that the bones of two young people were found buried in the Tower is all the confirmation they need to confirm that the boys were murdered and that their remains lie within Westminster Abbey. For others though, the issue of the bones raises questions. The bones were found in the seventeenth century and examined in 1933, when forensic examination of a body to identify it as we know it today, would not have even been dreamed of. Since then they have been subject to the most cursory of examinations and to a certain degree the findings appear to have been aimed at confirming they were the princes, rather than identifying who the bones belong to which is important. If you are trying to prove one theory, without considering others, you ignore all the information that contradicts the conclusion you want.

The questions over the bones led to a re-examination in the 1950's, again when many techniques commonly used today had still not been discovered. This re-evaluation was based not on the bones but on the paperwork from the initial investigation. The report does not confirm the age or gender of the remains. Despite developments in scientific techniques further examination of the bones has not been possible. Permission to exhume the bones has been refused as it has been deemed that this does not warrant disturbing the resting place of the two children. It is possible this is true, it is also possible that the discovery that the bones interred in Westminster Abbey as two princes, are in fact not the royal boys would prove embarrassing.

The fact that the bones were found in the Tower seems to support the account of Thomas More that the boys were murdered and buried in the Tower, leading to the conclusion that the bones do belong to the boys and they were indeed murdered. This approach requires us to ignore the part of More's account where he claims that Richard III was horrified that they had been buried in the Tower, so they were dug up and disposed of in water. For the bones to belong to Edward and Richard, this part of More's account must be inaccurate. If that part is inaccurate, how much more of his account is unreliable or misleading. Maybe the rumours reported by Vergil that the boys had been smuggled away are as credible as the account from More.

The threat from Perkin Warbeck and Lambert Simnel as Yorkist heirs to the throne are often dismissed. They are classed as pretenders and their value as evidence that the boys survived and continued to pose a threat to Henry VII is destroyed. It has been claimed that the Yorkists were so desperate to replace Henry VII that they would have happily replaced him with anyone and so where happy to back the two pretenders.

This argument requires us to ignore the existence of John de la Pole. The Earl of Lincoln, as another descendent from Richard Plantagenet and Cecil Neville had a stronger claim to the throne than anybody else. The supporters of the House of York did not need to rely on a false prince to win back the country, they already had somebody that they could back if indeed the boys were dead.

One of the main instigators behind the Simnel and Warbeck challenges was Margaret of Burgundy. She is believed to have been responsible for coaching them, for giving them the information they would need to convince others that they were who they were claiming to be. She was a sister of Richard III and an aunt to the boys, there could be not be better person to pass on the knowledge that nobody outside royal circles would have.

The only problem with this explanation is that Margaret had left England for Burgundy nearly two decades earlier. This meant that she had left the country before either of the boys was born. Since she had left England, Warwick had rebelled against her brother Edward IV, her other brother George, Duke of Clarence had been executed for treason and the Woodvilles had increased their grasp on power, especially in the household of the Prince of Wales. Whilst she may have confidently been able to coach the boys on general aspects of royal life, there had been so many changes since she left that whether she would have been able to teach them well enough to convince those that mattered is debatable. Of course, Burgundy became a haven for those that had opposed Henry VII and those of Richard III's supporters who survived the bloody slaughter at Bosworth fled here to figure out their next move. This included the person closest to Richard III, Francis Lovell, who would certainly have had more relevant knowledge of royal affairs to assist with preparing the boys.

In his account of what happened Vergil states that he believed that Margaret genuinely believed the boys to be who they claimed to be.[cxxxiii] This is certainly possible as she would have not really have known the boys. This would mean that they would have to have been coached by somebody else, to a standard that convinced Margaret of Burgundy that she was championing the cause of her nephews.

Margaret had supported her brothers when they were forced to flee at the hands of Warwick and had helped them to prepare for their return to England to take back control. Surely, with her knowledge of the Wars of the Roses she would have been aware that they stood the best chance against Henry VII with John de la Pole at the helm.

William Stanley was executed for claiming he would not take arms against Warbeck if he believed he was indeed Richard, Duke of York. Stanley was found out because of Henry VII's spy network. Sir Robert Clifford appeared to confirm that the boy was indeed Richard, Duke of York and he appeared to be a part of the group like Stanley refusing to fight for the king. Later it was claimed that Clifford was working for the king all along and only confirmed it was the boy to see who would not be loyal to Henry VII. He was pardoned for his part in the conspiracy and received a reward. The claim that the boy was one of the princes was made up to trap, confirming Warbeck was a pretender.

It seems equally possible that Clifford was convinced that Warbeck was Richard and when he believed he had been found out or was under suspicion, swapped sides to save himself, giving the king information about those who would support the challenger, in return for his own life.

Warbeck appeared to be successful in convincing other kings that he was who he was claiming to be. He was welcomed as a king in France and Scotland. France had previously supported Henry Tudor in his invasion of England but was now threatening his reign by accepting Warbeck as the son of Edward IV.

This could be used as evidence to suggest that at least the youngest boy survived as royalty around the world genuinely seemed to accept him for who he claimed to be. This has been dismissed as other king's trying to cause trouble and destabilise England. Certainly, Scotland and France were not England's allies and would not have been disappointed if another civil war broke out weakening their neighbour further. Therefore, this argument has a significant amount of merit. The problem lies with the decision of the King of Scotland to marry Warbeck to a member of his own family. Scotland was no friend of England but whether a king would go so far as to marry his kin to a lowly pretender to aid their cause is questionable.

The argument also does not explain why Henry's own emissary's, believed that he was the son of Edward IV. They clearly had no interest in causing distress to their king so are more likely to have genuinely believed him.

More significant is the fact that foreign officials referred to the boy as Henry's nephew, the Duke of York in official records. In June 1496, the Venetian Ambassadors in England wrote that Henry VII was 'in dread of being expelled from the kingdom by his nephew, the Duke of York'.[cxxxiv] These were papers that were not meant for Henry VII to read so there was no need to maintain any pretence if they were just trying to rattle him. If they genuinely believed him to be a fake, surely, they would have referred to him as such in official documentation. This writing suggests no doubt for them as to who was challenging Henry VII. Whilst it is possible that they were worried their papers may be intercepted, this is unlikely, and they would have had established routes for sending their papers back home.

Whilst many continue to pour scorn on any attempt to debate the possibility of the Princes in the Tower surviving their time in Richard III's care, it is clear that the evidence is not conclusive on either side and to understand the issue and keep the mystery alive, debate is the only way.

Conclusion – The Verdict of the Jury is….

The only conclusion I can reach on this murder investigation is that it is clearly not as simplistic as we may have been led to believe.

When I first started writing this book, I was told that I was expecting too much of the reader, asking them to be patient and to form their own ideas based on speculation. I disagreed then and I disagree now. For me it was not good enough for somebody to tell me that the boys died, and Richard III was responsible and that was that. Tell me why and tell me how. For years I read books that told me it had to have been Richard III that killed the boys as he was the one who had the most to gain and he was the one that had access to them. As I began to research this topic it became clear that so many people benefitted from the disappearance of the boys that have come to be known as the Princes in the Tower. The more I researched, the more suspects I was able to add to the list. Everybody in this book gained from the boys going missing. They may have benefitted in different ways and to different extents, but they were all better off once the boys were out of the way.

Many of those I looked at had reasons to exact revenge on Edward IV or their own grievances with what they considered to be the grasping, vulgar Woodville family.

After looking at all the evidence I am content to say that I do not know who if anybody murdered the Princes in the Tower. I don't need to. This was the topic that sparked my love of history and writing this book has only strengthened my love for the subject precisely because you don't need to know conclusively what happened.

What we need is the knowledge to debate, to wonder, to persuade. My history teacher at Secondary School told me that there were no wrong answers if you can defend your argument effectively. I have enjoyed considering why each of these people may have acted against the boys, how they could have achieved it and whether they would.

We may never know what happened to the Princes in the Tower, but I believe we can open the debate. We do not need to be told what happened in the past. We do not need to rely on others to evaluate the evidence for us and tell us what we need to know. History is an amazing subject that everybody has the right to enjoy and we all need to give ourselves the credit to take the facts and come to our own conclusions.

Epilogue – Walking in the Footsteps of Richard III

The beginning of my love affair with history started with that series, Discovery. The cassette tape that took me back in time, allowed me to develop an understanding of the character's involved. As part of the process of writing this book I wanted to try and recapture that emotion.

During my research I became aware that the Bosworth Battlefield Heritage Centre were conducting tours around the battlefield. This was an opportunity I had been waiting for. I was going to walk in Richard III's footsteps Given the amount of time that has passed since the events I have written about and also the lack of evidence from that period, this was a way to try and understand the period and figures I was writing about. I wanted it to take me back in time, like the Discovery tape had years before.

This time I had my own daughter who came to the Battlefield Heritage Centre with me, starting on her own journey of discovery with history.

I want my daughter to follow me in my love of history and this is an opportunity for a new generation to move away from the traditional views of historical figures and the certain views of historians. The new generation needs to continue to question. They need the facts, and the skills to analyse and evaluate evidence themselves, allowing them to come to their own views, allowing them to debate events and motivations.

This is what was going through my head as I arrived at the Bosworth Battlefield Heritage Centre, with my beautiful daughter, ready to follow the footsteps of the mysterious Richard III.

We set off on the walk at 9.30 in the morning. Our first stop was the Heritage Centre Monument at the top of Ambion Hill. This was the hill where it was believed Richard III stationed his troops. He had demonstrated he was an excellent soldier and surely would have taken the high ground so he could observe everything. This was why the Heritage Centre was built there. Stood on the hill it was easy to see why people had begun to doubt that this was the actual sight of the battlefield.
Serious investigation has concluded that the site of the Battlefield Heritage Centre is not the site of the battle. I would be shown this new site on my walk and the importance of the monument on Ambion Hill would then become clear.

Walking through the fields and climbing badly over various stiles, it was hard to imagine how it must have felt to be Richard III, Henry Tudor or any of the soldiers, trampling the same ground, heading towards bloodshed and an uncertain future.

It is hard to understand it because here in England most of us have not had to experience anything quite like the horrific battles from the wars of the medieval era.

On the walk everything is so ordinary it is like nothing had ever happened. Part of this is because of where the actual site of the battlefield is. The battlefield itself is owned by a farmer who does not want the land disturbed. There is no monument to show where the battle took place, where thousands were injured and killed.

The land itself is part of a working farm but the owner of the land has donated any historical items found on his land to be displayed in the Battlefield Heritage Centre.
This was when I realised how important the monument at Ambion Hill really is. At the actual site there is no memorial to commemorate the events of Bosworth, whereas Ambion Hill is a place that makes you stop and reflect.

Two important stops along the journey for me personally were two churches. The first church was as Sutton Cheney. The legend has grown that Richard III stopped here to pray before the battle. As with so many aspects of this mystery, there is no evidence to either confirm or deny.

Inside, the church is decorated with banners donated from the Richard III Society and they regularly hold services to remember Richard III there. It is highly possible that Richard III never attended this church. Yet to me this doesn't matter. As discussed previously, there is nothing at the battlefield to remember the people who died. This gives Sutton Cheney church a prominence that is sorely needed. It was the decisive battle between Lancaster and York, Henry, and Richard. It was the last battle that saw a reigning king killed in battle.

However, these were not the only people affected. Hundreds of people lost their lives that day. Women lost sons and husbands, whilst children would never see their fathers again. Although we cannot comprehend the scale of that now, I did feel some comfort from the fact that Sutton Cheney church allows people to remember those that gave their lives.

The second church that had an impact on myself was St James's Church in Dadlington. In the graveyard is a plaque announcing that some of the dead from the battle are buried there. This is the only known burial place of Bosworth's fallen. There must have been many more fatalities, but no other bodies have been discovered. There are several fields near where the battle took place. Regrettably, many of these fields have not been subject to archaeological investigation, which partly explains why no further bodies have been located. We may never know the secrets buried beneath the farms in these villages.

When I started this project, I felt frustrated about the way this period in history was treated. I was disappointed that old myths and unproven legends were being passed off as historical facts. Following the discovery of the remains of Richard III, there was a real opportunity to have a full, open debate about Richard III and about what we believe may have happened to the princes. Alternatively, the evil Shakespearean villain could again be rolled out to dramatic effect, making easy money from the new audience this story was now exposed to.

During the walk and later at the Bosworth Battlefield Heritage Centre I felt optimistic that people were finally seeing past the traditional image of Richard III. The church at Sutton Cheney was filled with symbols of Richard III and at the Heritage Centre my daughter was given tokens to vote for Henry VII or Richard III. My daughter was asked who she was going to vote for and answered 'Richard III'. The woman behind the till just laughed and confirmed that most people do.

Maybe this was a sign that the debate over Richard III was changing. You do not have to argue that he was perfect, but there must be an acceptance that he certainly isn't the absolutely evil tyrant he has been portrayed as for centuries.

With this optimism later that night I tuned into the documentary 'Who Killed the Princes in the Tower' presented by Dan Jones. Within two minutes, Dan Jones had confirmed that the princes were murdered in July 1483. Initially he stated it was most probably by Richard III, later he stated it was Richard III and towards the end referred to him as becoming a child killer.

This is clearly to state more than can possibly be known from the evidence we have. We know that the princes disappeared, we cannot confirm that they were killed, and we certainly cannot confirm who their possible killer was.

What I have tried to show in this book, is that there were a number of people who benefitted from the disappearance and instead of relying on lazy history, and being told what we should believe happened we are capable of looking at the facts and opening up the debate.

Notes

[i] John Ashdown-Hill, The Mythology of Richard III
[ii] Shakespeare, Richard III
[iii] Shakespeare, Richard III
[iv] Thomas More, The History of King Richard III
[v] Shakespeare, Richard III
[vi] John Rous, Historia Regum Angliae
[vii] Christ Church Letters, ed J.B Sheppard (Camden Society, 1877)
[viii] Francis Bacon, The History of the Reign of King Henry VII
[ix] Dominic Mancini, The Usurpation of Richard III
[x] Dominic Mancini, The Usurpation of Richard III
[xi] Thomas More, The History of King Richard III
[xii] Dominic Mancini, The Usurpation of Richard III
[xiii] Michael Jones -Psychology of a Battle
[xiv] Thomas More, The History of King Richard III
[xv] Dominic Mancini, The Usurpation of Richard III
[xvi] Polydore Vergil, English History
[xvii] Polydore Vergil, English History
[xviii] Thomas More, The History of King Richard III
[xix] John Rous, Historia Regum Angliae
[xx] Thomas More, The History of King Richard III
[xxi] Clements Markham, Richard III: His Life and Character Reviewed in the Light of Recent Research
[xxii] The Women of the Cousins' War: The Real White Queen and her Rivals – Philippa Gregory, David Baldwin and Michael Jones
[xxiii] Elizabeth Norton: Margaret Beaufort: Mother of the Tudor Dynasty
[xxiv] The Women of the Cousins' War: The Real White Queen and her Rivals – Philippa Gregory, David Baldwin and Michael Jones
[xxv] Letters of the Queens of England {1100-1547] – Anne Crawford
[xxvi] Elizabeth Norton: Margaret Beaufort: Mother of the Tudor Dynasty
[xxvii] Bernard Andre – The Life of Henry VII
[xxviii] Richard III as Duke of Gloucester and King of England - Caroline Halstead
[xxix] Letters of the Queens of England {1100-1547] – Anne Crawford
[xxx] J Fisher: The Funeral Service of Margaret Countess of Richmond and Derby
[xxxi] Elizabeth Norton: Margaret Beaufort: Mother of the Tudor Dynasty
[xxxii] The King's Mother: Memoir of Margaret Beaufort, Countess of Richmond and Derby – Margaret Domville
[xxxiii] The History of the Life and Reigne of Richard III - George Buck
[xxxiv] Richard III as Duke of Gloucester and King of England - Caroline Halstead
[xxxv] Memoir of Margaret, Countess of Richmond and Derby - Charles

Cooper
[xxxvi] Blood Sisters: The Women Behind the Wars of the Roses - Sarah Gristwood
[xxxvii] The Women of the Cousins' War: The Real White Queen and her Rivals – Philippa Gregory, David Baldwin and Michael Jones
[xxxviii] The Betrayal of Richard III: An Introduction to the Controversy – V B Lamb
[xxxix] J Fisher: The Funeral Service of Margaret Countess of Richmond and Derby
[xl] The History of the Life and Reigne of Richard III - George Buck
[xli] J Fisher: The Funeral Service of Margaret Countess of Richmond and Derby
[xlii] Francis Bacon, The History of the Reign of King Henry VII
[xliii] Memoir of Margaret, Countess of Richmond and Derby - Charles Cooper
[xliv] The History of the Life and Reigne of Richard III - George Buck
[xlv] Jones and Underwood – The King's Mother
[xlvi] Francis Bacon, The History of the Reign of King Henry VII
[xlvii] news.bbc.co.uk/2/hi/asia-pacific/667910.stm
[xlviii] Anne Neville: Richard III's Tragic Queen – Amy Licence
[xlix] Dominic Mancini, The Usurpation of Richard III
[l] Polydore Vergil, English History
[li] Cecily Neville: Mother of Kings - Amy Licence
[lii] Blood Sisters: The Women Behind the Wars of the Roses - Sarah Gristwood
[liii] Thomas More, The History of King Richard III
[liv] Dominic Mancini, The Usurpation of Richard III
[lv] The Stonor Letters
[lvi] Dominic Mancini, The Usurpation of Richard III
[lvii] Cecily Neville: Mother of Kings - Amy Licence
[lviii] Blood Sisters: The Women Behind the Wars of the Roses - Sarah Gristwood
[lix] Bosworth 1484: Psychology of a Battle - Michael Jones
[lx] https://www.independent.co.uk/news/world/americas/drill-sergeant-hell-grandmother-who-made-her-granddaughter-run-hours-until-she-died-sentenced-life-prison-10244405.html
[lxi] Bernard Andre – The Life of Henry VII
[lxii] The Memoirs of Philip de Commines - Philippe deCommynes
[lxiii] Polydore Vergil, English History
[lxiv] Francis Bacon, The History of the Reign of King Henry VII
[lxv] Francis Bacon, The History of the Reign of King Henry VII
[lxvi] Clements Markham, Richard III: His Life and Character Reviewed in the Light of Recent Research
[lxvii] Francis Bacon, The History of the Reign of King Henry VII
[lxviii] Jones and Underwood – The King's Mother
[lxix] Francis Bacon, The History of the Reign of King Henry VII

[lxx] Blood Sisters: The Women Behind the Wars of the Roses - Sarah Gristwood
[lxxi] Clements Markham, Richard III: His Life and Character Reviewed in the Light of Recent Research
[lxxii] Polydore Vergil, English History
[lxxiii] Calendar of State papers of Venice: Rawdon Brown
[lxxiv] The Lost Prince: The Survival of the Duke of York - David Baldwin
[lxxv] Dominic Mancini, The Usurpation of Richard III
[lxxvi] Thomas More, The History of King Richard III
[lxxvii] Polydore Vergil, English History
[lxxviii] Elizabeth of York: The First Tudor Queen - Alison Weir
[lxxix] Historical Notes of a London Citizen
[lxxx] The Survival of the Princes in the Tower: Murder, Mystery and Myth - Matthew Lewis
[lxxxi] The Princes in the Tower – Alison Weir
[lxxxii] The Memoirs of Philip de Commines - Philippe deCommynes
[lxxxiii] Ashmole MS. 1448.60
[lxxxiv] https://www.cbsnews.com/news/josh-powell-kids-die-in-alleged-murder-suicide/
[lxxxv] Richard III as Duke of Gloucester and King of England - Caroline Halstead
[lxxxvi] The Reign of King Henry VI – Ralph A Griffiths
[lxxxvii] Margaret Beaufort: Mother of the Tudor Dynasty - Elizabeth Norton
[lxxxviii] The Earls of Derby 1485 – 1985 – J.J. Bagley
[lxxxix] www.dailymail.co.uk/news/article-8057593/Man-60-killed-wife-son-17-years-apart-compares-deaths-losing-horse.html
[xc] John Rous, Historia Regum Angliae
[xci] Croyland Chronicle
[xcii] Anne Neville: Richard III's Tragic Queen – Amy Licence
[xciii] Blood Sisters: The Women Behind the Wars of the Roses - Sarah Gristwood
[xciv] The History of the Life and Reigne of Richard III - George Buck
[xcv] Blood Sisters: The Women Behind the Wars of the Roses - Sarah Gristwood
[xcvi] John Rous, Historia Regum Angliae
[xcvii] Polydore Vergil, English History
[xcviii] Anne Neville: Richard III's Tragic Queen – Amy Licence
[xcix] https://www.inquisitr.com/3428973/tami-huntsman-mom-torture-murder-children/
[c] Sean Cunningham – Richard III: A Royal Enigma
[ci] www.thesun.co.uk/news/6089157/nanny-yoselyn-ortega-trial-convicted-murder-killing-children/
[cii] Richard III's Beloved Cousyn: John Howard and the House of York – John Ashdown-Hill
[ciii] Richard III's Beloved Cousyn: John Howard and the House of York – John Ashdown-Hill

[civ] Richard III's Beloved Cousyn: John Howard and the House of York – John Ashdown-Hill

[cv] Thomas More, The History of King Richard III

[cvi] www.vanguardngr.com/2018/06/murdered-son-husband-housewife/

[cvii] Lovell Our Dogge: The Life of Viscount Lovell, Closest Friend of Richard III and Failed Regicide – Michele Schindler

[cviii] Lovell Our Dogge: The Life of Viscount Lovell, Closest Friend of Richard III and Failed Regicide – Michele Schindler

[cix] Lovell Our Dogge: The Life of Viscount Lovell, Closest Friend of Richard III and Failed Regicide – Michele Schindler

[cx] Lovell Our Dogge: The Life of Viscount Lovell, Closest Friend of Richard III and Failed Regicide – Michele Schindler

[cxi] The Dublin King: The True Story of Lambert Simnel and the Princes in the Tower

[cxii] Richard III - David Baldwin

[cxiii] The Lost Prince: The Survival of the Duke of York - David Baldwin

[cxiv] Thomas More, The History of King Richard III

[cxv] Historic Doubts on the Life and reign of King Richard III - Horace Walpole

[cxvi] Richard III: The Princes in the Tower, documentary

[cxvii] The King's Mother: Memoir of Margaret Beaufort, Countess of Richmond and Derby – Margaret Domville

[cxviii] Croyland Chronicle

[cxix] Red Roses: Blanche of Gaunt to Margaret Beaufort - Amy Licence

[cxx] The Princes in the Tower – Alison Weir

[cxxi] Francis Bacon, The History of the Reign of King Henry VII

[cxxii] Blood Sisters: The Women Behind the Wars of the Roses - Sarah Gristwood

[cxxiii] Bernard Andre – The Life of Henry VII

[cxxiv] www.thesun.co.uk/news/9186604/britain-youngest-double-killers-kim-edwards-inspired/

[cxxv] Francis Bacon, The History of the Reign of King Henry VII

[cxxvi] Historic Doubts on the Life and reign of King Richard III - Horace Walpole

[cxxvii] The Survival of the Princes in the Tower: Murder, Mystery and Myth - Matthew Lewis

[cxxviii] The Betrayal of Richard III: An Introduction to the Controversy – V B Lamb

[cxxix] The Dublin King: The True Story of Lambert Simnel and the Princes in the Tower

[cxxx] Historic Doubts on the Life and reign of King Richard III - Horace Walpole

[cxxxi] mattlewisauthor.wordpress.com/tag/jack-leslau/

[cxxxii] Clements Markham, Richard III: His Life and Character Reviewed in the Light of Recent Research

[cxxxiii] Polydore Vergil, English History

cxxxiv Calendar of State papers of Venice: Rawdon Brown

Bibliography
The Lost Prince: The Survival of the Duke of York - David Baldwin,
Richard III - David Baldwin
Elizabeth Woodville: The Mother of the Princes in the Tower - David Baldwin
Richard III: A Royal Enigma - Sean Cunningham
The Survival of the Princes in the Tower: Murder, Mystery and Myth - Matthew Lewis
The Betrayal of Richard III: An Introduction to the Controversy – V B Lamb
Richard III: His Life and Character - Clements Markham
The Anglica Historia of Polydore Vergil - Polydore Vergil
The Richard III Brief: Murderer or Misunderstood? - Carol Darbyshire
Croyland Chronicles
Westminster Bones: The Real Mystery of the Princes in the Tower – Richard Unwin
Anne Neville: Queen to Richard III - Michael Hicks
Edward V: The Prince in the Tower - Michael Hicks
Richard III and his Rivals: Magnates and Their Motives in the Wars of the Roses - Michael Hicks
Bosworth 1484: Psychology of a Battle - Michael Jones
The Women of the Cousins' War: The Real White Queen and her Rivals – Philippa Gregory, David Baldwin and Michael Jones
Richard III: From Contemporary Chronicles, Letters and Records - Keith Dockray
Richard III as Duke of Gloucester and King of England - Caroline Halstead
The House of Beaufort: The Bastard Line that Captured the Crown - Nathan Amin
Margaret Beaufort: Mother of the Tudor Dynasty - Elizabeth Norton
Bacon's History of the Reign of King Henry VII - Francis Bacon
Blood Sisters: The Women Behind the Wars of the Roses -

Sarah Gristwood
The Reign of King Henry VI – Ralph A Griffiths
Letters of the Queens of England {1100-1547] – Anne Crawford
Memoir of Margaret, Countess of Richmond and Derby - Charles Cooper
The King's Mother: Memoir of Margaret Beaufort, Countess of Richmond and Derby – Margaret Domville
Richard III and the Murder in the Tower -Peter A Hancock
Richard III and the Princes in the Tower - AJ Pollard
The History of the Life and Reigne of Richard III - George Buck
The Usurpation of Richard III - Dominic Mancini
Trial of Richard III – Richard Drewett and Mark Redhead
The Memoirs of Philip de Commines - Philippe deCommynes
Richard III: A Ruler and his Reputation - Horspool
Red Roses: Blanche of Gaunt to Margaret Beaufort - Amy Licence
Cecily Neville: Mother of Kings - Amy Licence
Elizabeth of York: The First Tudor Queen - Alison Weir
Lancaster and York: The Wars of the Roses - Alison Weir
The Woodvilles: The Wars of the roses and Englands Most Infamouds Family – Susan Higginbotham
The Yorkists: The History of a Dynasty – Anne Crawford
The Historical Collections of a Citizen of London in the

Fifteenth Century

RIII and Buckingham's Rebellion – Louise Gill

Elizabeth of Yprk: The Forgotten Tudor Queen - Amy Licence

Henry VII – S B Chrimes
Henry VII – Roger Turvey
Henry VII: The Maligned Tudor King – Terry Breverton
The Princes in the Tower – Alison Weir
England's Queens: The Biography – Elizabeth Norton
The Mythology of Richard III – John Ashdown-Hill
The Earls of Derby 1485 – 1985 – J.J. Bagley

Anne Neville: Richard III's Tragic Queen – Amy Licence
Last Champion of York: Francis Lovell, Richard III's Truest Friend – Stephen David
The Dublin King: The True Story of Edward, Earl of Warwick, Lambert Simnel and the Princes in the Tower – John Ashdown-Hill
The Dukes of Norfolk: Quincentennial History – John Martin Robinson
The Staffords, Earls of Stafford and Dukes of Buckingham: 1384-1521 – Carole Rawcliffe
Lovell Our Dogge: The Life of Viscount Lovell, Closest Friend of Richard III and Failed Regicide – Michele Schindler
Historic Doubts on the Life and Reign of King Richard III - Horace Walpole
The History of King Richard III – Thomas More
Richard III: Brother, Protector, King – Chris Skidmore.
Richard III's Beloved Cousyn: John Howard and the House of York – John Ashdown-Hill

Printed in Great Britain
by Amazon